THE
CLEAN & SIMPLE
DIABETES COOKBOOK

Flavorful, Fuss-Free Recipes for Everyday Meal Planning

BY JACKIE NEWGENT, RDN, CDN

American Diabetes Association.

Associate Publisher, Books, Abe Ogden; *Director, Book Operations*, Victor Van Beuren; *Managing Editor, Books*, John Clark; *Associate Director, Book Marketing*, Annette Reape; *Acquisitions Editor*, Jaclyn Konich; *Senior Manager, Book Editing*, Lauren Wilson; *Project Manager*, Lauren Wilson; *Composition*, Circle Graphics; *Cover Design*, Vis-à-vis Creative; *Photographer*, Renée Comet; *Printer*, Versa Press.

Printed in the United States of America
1 3 5 7 9 10 8 6 4 2

The suggestions and information contained in this publication are generally consistent with the *Standards of Medical Care in Diabetes* and other policies of the American Diabetes Association,
but they do not represent the policy or position of the Association or any of its boards or committees. Reasonable steps have been taken to ensure the accuracy of the information presented. However, the American Diabetes Association cannot ensure the safety or efficacy of any product or service described in this publication. Individuals are advised to consult a physician or other appropriate health care professional before undertaking any diet or exercise program or taking any medication referred to in this publication. Professionals must use and apply their own professional judgment, experience, and training and should not rely solely on the information contained in this publication before prescribing any diet, exercise, or medication. The American Diabetes Association—its officers, directors, employees, volunteers, and members—assumes no responsibility or liability for personal or other injury, loss, or damage that may result from the suggestions or information in this publication.

Madelyn L. Wheeler conducted the internal review of this book to ensure that it meets American Diabetes Association guidelines.

♾ The paper in this publication meets the requirements of the ANSI Standard Z39.48-1992 (permanence of paper).

ADA titles may be purchased for business or promotional use or for special sales. To purchase more than 50 copies of this book at a discount, or for custom editions of this book with your logo, contact the American Diabetes Association at the address below or at booksales@diabetes.org.

American Diabetes Association
2451 Crystal Drive, Suite 900
Arlington, VA 22202

DOI: 10.2337/9781580407052

Library of Congress Cataloging-in-Publication Data

Names: Newgent, Jackie, author. | American Diabetes Association.
Title: The clean & simple diabetes cookbook : flavorful, fuss-free recipes
   for everyday meal planning / by Jackie Newgent, RDN, CDN.
Other titles: The clean and simple diabetes cookbook
Description: Arlington, VA : American Diabetes Association, 2020. |
   Includes index.
Identifiers: LCCN 2019039549 | ISBN 9781580407052 (paperback) | ISBN
   9781580407274 (ebook)
Subjects: LCSH: Diabetes--Diet therapy--Recipes. | Cooking (Natural foods)
   | LCGFT: Cookbooks.
Classification: LCC RC662 .N495 2020 | DDC 641.5/6314--dc23
LC record available at https://lccn.loc.gov/2019039549

FOR AIDEN AND RHYUS

TABLE OF CONTENTS

ACKNOWLEDGMENTS

Many smart and creative people have helped make this book possible. I'm grateful to have the opportunity to thank them here for their generosity, time, commitment, passion, energy, and support.

THANK YOU:

- Rebecca, Don, and Jaime McLean, for being my favorite tasters.
- Jim and Sandi Newgent, for your honest feedback—and for providing me with two awesome nephews.
- Aiden and Rhyus (and Nibbles, the dog!), for your constant inspiration.
- My dear friends—you all know who you are—for your never-ending support, understanding, and love.
- Beth Shepard, for your guidance and friendship as my agent.
- Renée Comet, photographer, Lisa Cherkasky, food stylist, and Guilietta Pinna, prop stylist, for creatively and beautifully bringing this cookbook to life.
- All of the dedicated behind-the-scenes talent at the American Diabetes Association, including Lauren Wilson, Jaclyn Konich, MPH, RDN, and Victor Van Beuren.
- Baby Duke (my cat!), for being a constant source of joy and my occasional "sous chef."

INTRODUCTION

What are the keys to living well with diabetes? Cooking and eating nutritiously are at the top of that list. But they are often easier said than done. Maybe you find it challenging to determine the ideal dishes for a diabetes eating plan. Perhaps you don't feel fully confident of your kitchen skills. Maybe you just don't have that much (or any!) extra time to prepare healthy meals. Or perhaps you simply like to keep things easy.

There's no need to add stress to your diabetes-friendly lifestyle! That's where this cookbook steps in as your go-to recipe resource. *The Clean & Simple Diabetes Cookbook* helps you worry less and enjoy more; it provides guidance to help you prepare uncomplicated diabetes cuisine made with whole, natural ingredients. In fact, it's cuisine that everyone will appreciate.

What exactly will you find in this book? Over 100 recipes, including more than 50 main dishes. That's more than 7 weeks' worth of different entrées. All of the dishes in this book feature natural, flavorful, and highly appealing ingredients, and the recipes streamline the cooking process. Absolutely nothing is artificial! In other words, the recipes are "clean." Plus carbs are kept in check, so you can enjoy meals with 45 grams of total carbohydrate or less to fit into your personalized eating plan.

You'll love these additional friendly features, too. All recipes:

- contain 7 ingredients or fewer, including salt, pepper, and oil
- use common cooking equipment
- list simple-to-understand cooking instructions in a step-by-step fashion
- require just 15 minutes or less for prep time
- feature a complete nutrition analysis
- are easy, tasty, and healthy!

And there's more! These recipes are classified in three different categories based on cooking ease. You'll notice that there are symbols guiding you to the recipes that fit your culinary skill level or desire for simplicity.

Symbols for cooking ease:

Easy =
Cooking requires some skill (examples: stir-fry or more than one cooking technique)

Easier =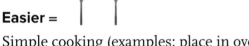
Simple cooking (examples: place in oven and bake, or cook while stirring)

Easiest =
Countertop cooking or no cooking (examples: combining in a blender or ingredient assembly)

You'll also appreciate that many of the recipes in this cookbook require no stove or oven use at all. Now that's cool—literally! Specifically, you'll find that more than three dozen recipes are classified as "easiest"—which is ideal if you have somewhat basic cooking skills or prefer straightforward, foolproof recipes that require little effort.

Another bonus feature is a meal prep guide with weekly menus. There are two complete sets of meal and snack options. One is designed for a family of four; the other is for when you're cooking for one. Most of the meals and snacks can be prepared in advance, so you have time-saving meals ready when you need them.

Whether you're a cooking newbie or just prefer simplicity from purchase to plating, *The Clean & Simple Diabetes Cookbook* is ready to assist. Consider it your diabetes-friendly guide to clean eating—helping you focus on mindfully eating more whole foods rather than overly processed foods. This book proves that easy, tasty, and healthy can all go together. I've had so much fun creating all of these recipes for you, and I can't wait for you to try them out!

–Jackie Newgent

A DIABETES-FRIENDLY LIFESTYLE

You're not alone! If you're living with diabetes or trying to prevent diabetes, know that there are millions of people on this planet that have been diagnosed with diabetes or prediabetes. According to the Centers for Disease Control and Prevention (CDC), 30 million adults and kids in the U.S. (that's about 1 in 10) have diabetes, and 90–95% percent of those people have type 2 diabetes. And an estimated 1 in 3 American adults has prediabetes (in other words, they're at risk for developing type 2 diabetes).

The good news is that diabetes is fully manageable with proper treatment and lifestyle changes, which include following a healthful eating plan. That's where this cookbook comes in handy. I developed all of the recipes in *The Clean & Simple Diabetes Cookbook* with the needs of people with diabetes in mind. So you can absolutely feel good about what you're eating by including any of these recipes into your diabetes-friendly eating plan.

EATING SMART

Before diving into the recipes, it's important to have at least a general understanding of what diabetes is and how food can be helpful in managing it. In a nutshell, diabetes is a chronic health condition. "Chronic" means long-lasting rather than something that's short-term. Having diabetes means your body isn't able to turn the food you eat into energy as well as the bodies of those without diabetes. The result is high blood glucose levels.

Two of the main forms of diabetes are simply called type 1 and type 2 diabetes. Type 1 diabetes is not nearly as common as type 2, affecting approximately 5% of those that have diabetes. Its cause is associated with an autoimmune reaction, and it's usually diagnosed when people are young. There is no cure for type 1 diabetes (at least not yet!), and it requires insulin for treatment. Type 2 diabetes is more common, affecting approximately 90–95% of those that have diabetes. It's generally diagnosed during adulthood, though a growing number of younger people are developing type 2 diabetes. It can be prevented or treated by aiming for or maintaining a healthy weight, eating well, and leading an active lifestyle. Medication may also be part of the treatment plan. One other form of diabetes is called gestational diabetes, which some people develop during pregnancy.

Because type 2 diabetes is the most common form of the disease, the information in this cookbook is geared towards this population. However, the recipes are beneficial for people with all types of diabetes—as well as for people who do not have diabetes. Personally, I have a family history of diabetes, so I eat diabetes-friendly recipes to try to prevent it!

Eating right *and* cooking right play essential roles in managing weight. Maintaining a healthy weight—or losing weight if overweight—is often a key strategy for managing type 2 diabetes. The types of foods you eat, when you eat them, and how much of them you eat can all affect your body weight and blood glucose levels. Following a meal plan or eating pattern developed for you by a registered dietitian nutritionist is an effective strategy for weight and diabetes management.

What about carbohydrates? In addition to eating healthfully overall, limiting the total carbohydrate (or carbs, for short) you eat at meal and snack times is one of the most important aspects of eating well for diabetes. Simply put, the carbohydrates you eat have a direct impact on your blood glucose. The goal isn't to go low-carb; it's to eat the right amount of carbs for your body while spreading them out throughout the day. Your physician, a registered dietitian nutritionist, or another member of your diabetes care team can help you determine carbohydrate goals that are right *for you*. There isn't one specific amount of carbs per day or per meal that works for everyone with diabetes. Carbohydrate goals need to be individualized based on factors such as activity level, weight (or body fat level), age, how long you've had diabetes, and whether or not you take medications. For instance, aiming for a maximum of 45 grams of total carbohydrate for a meal may be a good goal for you—though, if you're highly active, including more carbohydrates may be necessary, especially when planned in accordance with your activity. Always follow the advice of your diabetes healthcare practitioner.

Where do you find carbs? They're in much of our food supply! Foods with carbs include vegetables, fruits, grains, dairy, beans, and also breads, pastas, sweets, and sodas. The carbohydrate in all of these foods affects your blood glucose levels, but some of these food choices are better for you than others. Carbohydrate foods can be rich in fiber, vitamins, and minerals and low in added sugars, fats, and sodium, but it is important to focus on the quality of carbohydrates you consume. Your best bet is to choose carb-containing foods that are the least processed. Less processing can mean more fiber, which can be beneficial for blood glucose management. For instance, aim to choose whole grains instead of refined grains and whole fruits instead of fruit juice. When it comes to vegetables, going for nonstarchy vegetables (some examples are salad greens, broccoli, cauliflower, asparagus, tomatoes, onions, carrots, and many more) rather than starchy vegetables (for example, corn, potatoes, peas, winter squash) when possible can be beneficial, too. That means enjoying cauliflower or asparagus more often than potatoes or peas. When you do want starchy vegetables, just be sure to account for their higher carbohydrate count.

Of course, sugar is a form of carbohydrate, too. While it's not necessary to eliminate sugar from your diet, try your best to forgo added sugars whenever possible. Added sugars are simply the sweeteners (such as sugar, corn syrup, brown sugar, honey, and others) that are added to some foods for desired sweetness. Unfortunately, they are a form of "empty" calories—meaning they provide minimal or no nutritional benefit. Major sources of added sugars include sodas, energy drinks, fruit drinks, baked goods, candy, and desserts (such as ice cream). When in doubt, read food labels to check for added sugars. Luckily, having diabetes doesn't mean you must say "no" to dessert. But when you do want to include an occasional sugary food in your meal plan (hello, birthday cake!), make sure to actually plan it in so that you stay within the range of total carbohydrate that's right for you.

CREATE YOUR PLATE

Finding the right diabetes eating plan for you is more about aligning with your personal preferences and goals, not simply following a popular diet. Many different eating patterns are considered effective for people with diabetes. There are benefits to carb-counting as well as to following a Mediterranean or DASH diet. (DASH actually refers to Dietary Approaches to Stop Hypertension.) Going vegetarian or vegan may be effective for some people with diabetes, while others may be successful with a low-carb eating plan. Above all, it's important that your plan is personalized for you (by a member of your diabetes care team) to meet your unique needs. Your personal eating plan may not fit perfectly within any of those eating patterns mentioned above, or it may be a combination.

No matter which eating pattern you follow, using the Diabetes Plate Method (also sometimes called Create Your Plate) can be helpful for everyone. It can be utilized in coordination with your diabetes eating plan—or even on its own—for effective management of diabetes or weight loss. It was created by the American Diabetes Association to basically show what healthful portions look like on a plate. Using this simple method, you'll be able to enjoy a diabetes-friendly eating style—no carbohydrate counting or special equipment required!

Here's what you do: First, assess the size of your dinner plate. Our portion sizes tend to be proportional to the size of our dinner plate (i.e., smaller plate = smaller portions). A 9-inch plate is a good place to start—that's about the width of a piece of paper. Next, draw an imaginary line down the middle of your plate. Fill half of your plate with nonstarchy veggies, like leafy salad greens, zucchini, or peppers. That's the most important part . . . and the simplest! Then you'll divide the other half of the plate into two sections; fill one section with carb-rich foods such as whole grains, starchy veggies, fruit, or milk/yogurt, and the other section is where you'll place your

protein food, such as chicken or a plant-based protein source like black beans. That's the plate! From there, based on your own eating plan, you may add a serving (or another serving) of fruit or dairy, some healthy fats, and a calorie-free beverage. Of course, mixed meals count, too, like when you build a bowl, or make a stir-fry or casserole. Just keep these proportions in mind: 2 parts nonstarchy vegetables, 1 part carb-rich foods, 1 part protein-rich foods.

GOING PLANT-BASED

How about a plate without meat? If you've dabbled with the idea of going vegetarian or vegan, keep dabbling. Following a plant-based eating pattern can have significant benefits for protecting your health. In fact, a review of the research suggests that when following a plant-based diet, people with type 2 diabetes were able to better manage their condition, including their HbA1c (more commonly known as A1C) levels, total cholesterol, and weight, as well as boost their mood and quality of life.

In general, a plant-based diet includes vegetables, fruits, whole grains, legumes, nuts, and seeds and excludes most or all animal products. Some people who follow a plant-based eating pattern choose to eat dairy and eggs; research finds A1C levels can still be improved by following a vegetarian diet that includes dairy and eggs.

While you don't have to become a vegan (excluding all animal products from your diet), try adding some vegan meals to your meal plan, with easy entrées like No-Brainer Bean Burrito Wrap (page 128), Veggie Lo Mein (page 134), Overstuffed Veggie & Hummus Sandwich (page 136), or "Steak" Fajitas (page 152). (Hint: Check out the list of vegan recipes in the index on page 335.) You might already do it some of the time without realizing it. A peanut butter and jelly sandwich, spaghetti marinara, and a bean and veggie burrito can all be made vegan! There's recent research that suggests a therapeutic potential of eating vegan meals for improving parameters associated with type 2 diabetes.

What are other benefits of plant-based eating? By eating mostly plants, you'll naturally be able to eat a significant amount of nutrients—including vitamins, minerals, antioxidants, fiber, and healthy (unsaturated) fats—which may play a protective role when you have diabetes. One special type of nondigestible fiber found in plants is prebiotic fiber; it feeds probiotics (the "good" bacteria in your gut) to potentially help protect your health. Studies suggest there may be a promising connection between having a healthy intestinal microbiome ("good" gut) and diabetes health.

Fortunately, *The Clean & Simple Diabetes Cookbook* includes an entire chapter on plant-based main dishes (see Main Dishes: Plant-Based on page 127) to help you incorporate some plant-based meals into your eating plan. Some are vegan (containing no animal products), and others are lacto-ovo vegetarian (containing dairy and/or eggs). And all are easy to make, of course!

YOUR PERSONAL CHECKLIST

Remember that there's not just one eating pattern or meal plan that's right for everyone with diabetes. The more personalized your meal plan is to your lifestyle, preferences, and goals, the better. You are unique! With that said, there are many nutrition-related tips that may be helpful for everyone with diabetes. I've created a list of some of the most important strategies for managing diabetes; this list may be especially helpful if you're new to diabetes or need a refresher. You can use it like an ongoing checklist. If you feel overwhelmed by the thought of putting all these strategies into action, simply pick three tips at a time. Once they become good habits, focus on three more. Please note that this list is just a starting point and is not a substitute for routine visits with your diabetes care team. Be sure to follow the guidance of your physician, registered dietitian nutritionist, and/or diabetes educator.

- **Check your blood glucose levels regularly.** Maintaining blood glucose levels within a certain range (your physician can help you determine what that range should be) can help prevent complications from diabetes, such as hypoglycemia, heart disease, neuropathy, or retinopathy. What you eat has a big effect on your blood glucose levels, and so do stress, exercise, sleep, and illness. Checking your blood glucose regularly helps you understand how your body reacts to these different factors so you can better manage your blood glucose. Ask your physician or diabetes care team for details about checking your blood glucose.

- **Know your A1C level.** A1C is an indicator of your "average" blood glucose over the past few months. Ask your physician about your A1C level and see if he or she can suggest a goal level for you.

- **Choose whole grains.** Think wholesome! Choose whole-grain versions of grain-based foods, like whole-grain bread, oatmeal, brown rice, or whole-wheat pasta. You'll get more naturally occurring plant nutrients and fiber from whole-grain foods than the refined versions. The goal is to come as close as possible to 100% of your grain foods being from whole grains.

- **Stick to a regular schedule.** First of all, don't skip breakfast! Be sure to balance out your food choices, especially carbohydrate-rich foods, throughout the day, rather than eating large quantities once or twice a day. This can help you better manage your blood glucose levels—and potentially prevent overeating. Follow this rule of thumb: Don't go more than 5 waking hours without something to eat. So if lunch is at noon and dinner is at 7:00 pm, you'll need to plan a snack during that 7-hour span of time.

- **Choose to chew.** In other words, pick whole fruit instead of fruit juice, whenever possible. You'll get more chewing satisfaction and fiber. If you do drink juice, use a small juice glass, not a large water glass. And choose 100% juice, such as 100% orange juice or 100% pomegranate juice, not just a fruity drink that contains only some (or no!) real fruit juice.

- **Go halfsies.** Aim to always fill half of your plate (or bowl) with nonstarchy veggies. Choose from any of these nonstarchy favorites: asparagus, beets, broccoli, Brussels sprouts, carrots, cauliflower, cucumber, eggplant, leafy greens, mushrooms, okra, onions, pea pods (snow peas), peppers, spinach, tomatoes, yellow summer squash, or zucchini. Add on to this list as you wish.

- **Try fat swapping.** Choose foods that are rich in healthy (unsaturated) fats—such as extra-virgin olive oil, avocados, nuts, seeds, and salmon—in place of foods that are high in saturated fats—such as butter, lard, bacon, ribs, and heavy cream. Making healthy fat swaps can be helpful for diabetes management and may help play a role in lowering A1C. For instance, try spreading avocado instead of butter onto whole-grain toast.

- **Shrink your sodium intake.** According to the CDC, Americans consume more than 3,400 milligrams (mg) of sodium a day on average. That's well over the suggested 2,300 mg per day—which is almost the amount of sodium in 1 teaspoon of salt. Ask your physician or registered dietitian nutritionist if you need to modify your sodium intake below 2,300 mg per day. Reducing the amount of sodium in your diet may help reduce blood pressure, which could reduce your risk for stroke or heart attack. But since sodium (salt) provides flavor; don't go too low—it's important to still enjoy your food!

- **Do desserts wisely.** Dessert is not a "no-no." It's fine to occasionally plan a serving of dessert into your diet. Enjoy a petite-portioned sweet, like a small oatmeal cookie or a thin sliver of pumpkin pie. Focus mainly on desserts that include nutrient-rich ingredients, such as whole grains, fruits, vegetables, or nuts. You'll find several dessert options in *The Clean & Simple Diabetes Cookbook* (see Desserts & Drinks on page 297) that are made with whole fruits, nuts, and other wholesome ingredients. Most contain no added sugars . . . and are still deliciously sweet!

- **Steer clear of sugary beverages.** Examples of sugary drinks include regular sodas, energy drinks, sweet tea, regular lemonade, fruit punch, and some coffee shop concoctions. To quench your thirst, drink calorie-free beverages, like flat or fizzy water, unsweetened tea, or black coffee. If you drink alcoholic beverages, do so in moderation (no more than one drink a day for women or two drinks a day for men) and account for them in your diabetes eating plan.

- **Just do the best you can.** Perfection isn't a requirement for following a diabetes-friendly eating plan. No one is perfect. And no eating plan is perfect. But always try to be mindful of what you're eating. Try to eat while sitting, eat at a table, and eat from a plate or bowl instead of out of a bag. Aim for distraction-free dining—for example, put that mobile device out of sight while eating. (Well, try to at least!)

- **Move it!** In addition to a eating well, exercising is key to managing diabetes. Regular activity can be beneficial for lowering blood glucose, managing weight, reducing blood pressure and cholesterol, and more. You don't have to run a marathon. Walking is always a good idea. You can break up activity sessions throughout the day, too.

A STEP-BY-STEP GUIDE TO EASY COOKING FOR DIABETES

DIABETES COOKING SIMPLIFIED

Hooray for simplicity! But watch out for over-simplicity. While some people may rely on ultra-processed convenience foods or quick-service foods to streamline mealtimes, that's not the best approach if you have diabetes or prediabetes, or if you can greatly benefit from following a healthful eating plan.

Does that mean you need to spend more time and effort in the kitchen? Nope! Diabetes-friendly and clean-eating food prep can absolutely be easy, especially if you know the right culinary tweaks to try. Enjoying the recipes in *The Clean & Simple Diabetes Cookbook* will naturally help you learn those tweaks. But no matter what you make,

following these six savvy strategies for simplifying your cooking will help.

1. **Have a plan.** If you know what you plan to eat for meals and snacks, that will help guide your grocery shopping—so you'll have the ingredients you need right when you need them. You'll be more likely to stick to a healthy eating pattern if you have a plan, too.

2. **Be an organizer.** Even if you're someone who doesn't mind being a bit unorganized, having an organized kitchen will help make the cooking process quicker and more enjoyable. You can never be too organized, even if that means alphabetizing spices. (I admit, I do that!)

3. **Stock up.** Do keep a well-stocked pantry, fridge, and freezer, but don't overstock (which may lead to food waste). Make sure

you have some pantry staples with long storage lives on hand (such as canned foods, brown rice and other grains, oatmeal, whole-grain pasta, etc.), so you can shorten your shopping list, minimize your shopping time, and be able to make quick-fix dishes when you need something fast. See Nutritious Food Staples on page 16 for a list of suggested items.

4. **Smartly incorporate convenience.** When you're simplifying the cooking process, it's okay to include convenient, minimally processed ingredients. Just opt for natural products, rather than those with synthetic preservatives or artificial anything. For instance, buy bottled lemon juice (not from concentrate) so you don't need to juice whole lemons, or choose canned beans so you don't need to soak and cook dry beans in advance. Check the ingredient list of these products—ideally the list will read more like a recipe than a science experiment.

5. **Choose easy.** In other words, don't make things more difficult for yourself. Easy recipes with seven ingredients or less (like you'll find in this cookbook!) can be just as healthy and tasty as difficult recipes that call for lots of ingredients. Make your ingredients count by focusing on good-quality and in-season ingredients for the best flavors from the get-go. Keep calorie-free or very, very low-calorie flavorings handy, such as spices, vinegars, and hot sauce. They'll help punch up the appeal of relatively plain cuisine in seconds. See the Easy Cooking "Rules" on page 18 and High-Flavor Tips on page 19 for more specifics.

6. **Meal prep.** Ideally, pick a couple days a week to prep meals and snacks for later on—or at least part of them. What are you doing Sunday and Wednesday from 7:00 to 8:00 pm-ish? If you're busy then, pick other time slots . . . even if it's just 15 minutes. Pre-prepping (for example, slicing veggies) and pre-cooking (such as roasting veggies) for your weekly meals when you have time, enables you to spend far less time and effort the rest of the week (when you may not have extra time). See Meal Prep: Make-Ahead Weekly Menus on page 31 to get started.

IN YOUR GROCERY CART: AISLE-BY-AISLE

Once you've got an eating plan, you can then create a shopping list to match. Otherwise, it's just you and your grocery cart (or basket) meandering down the aisles of the supermarket. If you don't walk in with a plan, it's easy to veer off the course of a healthy shopping trip. When you've got a shopping list, your grocery experience can go more smoothly and strategically. However, some nutritional roadblocks may still pop up as you stroll down the aisles. So try these quick tips for smart shopping. They're especially helpful when deciding between similar products.

Breads

- Simply put, buy bread that's made from 100% whole grains. Wheat bread doesn't necessarily mean whole-wheat bread; look for the actual term "whole wheat" on the packaging. Also, multigrain doesn't necessarily mean whole grain; look for any term that refers to a whole grain on the packaging, such as "whole wheat," "rolled oats," or "brown rice." Ideally, choose thin-sliced breads, even if you need to buy fresh bakery loaves and thinly slice them yourself.
- Not all buns, English muffins, and pita breads are sized equally. When comparing products, keep it simple and choose the one that's lower in total carbohydrate, but (preferably) higher in dietary fiber per serving. And, of course, go for whole-grain varieties.
- Choose tortillas that are the right size for your needs. If the tortillas you find are larger than a recipe requires, trim them to fit. (Hint: Tortilla scraps can be baked and enjoyed as salad or soup croutons!) And again, go for whole-grain options. Better yet, look for sprouted-grain tortillas. Sprouting reduces some of the starch content in grains, which could increase the ratio of other nutrients, including protein.

Packaged & Canned Foods

- Select salad dressings and condiments that contain no added sugars or are sweetened with fruit. If you can't find any in stores, here are a couple recipes to try: Easy Dijon Vinaigrette (page 290) and Fruit-Sweetened BBQ Sauce (page 286).
- Choose low-sodium soups, beans, tomatoes, and other canned foods when recipes call for low-sodium varieties. Otherwise, know that a recipe may rely on the sodium within a product for taste . . . or so you won't otherwise need to add any salt to a recipe.
- Pick cereals and snacks that are made with wholesome ingredients, such as whole grains, nuts, or seeds. Read the first few items on the ingredient list to double-check. Aim for at least 3 grams of dietary fiber per serving.

Beverages

- Always check the grams of total carbohydrate and sugar listed on sodas and energy drinks. Some may sound healthy, but they may just be bubbly drinks with different types of added sugar. For instance, a "natural" soda may contain cane sugar, but that's still sugar. It's best to choose sugar- and calorie-free beverages instead of sugary beverages.

- Regular water and sparkling or seltzer water provide zero calories. Note that tonic water contains sugar—12 fluid ounces of tonic water provides 32 grams of total carbohydrate, all of which is from sugar.
- When buying juice, read the ingredient list to make sure it's real, 100% fruit juice. Some fruity drinks may disguise themselves as juice, but many contain little or no actual fruit. Also, stock up on bottled lemon and lime juice (not from concentrate); I use them liberally in my recipes for an easy way to punch up taste.

Bulk Bins

- Bulk bins are a great way to save money and buy exactly what you need. If your local store has a bulk section, you can usually find grains, nuts, dried beans, dried fruit, and other pantry staples.
- Scoop up nuts and seeds that are raw or roasted and unsalted or lightly salted. Even though it's tempting, steer clear of those that are labeled "honey roasted" or "salted."

The plainer versions tend to be more versatile in recipes anyway!

- Buy dried fruit that contains no added sugar and no added preservatives (such as sulfur dioxide). Without preservatives, some dried fruits may look different than you expect them to. For instance, when not preserved, dried apricots should look naturally brownish instead of neon orange.
- Go for grains and grain foods from the bulk bins that are whole rather than refined. That means selecting brown rice rather than white rice and whole-wheat couscous rather than "white" couscous.

Dairy & Eggs

- You can choose lower-fat cheeses if you like lower-fat cheeses. Otherwise, choose regular, high-flavor cheeses, like sharp cheddar or blue cheese; you'll be able to use just a small amount of these cheeses for full flavor and enjoyment.
- Grab regular, Greek-style, and/or Icelandic-style yogurts that provide 0 grams of added sugars. That way you can manage what's being added to them. For instance, if you want strawberry yogurt, buy plain yogurt with no added sugars and add your own fresh strawberries. Greek yogurt and Icelandic yogurt (or skyr) can be used interchangeably; they're both strained yogurts

and will have a thick texture. Keep an eye out for newer plant-based versions of yogurt, too; but know that many of these products are lower in protein than traditional dairy versions.

- Buy eggs based on freshness, not color. Brown and white eggs are equally nutritious. Don't rely on egg substitutes. Egg white–based egg substitutes provide no cholesterol and are low in calories, but they naturally provide less overall nutrition than whole eggs because they're yolkless.

Poultry & Fish

- Pick poultry based on the type needed rather than what you might normally purchase. If a recipe calls for boneless, skinless chicken thighs, buy thighs and not breasts. Recipes are created using a specific type of poultry based on taste, nutrition, cooking characteristics, and/or overall appeal. Do also try to pick chicken and turkey that's free of antibiotics—that'll generally be noted on the front of the package. Or look for poultry with the USDA organic seal if that option fits into your budget.
- At the deli counter, request "natural" deli meat, like turkey breast that is *not* preserved with nitrates or nitrites. If that's not available in the deli, peruse the packaged deli meat section; packaged organic and natural

deli meats, such as Applegate Organics or Applegate Naturals, are free of these potentially harmful preservatives.

- Select the freshest fish available. Fresh fish will smell ocean-fresh, not fishy! Use it the same day you buy it if possible—or no longer than 24 hours after purchasing (if it's kept properly chilled).

Fresh Produce

- Fill up your shopping cart or basket with a variety of vegetables. Ideally, they'll be mostly nonstarchy varieties, such as broccoli, cauliflower, bell peppers, and zucchini (these are just a few examples). Choose the exact amounts needed for recipes, when possible, by weighing them on a scale in the produce section. This can help you avoid overbuying and curb food waste.
- Choose a variety of fruits—but just the amount you have planned to eat with your meals and snacks. Pick fruits that are in season for the best nutrition and flavor. In-season options are typically the cheapest and most abundant, too!
- If you're feeding a family, bulk bags of fruits and vegetables may be cheaper by the pound. But make sure you will actually use all of the produce you're purchasing. Otherwise, you may end up overeating or having to throw some of it away.

- Don't skip past the pre-prepped produce area. Even if it costs a bit more, it may be worth it if you don't have the time to or prefer not to slice or dice certain vegetables or fruits yourself. It can also be a wise choice when the pre-prepped amount is just what you need and will keep you from having excess produce hanging around.

Frozen Foods
- Buy frozen fruits and vegetables if you're unable to find fresh versions—or when the fresh versions are out of season. Frozen fruits and vegetables are packed at their peak of ripeness, nutritional value, color, and flavor.
- For frozen fruit, check the ingredients to make sure there is no added sugar.
- For frozen vegetables, choose packages that are *just* the vegetable, with no added salt, butter, cream, or sauces. Check the ingredients to make sure.
- If you can't find fresh fish or you don't plan to use fresh fish within 24 hours, frozen fresh fish fillets are a great option . . . but steer clear of the fried and breaded varieties.

Hint: Once you've added the last item to your shopping cart or basket, stop and take a look. Ideally, it'll look a bit like the Diabetes Plate Method approach to meal planning—about half nonstarchy vegetables, a quarter protein foods, and a quarter carbohydrate foods such as whole grains, starchy vegetables, fruit, and milk/yogurt.

IN YOUR KITCHEN

Having a well-stocked kitchen can help simplify the preparation of meals and snacks in your diabetes-friendly eating plan. You'll want to have a variety of nutritious food staples on hand. And you'll want to have at least a basic stash of the right types of kitchen tools and countertop small appliances. Couple these staple ingredients and tools with some easy cooking "rules" and high-flavor tips, and you'll be all set to make delicious diabetes-friendly cuisine with ease.

Nutritious Food Staples
Stock up on these ingredients for a health-promoting pantry, fridge, and freezer. Doing so will help make following the recipes in this cookbook (and beyond!) even easier and breezier. Hint: Remember to practice "first in, first out"—also known as FIFO—to make sure you use the oldest ingredients first.

- **Pantry or counter:** Nonstarchy veggies (such as grape tomatoes, English cucumber, onions, and garlic), fruits (such as avocados, bananas, and oranges), canned tomatoes, pumpkin, and beans, cans or pouches of low-mercury tuna, nuts and seeds, heart-healthy oils (such as extra-virgin olive oil), dried fruits (such as dried, unsulfured apricots), whole grains (such as brown rice and quinoa), pulse/legume pastas or whole-grain pastas, low-sodium vegetable and chicken broths, vinegars, tamari (soy sauce), hot sauce, pure vanilla extract, dried herbs and spices (a variety!), and sea salt

- **Fridge:** Nonstarchy veggies (such as bell peppers, cauliflower, zucchini, ginger-root, and packaged leafy greens), various berries, eggs, plain 0% fat Greek yogurt, fat-free milk or plain unsweetened plant-based milk, bottled lemon and lime juices (not from concentrate), unsweetened applesauce, unsweetened ketchup, salsa, fruit-sweetened fruit spreads (jams)
- **Freezer:** Frozen vegetables and legumes (such as sliced okra, peas, and black-eyed peas), frozen fruits (such as peach slices, dark sweet cherries, strawberries, raspberries, and blueberries), frozen fish (such as salmon and barramundi fillets), boneless, skinless chicken breasts and thighs, and ground turkey (packaged in recipe-sized portions)

Healthy Kitchen Tools

The majority of the recipes in this book require basic kitchen tools that you'll likely already have.

But stocking your kitchen with a variety of healthy cooking gadgets is an excellent idea. If you have most of the tools listed in the seven categories below on hand, you should be prepared to make anything in this cookbook—and beyond. If you don't have some of these tools, add them to your shopping list as needed. Better yet, you can add them to your birthday and holiday gift list so someone else can treat you!

- **Measurers:** Liquid measuring cups, dry measuring cups, measuring spoons, and a small kitchen scale
- **Knives, graters, peelers, and cutters:** Chef's knives, a bread knife, a pizza cutter, a vegetable peeler, a Microplane zester/grater, a box grater, kitchen shears/scissors, and a can opener
- **Non-cutting hand tools:** Cooking spoons (including flexible, spoon-shaped spatulas and a large slotted spoon), a spatula/turner, a whisk, a culinary/pastry brush, long-handled tongs, and an ice cream or cookie scoop
- **Pans and skillets:** Baking sheets/pans (including a large rimmed baking sheet, a 9 × 13-inch baking pan, and an 8-inch round cake pan), cast-iron or other stick-resistant skillets (at least one large and one small), saucepans with lids (at least one

large and one small), a wok (or a large, deep skillet), and a grill pan (or grill)

- **Glasses and jars:** Jars with lids (ideally one 8-ounce-capacity jar, two 12-ounce-capacity jars, and one 16-ounce-capacity jar), 6 juice glasses, and 1 champagne flute
- **Bowls and ramekins:** Mixing bowls (various sizes), microwave-safe ramekins or small dishes (one 1-cup-capacity ramekin and four 3/4- or 1-cup-capacity ramekins)
- **Countertop small appliances:** A blender, a food processor, an electric mixer (hand held is fine), a microwave, and a toaster
- **Other tools:** Cutting boards, a cooling rack, a mesh strainer (standing or hand held), an instant-read (meat) thermometer, a cocktail shaker with strainer, and reusable skewers (7 inches or longer)

Easy Cooking "Rules"

When it comes to cooking, I personally like to toss out the rule book and have fun in the kitchen. You never know what you can create when you have extra nonstarchy veggies on hand that need to be used up before they "go bad" and you're in an experimental mood. That said, I've provided some tips (which I loosely call "rules") that can actually help make the cooking process go more smoothly. These "rules" apply whether you're being playful or want to follow a recipe precisely as written . . . or both!

1. **Get moody!** Create an atmosphere in which you'll enjoy cooking. Turn on your favorite music, an audiobook, or a podcast. Clear the clutter from the kitchen. Have some potted herb plants in your windowsill. Pour yourself a beverage and get cooking. (Hint: My moody thing is to sip on unsweetened iced peppermint tea as I cook!)

2. **Read it before you make it.** When following a recipe, especially a new one, read through the entire recipe in advance so there are no surprises halfway through. For instance, if you need pre-cooked chicken for a recipe, you don't want to figure that out in the middle of preparation when you've got raw chicken sitting in front of you. Or if something needs to be thawed in advance, it's no fun finding it solidly frozen when you're ready to start cooking.

3. **Use *mise en place* (MEEZ ahn plahs).** It's a French term that basically means to have everything gathered, prepped, measured out, and organized before you begin to cook. In English, another way to say it is . . . "Get your stuff together!" It truly makes the cooking process go more smoothly and (hopefully) error-free.

4. **Avoid guesstimating sizes.** Unless you're a size savant, when given a food size or a guide to food size (for example, "1/2-inch-thick slices"), get out the ruler! Measuring

will help ensure that the recipe works just as it's written. The same thing applies to food weights. Having a small kitchen scale is highly useful for healthy cooking and baking.

5. **Multitask cooking steps—but only if you want to.** For instance, make pasta at the same time you're making the sauce; it'll save time. But if that stresses you out, know that you can make them separately—it'll still work!

6. **Have a pre-plan.** Whatever you can do in advance to make cooking more efficient, do it! Portion out ingredient amounts when you have extra time beforehand. If a recipe you often make calls for a few spices, make a recipe-specific spice mixture in advance and label it. Batch-prepare commonly used items; for instance, you can pan-toast lots of nuts in advance and store in a jar in the fridge to be used in recipes as needed. Or if you often eat chicken, buy family-sized quantities, portion out what you need for recipes you'll soon prepare, and freeze. (Hint: Use your freezer well!) And let one meal help inform the next. In other words, if a recipe uses part of a rotisserie chicken, plan to make another dish that uses other parts of the chicken the next day. Or, if you're a fan of pre-prepping, you can prepare entire make-ahead meals. (See Meal Prep: Make-Ahead Weekly Menus on page 31 for a meal-prep plan.)

7. **Don't be a "rule" follower!** OK, so I couldn't resist adding this one in this list of "rules"! It's A-OK to add your own twist to recipes. If you like things spicy, go ahead and pepper up your plates. If you're an artist at heart, plate your food in your own artsy way. If you hate cilantro, use scallions or chives in its place. Just try not to stray too far from a recipe as written, especially when it comes to the type and amount of carbohydrate-based ingredients.

8. **Get schooled.** If you feel your chopping, dicing, mincing, and slicing skills aren't so polished, take a knife skills class at a nearby cooking school or cooking store. There are even some basic online classes available, if you can't do it live. When you know the best way to hold and use a knife for food prep, it makes the entire cooking experience go more quickly and enjoyably.

High-Flavor Tips

Easy cooking can and should still be flavorful cooking. In the recipes within *The Clean & Simple Diabetes Cookbook*, I've incorporated some high-flavor strategies so you don't have to change a thing (unless you want to!). But when you're cooking without a recipe, try these tips to make sure everything is tasty.

- **Splash with acid.** Culinary acids include vinegars, lemon juice, and lime juice. Adding a splash or squirt of one of these acids to your dishes can add a lively pop of flavor. They can balance the bitterness found in some vegetables, like dark leafy greens. And they may help you use a little less salt thanks to the zing they provide. When it comes to determining what type of acid to use, treat it like wine pairing or color matching. Pair balsamic vinegar with a tomato dish or pair lemon juice with a fish or chicken dish.

- **Kick up the "heat!"** While you don't want everything to taste like hot buffalo chicken wings, adding a hint of hot sauce, crushed red pepper flakes, or other spicy ingredients can add an element of flavor to a dish when you think it needs some oomph. Just a drop or pinch may pack enough pow to take a lackluster dish to more of a wow!

- **Bring on the browning.** Sometimes when in a rush, the taste of your food may be underperforming because of under-browning. Aim to be a little more zen and enjoy the art of cooking by allowing your foods to brown. For instance, when roasting cherry tomatoes or grilling bell peppers, don't just wait until they look like they're cooked through, go for some brownness—also called caramelization. Browning can help bring out the natural sweetness of vegetables, so they provide full sweet-savory appeal rather than having just a slight savory taste. Browning also enhances the sweetness of fruits—so consider grilling fruits, like peaches or bananas, too.

- **Get toasty.** Similar to the concept of browning vegetables, take the time to pan-toast nuts, like sliced almonds, if they're not already toasted/roasted. It'll make them taste extra nutty—so you get lots of nuttiness in a small amount of the ingredient. You can pan-toast whole spices, too. Once a spice, like cumin seeds or coriander seeds, becomes fragrant in a hot skillet, grind it in a coffee or spice grinder. It'll be way tastier than if you've had a pre-ground spice sitting in your pantry for a year (or more)!

- **Make your liquids count.** Rather than plain ol' water, consider using low-calorie, highly flavored liquids for some of your cooking. For instance, cooking brown rice or other whole grains in low-sodium vegetable or chicken broth will provide more savoriness. Poaching (simmering) chicken in unsweetened jasmine green tea will impart a delightful floral accent, which will be lovely when using the chicken for chicken salad. Also, try drizzling in tea instead of water when you need to thin a recipe, like when blending thick hummus or other dips.

- **Up the umami.** Umami is the fifth sense of taste. It refers to savoriness. By using ingredients that are rich in umami, you'll get more flavor and deliciousness from healthful cuisine, even if it's lower in sodium. Try including these umami-rich ingredients in your diabetes-friendly eating repertoire: mushrooms, naturally brewed tamari (soy sauce), shrimp, green tea, aged Parmesan cheese, and fully ripened tomatoes. (Hint: To get the most umami, don't refrigerate your tomatoes!)

- **Drop in the extracts.** When adapting recipes to make healthier versions of cakes, cookies, brownies, or other desserts, you'll often use less sugar or fat—or both. Doing so also cuts the flavor. But you can still get full enjoyment from these recipes by adding a pure flavor extract—or more extract than the recipe calls for. For instance, go heavier on pure vanilla extract (by using 1 1/2 instead of 1 teaspoon, for example) or add a few drops of pure almond or pure peppermint extract for flavor intrigue.

- **Embrace smelliness.** The majority of what you're tasting when you eat is actually thanks to your sense of smell. So make your food smellier—in a good way! To get more aroma, sauté with aromatics, such as garlic and gingerroot. Finish a dish with fresh herbs, when that works with the dish. Use sharper and smellier cheeses, like sharp cheddar and blue cheese. And serve dishes at warmer temperatures; for example, serve a sandwich toasted rather than chilled.

- **Sprinkle with zest.** Reaching for the salt shaker can become almost an automatic reflex. But one of the best ways to make food more interesting is not by simply adding salt; instead try sprinkling a dish with orange, lemon, or lime zest (that's the grated, colorful part of the citrus peel). It provides a vibrant burst of citrusy goodness. Even though it's not related to salt, lemon or lime zest can seem salty, as when lemon zest is sprinkled onto a pasta dish kind of like it's Parmesan cheese.

- **Don't forget the salt.** Sometimes a dish may actually need salt. In fact, "salty" is a sense of taste—so there is no true replacement for it. Keep in mind that when you're starting with plenty of plant-based and other wholesome ingredients, they may have little or no sodium to start. So don't fear salt; just use it wisely. Keep in mind, 1 teaspoon of salt has about 2,300 mg of sodium; so even a tiny 1/8-teaspoon pinch of salt will add about 300 mg of sodium to your dish.

ESSENTIAL COOKING HOW-TO'S

When you have solid skills in the kitchen, it can make cooking diabetes-friendly cuisine easier and more enjoyable. Here are some basic techniques that'll be especially helpful as you prepare the recipes found in *The Clean & Simple Diabetes Cookbook*! These "how-to's" are based on classic culinary techniques—some with an easier twist. While using these techniques, remember to keep good food-safety practices in mind. Wash and dry all produce before prep, even if you're not eating the peels. Always remember to keep ready-to-eat foods away from raw meat, poultry, and fish—ideally using separate cutting boards. And wash your hands often.

How to mince garlic

1. Place an individual garlic clove onto a cutting board. Place the flat side of a chef's knife on top of the clove and firmly press down on the knife with the palm of your hand—but not so firmly that you completely smash the garlic. Then peel off the garlic skin.

2. Next, grip the knife by the handle, place just the point of the knife onto the cutting board, and place three fingers on top of the knife towards the point. Continuously cut down several times onto the garlic, while lifting up the handle of the knife and always keeping the point of the blade on the cutting board, until the garlic is very finely chopped.

How to slice an onion

1. Using a chef's knife, cut the whole onion in half on a cutting board.

2. Lay each half cut side down on the cutting board. Working with one half at a time, hold the root end of the onion, and slice about 1/2 inch off the other end. (Hint: For best results, always keep the root end on while working with the onion—it holds the onion together.) Then, peel off the skin.

3. Working from the cut end, slice down to form thin or thick slices, as needed, until you reach the root end. Slicing works best if you firmly hold the onion half down with your hand, with your fingertips tucked inward, and using your knuckles as a guide for the side of the knife.

How to dice an onion

1. Using a chef's knife, cut the whole onion in half on a cutting board.

2. Lay each half cut side down on the cutting board. Working with one half at a time, hold the root end of the onion, and slice about 1/2 inch off the other end. (Hint: For best results, always keep the root end on

while working with the onion—it holds the onion together.) Then, peel off the skin.

3. Firmly place your palm on top of the onion half. With your knife blade parallel to the cutting board, cut into the onion, all the way to the root end, but without cutting through the root end, about two or three times. (Note: If this seems too challenging or confusing, you can skip this step.)

4. Then, slice downward lengthwise several times to make thin or thick slices, but without cutting through the root end. Then slice downward several times crosswise (or widthwise) to make dices.

How to grate fresh gingerroot

1. Break off a piece of gingerroot based on the amount you'll need for the recipe. Scrape off the gingerroot skin with a regular spoon. You can also use a paring knife, but you'll lose more ginger that way. For easier grating, leave a little bit of skin on the top portion of the piece you'll be grating to make it easier to hold onto.

2. Grate the gingerroot using a Microplane zester/grater. Do this by holding the zester/grater by the handle and standing it up almost vertical with the end of the blade on the cutting board. Grate the piece of ginger up and down against the grater as needed.

For best results, slightly rotate the ginger after every five up-and-down gratings.

3. To remove the grated gingerroot from the back of the zester/grater blade, simply smack it against your cutting board, and the grated gingerroot should drop onto the cutting board.

Use this general guide for the size you'll want to start with to yield various grated amounts:

- 1 large thumb-sized piece fresh gingerroot = 1 tablespoon grated
- 1 thumb-sized piece fresh gingerroot = 1 1/2 teaspoons grated
- 1 finger-sized piece fresh gingerroot = 1 teaspoon grated
- 1 small finger-sized piece fresh gingerroot =1/2 teaspoon grated

How to slice a bell pepper

1. Stand a bell pepper upright on a cutting board. Start with the blade of your knife just outside of the stem part of the pepper, then cut down the side of the pepper. Cut off the rest of the sides of the pepper, keeping the stem and all of the seeds inside intact. Then cut off the bottom piece of the bell pepper. You should have four or five large pieces.

2. To slice, work with one piece of pepper at a time, laying smooth (skin) side down on the cutting board. With the chef's knife, hold the piece down on one side, while you cut down several times to make thin or thick slices (as needed) starting from the other side. Don't completely pick your knife up off the cutting board between slices. Rather, after cutting down through the pepper piece to make a slice, keep the entire cutting blade on the cutting board, and slide the knife away from you on the cutting board while making sure you've completely cut the pepper though to make a slice.

3. To dice the pepper, hold several slices together with one hand; with your other hand, cut perpendicular to the slices to create small pieces.

How to cut a cucumber

1. There's no need to peel a cucumber before cutting; the skin and seeds are 100% edible. One way to cut a cucumber is to make coins. Place the cucumber on a cutting board. Using a chef's knife, slice it crosswise into thin or thick slices (as needed). However, the cucumber can roll around on you when you make coin shapes. If you don't need perfectly round slices for a recipe, you can make half-moon or quarter-moon shapes instead.

2. To make half-moons, cut the whole cucumber in half lengthwise. This will form two long halves. Place them cut side down on the cutting board. Working with one piece at a time, cut it crosswise into thin or thick slices.

3. To make quarter-moons, cut the whole cucumber in half lengthwise; then cut each of those pieces in half lengthwise. This will result in four long cucumber pieces. Working with one or two pieces at a time, cut it/them crosswise into thin or thick slices. These quarter-moon pieces can also be used as "cubes" when you don't need perfect square shapes.

How to prep asparagus

1. Hold one asparagus spear with both hands near the bottom of the stalk. Then bend the spear until the woody end of the stalk is snapped off. Rather than doing this for every spear, simply cut each asparagus spear in the same spot as that first spear naturally snapped. You can compost (or discard) the woody stems.

2. If you're preparing a recipe where you need chopped (cut) asparagus, be sure to keep the tips separate after chopping. If you're making a stovetop dish, like a stir-fry, it's best to add the tips in after the thicker parts of the asparagus so the tips don't get overcooked.

How to cut an avocado

1. There are various ways to cut an avocado. But the following method is the safest and easiest. Place the avocado on a cutting board. Place your palm firmly on top. Hold your chef's knife parallel to the cutting board, and cut into the avocado, like you plan to halve it, until you hit the seed. Then, while keeping the avocado on the cutting board, rotate the avocado holding the knife in place until it's cut all the way around. Remove the knife.

2. Twist the avocado halves in opposite direction to separate. Remove the seed. The safest way to do so is by scooping it out with a spoon. (You can compost or plant the seed!)

3. Place the avocado halves, cut side down, on the cutting board. Cut each in half lengthwise. You'll then have four avocado quarters.

4. Next, peel them; you can do it with your fingers—no knife or spoon required. Now, your avocado is recipe ready. Slice or dice each quarter as needed.

Hint: If only using a portion of the avocado, keep the part you're not using in its peel. To prevent the avocado flesh from browning, place it cut side down in a sealable bowl. Add cold water to cover the cut surfaces, seal, and store in the refrigerator for up to 3 days. Keeping the seed in the avocado, if possible, may also help prevent browning. But don't worry if you didn't save the seed; keeping it in the avocado only helps protect the fleshy part of the avocado that it's actually touching . . . so leaving the seed in is kind of like putting sunblock on your right arm, but not your legs or left arm! Your best bet is to protect the entire flesh by covering with water, with or without the seed.

How to make hard-boiled eggs

1. Remove the number of eggs you need from the refrigerator about 15 minutes before you plan to boil them.

2. In a medium saucepan, bring about 6 cups of water to a boil over high heat. Reduce heat to medium high, then quickly (yet gently) add up to six large eggs, one at a time, to the water using a large slotted spoon. Boil the eggs for exactly 10 minutes, making sure the eggs are completely covered with boiling water.

3. Quickly transfer the boiled eggs to a bowl of cold water that's filled with ice. Let the eggs cool for at least 15 minutes.

4. Crack and peel the boiled eggs as needed. You can store unpeeled hard-boiled eggs in the refrigerator for up to 1 week.

How to fry eggs

1. In a cast-iron or other stick-resistant skillet, heat a little oil (such as 1/2 teaspoon of

avocado oil or sunflower oil per egg) until fully heated over medium-high heat.

2. Carefully crack a large egg directly into the hot skillet. Or, if uncomfortable with that approach, crack the egg into a small bowl, then pour the egg from the bowl into the skillet. (Note: If frying several eggs, consider frying the eggs in batches or in two skillets so the eggs don't run together.)

3. Fry until the yolk is done as desired and egg-white edges are browned, about 2 1/2 minutes. This results in a "sunny side up" egg. If you prefer, flip the egg over using a spatula/turner and fry for about 1 minute more for an "over easy" egg (yolk and some white are still runny); 1 1/2 minutes more for an "over medium" egg (white is completely set, but yolk is still runny); or 2 minutes more for an "over well" egg (white and yolk are completely cooked through and set).

Note: The consumption of undercooked eggs may increase the risk of foodborne illness.

25 OF THE EASIEST-EVER THREE-INGREDIENT RECIPE IDEAS

Gather three ingredients and combine. Yes, it can really be that simple to make nutrient-rich dishes with great taste! I personally like to call it "no-brainer cuisine." So here are 25 ideas to prep when you need something healthy and filling pronto. Even if you don't need something that quickly, you can plan ahead and include any of these no-recipe-required dishes into your diabetes-friendly eating repertoire. I've included bonus items with these recipes just in case you're a fan of four-ingredient dishes from time to time, too. You can make these ideas even easier by using store-bought, pre-prepped items as you wish— just try to choose healthful options whenever possible, such as preservative-free or no-sugar-added versions of store-bought ingredients. Ready? Set? Go!

APPS & SNACKS

Almost Cowboy Caviar
In a bowl, stir together equal amounts of canned, drained, no-salt-added black beans, thawed frozen sweet corn, and pico de gallo (fresh chunky salsa).

Bonus: Stir in diced avocado.

PB&J Yogurt Snack Sundae
In a glass, layer plain 0% fat Greek yogurt, a dollop of no-sugar-added peanut butter, and a dollop of fruit-sweetened strawberry fruit spread (jam).

Bonus: Stir a few drops of pure vanilla extract into the yogurt before layering.

Cheese & Grape Kebabs

Cut string cheese into coins, arrange on bamboo picks or reusable skewers with grapes (or grape tomatoes), and drizzle with aged balsamic vinegar.

Bonus: Add fresh whole basil leaves onto the skewers.

Apple Stack

Core a small apple and cut into 4 round slices, spread the top of 3 of the slices (not the top slice) with natural, unsweetened peanut butter, sprinkle with no-sugar-added granola, and restack the slices into an apple shape.

Bonus: Sprinkle the slices with ground cinnamon.

Grilled Figs & Goat Cheese

Cut fresh figs in half, brush the cut sides with a little avocado oil or sunflower oil, grill until grill marks form, and serve sprinkled with crumbled goat cheese.

Bonus: Sprinkle with balsamic vinegar or sliced fresh basil.

MAIN DISHES

Avocado & Hummus Toast

Toast a slice of whole-grain bread, and top with hummus and a few avocado slices.

Bonus: Drizzle with hot pepper sauce.

Peanut Noodles

Prepare whole-wheat noodles of choice, rinse with cold water to cool, toss with a drizzling of bottled natural Asian peanut sauce, and then toss in a large handful of fresh coleslaw mix.

Bonus: Sprinkle with fresh cilantro, shelled edamame, or peanuts.

Grilled Salsa Chicken & Beans

Grill or pan-grill boneless, skinless chicken breasts or thighs until well done, smother with salsa verde, and sprinkle with canned, drained, low-sodium black beans.

Bonus: Top with grilled cherry tomatoes or fresh cilantro.

Pulse Pasta Pesto

Boil red lentil or garbanzo bean/chickpea pasta until done. Drain, quickly rinse with cold water just to stop the cooking, and drain again. Toss with a dollop of jarred pesto sauce and lots of grape tomatoes.

Bonus: Add lemon zest (grated lemon peel).

Chicken & Guacamole Taco

Stuff each soft or crispy corn tortilla with shredded rotisserie chicken breast and a big dollop of guacamole of choice.

Bonus: Stuff with shredded lettuce of choice and/or drizzle with taco sauce.

Hummus Wrap
Spread hummus of choice onto a whole-grain tortilla, top with fresh baby salad greens, and wrap.

Bonus: Splash with lemon juice or harissa sauce.

Asian-Style Egg on Rice
On top of a small bed of steamed brown rice, place a fried egg, and drizzle with naturally brewed tamari (soy sauce).

Bonus: Sprinkle with sliced scallions.

Turkey & Cheddar Quesadilla
Lightly top a whole-grain tortilla with shredded sharp cheddar, top with leftover roasted turkey (think Thanksgiving!), fold in half, and cook in dry skillet over medium-high heat until toasted.

Bonus: Top with a dollop of cranberry sauce or tuck in a few thin apple slices.

Egg Salad Tartine
Toast one slice of whole-grain sourdough or rye bread, top with a small handful of fresh baby arugula, then a scoop of deli-prepared egg salad, and serve open-face style.

Bonus: Grill instead of toast the bread or sprinkle with a pinch of smoked paprika.

Grilled Turkey Parm Burger
Grill a ground turkey or chicken burger. A couple minutes before removing from the grill, top with marinara sauce of choice and a slice of part-skim mozzarella cheese.

Bonus: Serve on steamed zucchini noodles ("zoodles") or a grilled slice of whole-grain bread.

Latin Shrimp Stack
Add a few large dollops of warm refried black beans (from a can) to the center of a plate, top with a few dollops of guacamole of choice, and arrange cocktail-style shrimp on top.

Bonus: Splash with lime juice or garnish with fresh cilantro.

Tapenade Chicken Skewers
Toss boneless, skinless chicken thigh cubes with olive tapenade (olive spread) to lightly coat the chicken. Arrange on reusable skewers with red bell pepper cubes (or whole cherry tomatoes). Grill until well done.

Bonus: Sprinkle with crumbled feta cheese after grilling.

Mac & Cheese & More
Combine equal parts warm macaroni and cheese (such as healthy frozen entrée mac & cheese) and baby spinach that's been wilted in a skillet or microwave, and sprinkle with freshly ground black pepper.

Bonus: Drizzle with hot pepper sauce or sprinkle with crushed red pepper flakes.

Savory Pizza "French Toast"

Soak a leftover slice of veggie pizza in a whisked egg. Cook in a stick-resistant skillet over medium heat (cheese side down first) until browned. Top generously with diced fresh tomato.

Bonus: Sprinkle with thinly sliced fresh basil.

SALADS, SOUPS & SIDES

Burrito Entrée Salad

Microwave a frozen bean burrito according to package directions and cut crosswise into 6 slices. Arrange on fresh mixed salad greens, and dress with salsa verde or tomato-based salsa.

Bonus: Sprinkle with fresh cilantro leaves.

Tomato & Mint Salad

Attractively arrange slices of vine-ripened tomato onto a salad plate, sprinkle with whole fresh mint leaves, and squirt with lemon juice to taste.

Bonus: Drizzle with extra-virgin olive oil or sprinkle with toasted pine nuts.

Creamy Cauliflower Soup

Add finely chopped cauliflower to a saucepan, just cover with low-sodium chicken broth, and cook, covered, over medium heat until cauliflower is mushy. Blend the mixture, adding seasoning or herbs of choice.

Bonus: Drizzle with extra-virgin olive oil or top with a small pat of unsalted butter.

Black Bean Soup

Combine equal parts canned, rinsed, and drained black beans, canned diced tomatoes with chilies, and low-sodium chicken broth in a saucepan. Simmer for about 10 minutes, and serve as is or blended.

Bonus: Top with a dollop of low-fat quark or plain 0% fat Greek yogurt.

Peppered Corn

In a dry stick-resistant skillet over medium-high heat, combine equal amounts of thawed frozen corn and finely diced fresh red and green bell peppers. Cook, while stirring, until cooked through.

Bonus: Stir in thinly sliced scallions or squirt with lime juice.

Cheesy Sweet Potato Fries

Cut sweet potatoes into strips, lightly toss with avocado oil or sunflower oil, place on an unbleached parchment paper–lined baking sheet, and sprinkle with grated Parmesan. Bake in 375°F oven until crisp.

Bonus: Season with freshly ground black pepper or cayenne pepper.

MEAL PREP: MAKE-AHEAD WEEKLY MENUS

From purchase to plating, here you'll get to enjoy easy meals for any time of year based on a mix of quick-to-fix recipes along with no-brainer ideas. But the trick here is that you don't need to cook every day!

BASICS OF MEAL PREPPING

Meal prepping simply means preparing your meals or parts of your meals ahead of time instead of preparing each meal just before you eat it. Meal prep can save you time, reduce waste, and help you stick with your healthy eating plan. There are many ways to meal prep. One is to do "big batch" cooking. That refers to preparing a large quantity of a few simple dishes—such as steamed brown rice, a mixture of roasted vegetables, or grilled chicken breasts—and enjoying them in meals sporadically throughout the week.

Batch cooking is a great idea and works especially well with dishes that freeze well. Definitely embrace this method of meal prepping as you wish!

For the menus in this section, I'm focusing on another meal-prep method: make-ahead meals. It's the most comprehensive way to make sure you're able to easily stick to a healthful eating plan. I've included all of the recipe guidance you need for preparing these simple meals. Ideally, anything that can be made in advance should be made in advance. Once prepped, anything that's not shelf-stable should be stored in the fridge (and occasionally the freezer) as needed.

I advise 2 prep days a week so your make-ahead meals stay fresh. Refrigerated meals should ideally be eaten within 3–4 days. Set aside Sunday and Wednesday to do as much of the cooking for the entire week as possible. (I've indicated those prep times on the menus for you.) If those days don't work well for you, pick the days that do. Since the meals are easy to make, it won't require all day; but do set aside a couple hours on each of these 2 days. And if you're able to get someone else to help, it'll be faster and more fun.

Don't worry if you don't always have extra time for meal prepping a couple days per week; just aim to do whatever you can in advance. For instance, you can make all of the lunches for you (and your family) in advance a couple days a week, so you don't need to worry about those during workdays. And if you're simply not the meal-prepping type and prefer to do all of your cooking only as needed from day-to-day, you can still follow these menus!

Other Meal-Prepping Advice

Before getting started meal prepping, make sure you have a well-stocked pantry so that all you need to purchase each week at the market are fresh and frozen items. Make sure you have plenty of containers in which to store your make-ahead meals, too. If necessary, they can be stored in family-style portions rather than individual portions so you can use fewer containers.

Of course, make sure you also have the space in the fridge for your make-ahead meals. Label everything with what's in the container along with the date.

What about if you dine out? There may absolutely be times that you and your family dine out instead of enjoying a make-ahead meal. Or perhaps you're going to be out of town for a few days and won't be eating at home. If that's the case, consider which meals may freeze well, then prepare and freeze accordingly. Or just have a part-week plan; maybe you do your meal-prepping on Sunday evening that week and skip it on Wednesday evening, for instance.

MENU DETAILS

In this section, you'll find 2 weeks of detailed meal-prep menus designed for a family of four as well 2 weeks of detailed meal-prep menus for one. If you're cooking for two, you can just double everything on the "cooking for one" menus. Or you can follow the "Cooking for Four" menus and plan to use your freezer wisely, saving the extra portions for when you need them. Freezer meals should ideally be eaten within 2 months. After finishing the 2 weeks of menus, you can simply put them on repeat!

By the way, if you're not sure that you want to jump in with both feet by putting this 2-week menu plan into rotation, you can first begin by just picking 2 days of menus; then, you can rotate those same menus throughout the week. Then, for the next week, pick two different menus. And so on.

Any dishes you've prepared ahead of time that need to be served hot can be reheated in the microwave until steamy. Feel free to give menu items your own special touch by adding (for example) herbs, spices, or a splash of lemon or lime juice, vinegar, or hot sauce. Try to plate your foods attractively; don't just eat straight out of a storage container! We eat with our eyes, too. Finally, be sure to plan for calorie-free beverages, such as water or unsweetened tea, to enjoy along with every meal and snack, too.

Tips for What to Make and When

Make Your Shopping List and Go Shopping:

To save time, aim to do your meal-prep grocery shopping one day each week, such as Sunday morning (for example). Make your shopping list based on the weekly menus. Check first to see what you have in your pantry. Restock staple pantry ingredients that you're low on. And buy all fresh and frozen items for the week. However, it's OK to wait to buy certain items until they're needed so they stay fresh, like fish. Remember to save your grocery list so you can easily shop for your meal plan the next time you use these same menus.

What to Make on Sunday:

Prepare meals and snacks for Sunday (dinner only—to enjoy that evening), Monday, Tuesday, and Wednesday (breakfast, lunch, and snacks only). Ideally prepare dishes with the longest cooking times first, saving the no-cook items for last.

What to Make on Wednesday:

Prepare meals and snacks for Wednesday (dinner only—to enjoy that evening), Thursday, Friday, Saturday, and Sunday (breakfast, lunch, and snacks only). Ideally prepare dishes with the longest cooking times first, saving the no-cook items for last.

(Note: These menus are designed based on Sunday and Wednesday prep days. However, you don't need to prep your meals on Sundays and Wednesdays, if that's not ideal for you. The guidelines above can be adapted to fit your meal-prep schedule.)

Other Tips

- You don't need to cook entire recipes one at a time. When two or more meals or snacks use the same ingredient, like an onion, pre-prep that ingredient for all meals or snacks at the same time to save time. The same rule applies if you're serving the same dish for two (or more) separate meals or snacks.
- There are some foods that are best when not prepped in advance. For instance, a pre-sliced avocado can brown, and pre-tossed salads can wilt. Always wait until serving time to prepare dressed leafy salads.
- When reheating pre-prepared meals, adding a splash of water may help moisten certain recipes, especially when they include grains, poultry, or meat.

WEEKLY MENUS

Per serving, each meal provides 340–520 calories and a maximum of about 60 grams of total carbohydrate; each snack provides 100–210 calories and a maximum of about 21 grams of total carbohydrate. Two snack options are provided each day—include one or both snacks, if your meal plan includes snacks, at the time(s) best for you. The daily totals for calories and carbohydrate listed for each day are *per serving* and include *all three meals and both snacks*. For any ingredient in these menus, be sure to choose no-sugar-added and lower-sodium options when possible.

Do check with your registered dietitian or other diabetes healthcare provider to make sure these meal plans meet your individualized needs—or ask your provider for guidance on how to adjust these menus so that they're personalized just for you. Once you get the hang of following the meal plans, try creating additional menus of your own. Now, let's get started!

TWO WEEKS OF MENUS WHEN COOKING FOR FOUR

SUNDAY

Breakfast (410 calories and 31 grams of total carbohydrate):

- No-cook breakfast platter (serves 4): 3 cups low-fat cottage cheese + 4 cups sliced fresh or thawed frozen peaches + 1 1/3 cups shelled, roasted, unsalted pistachios | Arrange all ingredients on a platter.

Lunch (470 calories and 43 grams of total carbohydrate):

- **Tuscan Turkey Sausage Stew** (page 280)
- Dressed tomatoes (serves 4): 1 pint cherry or grape tomatoes, halved + 1 tablespoon extra-virgin olive oil + 2 teaspoons red wine vinegar | Toss all ingredients together at serving time.

HINT: IT'S PREP TIME!

Dinner (390 calories and 22 grams of total carbohydrate):

- **Pan-Grilled Curry-in-a-Hurry Chicken Thighs** (page 192)
- Sautéed peppers (serves 4): 2 teaspoons avocado oil or sunflower oil + 2 large red bell peppers, sliced + 4 lime wedges | Heat oil in a skillet over medium-high heat. Sauté the peppers until lightly browned. Serve with lime.
- Avocado (serves 4): 1 Hass avocado, sliced
- Fruit (serves 4): 5 kiwifruits, sliced, or 4 fruit servings of choice

Snack 1 (170 calories and 16 grams of total carbohydrate):

- Veggies and guacamole (serves 4): 1 pound baby carrots + 1 cup store-bought guacamole

Snack 2 (140 calories and 15 grams of total carbohydrate):

- Fruit and cheese (serves 4): 4 small apples + 4 pieces string cheese

Daily Total (including snacks): 1,480 calories and 127 grams of carbohydrate per serving

MONDAY

Breakfast (390 calories and 38 grams of total carbohydrate):

- Savory Greek yogurt (serves 4): 32 ounces plain 0% fat Greek yogurt + 2 tablespoons extra-virgin olive oil + 1/2 cup roasted, salted chickpea snacks + 1/4 cup fresh mint leaves + 1/2 English cucumber, sliced + 4 ounces whole-grain pita chips | Divide the yogurt evenly among 4 jars or small bowls with lids, top with the olive oil, chickpea snack, and mint leaves; serve the cucumber sliced and pita chips on the side.

Lunch (340 calories and 28 grams of total carbohydrate):

- Deli quesadillas (serves 4): 4 (8-inch) whole-grain tortillas + 4 ounces natural reduced-sodium turkey breast + 3/4 cup shredded Gruyère or other cheese + 1 tablespoon avocado oil or sunflower oil | Top each tortilla with the cheese and turkey. Fold, brush with the oil, and cook (in batches) in a skillet over medium-high heat until the cheese just melts.
- Side salad (serves 4): 1 (5-ounce) package fresh baby salad greens (mesclun) + 3 tablespoons no-sugar-added vinaigrette of choice | Toss ingredients together at serving time; serve on the side or on top of the quesadillas.
- Fruit (serves 4): 4 small apples

Dinner (440 calories and 42 grams of total carbohydrate):

- **"Vintage" Vegetable & Chicken Bake** (page 196) (Note: Recipe makes 8 servings, so it's on Tuesday's menu, too.)
- Veggies and hummus (serves 4): 2 large red or orange bell peppers, sliced + 1 1/2 cups hummus

Snack 1 (160 calories and 17 grams of total carbohydrate):

- Fruit and nuts (serves 4): 2 cups

red seedless grapes + 1/2 cup whole roasted or smoked almonds

Snack 2 (160 calories and 13 grams of total carbohydrate):

- Veggies and dip (serves 4): 1 pound baby carrots + 1/2 cup natural Caesar or ranch dressing

Daily Total (including snacks): 1,490 calories and 138 grams of carbohydrate per serving

TUESDAY

Breakfast (430 calories and 46 grams of total carbohydrate):

- Yogurt bowl (serves 4): 48 ounces plain 0% fat Greek yogurt + 2 cups thawed frozen raspberries or sliced strawberries + 2 cups no-sugar-added granola + 2 tablespoons roasted, unsalted sunflower seeds | Divide the yogurt evenly among 4 bowls or jars, then top with the berries, granola, and seeds.

Lunch (460 calories and 51 grams of total carbohydrate):

- Hummus wrap (serves 4): 4 (8-inch) whole-grain tortillas + 1 1/3 cups hummus + 2 cups baby salad greens (mesclun) + 4 teaspoons lemon juice | Top each tortilla with 1/3 cup hummus, 1/2 cup greens, and 1 teaspoon lemon juice, and wrap.
- Veggies (serves 4): 1 pound baby carrots
- Seeds (serves 4): 3/4 cup roasted, unsalted sunflower seeds

Dinner (440 calories and 43 grams of total carbohydrate):

- **"Vintage" Vegetable & Chicken Bake** (page 196)
  (Note: Recipe makes 8 servings, so it's on Monday's menu, too.)
- Fruit and yogurt (serves 4): 2 cups thawed frozen raspberries or sliced strawberries + 32 ounces plain 0% fat Greek yogurt

Snack 1 (170 calories and 17 grams of total carbohydrate):

- Veggies and hummus (serves 4): 4 cups sliced English cucumber + 1 1/2 cups hummus

Snack 2 (190 calories and 19 grams of total carbohydrate):

- Fruit and nut butter (serves 4): 2 medium bananas, halved + 1/3 cup natural, unsweetened peanut butter

Daily Total (including snacks): 1,690 calories and 176 grams of carbohydrate per serving

WEDNESDAY

Breakfast (390 calories and 46 grams of total carbohydrate):

- Avocado and egg toast (serves 4): 4 slices whole-grain bread, toasted + 2 Hass avocados + 2 teaspoons lemon juice + 5 large hard-boiled eggs, sliced | On each slice of toast, mash 1/2 avocado, drizzle with 1/2 teaspoon lemon juice, and arrange slices from 1 hard-boiled egg on top.
- Fruit (serves 4): 4 cups red seedless grapes

Lunch (340 calories and 34 grams of total carbohydrate):

- Deli-style chicken salad sandwich

halves (serves 4): 4 slices whole-grain bread, halved + 1 1/3 cups deli-prepared chicken salad + 2 cups fresh baby arugula | Serve the chicken salad and arugula in between the bread halves
- Fruit and yogurt (serves 4): 2 cups fresh or thawed frozen cherries + 24 ounces plain 0% fat Greek yogurt

HINT: IT'S PREP TIME!

Dinner (400 calories and 27 grams of total carbohydrate):

- **Korean BBQ–Inspired Baked Salmon** (page 170)
- Veggies (serves 4): 1 pound fresh baby spinach, wilted in the microwave or a skillet
- Grains (serves 4): 1 1/2 cups cooked brown rice or whole-wheat couscous

Snack 1 (160 calories and 17 grams of total carbohydrate):

- Fruit and nuts (serves 4): 2 cups red seedless grapes + 1/2 cup whole roasted or smoked almonds

Snack 2 (160 calories and 13 grams of total carbohydrate):

- Veggies and dip (serves 4): 1 pound baby carrots + 1/2 cup natural Caesar or ranch dressing

Daily Total (including snacks): 1,450 calories and 137 grams of carbohydrate per serving

THURSDAY

Breakfast (400 calories and 45 grams of total carbohydrate):

- Toasted PB&J sandwiches (serves 4): 8 slices whole-grain bread, toasted + 1/2 cup natural, unsweetened peanut butter + 1/4 cup fruit-sweetened strawberry fruit spread (jam)
- Veggie (serves 4): 4 cups celery sticks

Lunch (440 calories and 9 grams of total carbohydrate):

- Protein-powered chef salad (serves 4): 8 cups packed fresh baby salad greens (mesclun) + 2 tablespoons extra-virgin olive oil + 2 tablespoons lemon juice + 1 pound pre-cooked (rotisserie) chicken, both white and dark meat + 4 hard-boiled eggs, sliced + 2/3 cup trail mix | At serving time, toss the salad greens with the oil and lemon juice. Top with the chicken, eggs, and trail mix.

Dinner (360 calories and 40 grams of total carbohydrate):

- **Salsa, Chicken, Sweet Potatoes & Black Beans** (page 98)
- Seeds (serves 4): 3 tablespoons pumpkin or sunflower seeds (to sprinkle on entrée)

Snack 1 (150 calories and 19 grams of total carbohydrate):

- **Buffalo Garbanzo Snackers** (page 70) | Ideally prepare at snack time.

Snack 2 (190 calories and 12 grams of total carbohydrate):

- Munchies (serves 4): 1 1/3 cups trail mix

Daily Total (including snacks): 1,540 calories and 125 grams of carbohydrate per serving

FRIDAY

Breakfast (390 calories and 46 grams of total carbohydrate):

- Bagel breakfast (serves 4): 4 ounces Neufchâtel (light cream cheese) + 2 bakery-style whole-grain "everything" or other whole-grain bagels, halved and toasted + 1/2 English cucumber, thinly sliced | Spread the Neufchâtel onto the toasted bagel halves and arrange the cucumber slices on top.
- Munchies (serves 4): 1 cup trail mix

Lunch (410 calories and 47 grams of total carbohydrate):

- PB&J sandwiches (serves 4): 8 slices whole-grain bread + 1/2 cup natural, unsweetened peanut butter + 1/4 cup fruit-sweetened strawberry fruit spread (jam)
- Veggies (serves 4): 1 1/2 English cucumbers, sliced

Dinner (390 calories and 43 grams of total carbohydrate):

- **Caramelized Cauliflower & Herbs on Bed of Hummus** (page 148)

- Veggies (serves 4): 12 ounces frozen shelled edamame, boiled
- Fruit (serves 4): 2 cups red seedless grapes

Snack 1 (200 calories and 10 grams of total carbohydrate):

- Cottage cheese platter (serves 4): 2 cups low-fat cottage cheese + 1 pint cherry or grape tomatoes + 1/2 cup whole roasted or smoked almonds

Snack 2 (190 calories and 19 grams of total carbohydrate):

- Fruit and nut butter (serves 4): 2 medium bananas, halved + 1/3 cup natural, unsweetened peanut butter

Daily Total (including snacks): 1,580 calories and 165 grams of carbohydrate per serving

SATURDAY

Breakfast (390 calories and 46 grams of total carbohydrate):

- Bagel breakfast (serves 4): 4 ounces Neufchâtel (light cream cheese) + 2 bakery-style whole-grain "everything" or other whole-grain bagels,

halved and toasted + 1/2 English cucumber, sliced | Spread the Neufchâtel onto the toasted bagel halves and arrange the cucumber slices on top.
- Munchies (serves 4): 1 cup trail mix

Lunch (390 calories and 43 grams of total carbohydrate):
- **Caramelized Cauliflower & Herbs on Bed of Hummus** (page 148)
- Veggies (serves 4): 12 ounces frozen shelled edamame, boiled
- Fruit (serves 4): 2 cups red seedless grapes

Dinner (370 calories and 43 grams of total carbohydrate):
- **Tuscan Turkey Sausage Stew** (page 280)
(Note: Recipe is on Sunday's menu, too.)

- Dressed tomatoes (serves 4): 1 pint cherry or grape tomatoes, halved + 1 tablespoon extra-virgin olive oil + 2 teaspoons red wine vinegar | Toss all ingredients together.

Snack 1 (180 calories and 20 grams of total carbohydrate):
- Fruit and yogurt (serves 4): 2 cups thawed frozen raspberries or sliced strawberries + 32 ounces plain 0% fat Greek yogurt

Snack 2 (130 calories and 14 grams of total carbohydrate):
- Veggies and hummus (serves 4): 8 ounces baby carrots + 1 cup hummus

Daily Total (including snacks): 1,460 calories and 166 grams of carbohydrate per serving

SUNDAY

Breakfast (400 calories and 33 grams of total carbohydrate):

- **Party Pan Chicken Sausage Frittata** (page 114)
  (Note: Recipe makes 8 servings; it was on Saturday's menu, too.)
- Avocado and egg toast (serves 4): 4 slices whole-grain bread, toasted + 2 Hass avocados + 2 teaspoons lemon juice | On each slice of toast, mash 1/2 avocado and drizzle with 1/2 teaspoon lemon juice. Ideally prepare at breakfast time.
- Fruit (serves 4): 1/2 cup dried, unsulfured apricots or figs

Lunch (380 calories and 47 grams of total carbohydrate):

- **Turkey Jambalaya** (page 102)
- Wilted spinach (serves 4): 1 tablespoon extra-virgin olive oil + 1 (5-ounce) package fresh baby spinach + 1/8 teaspoon sea salt + 4 lemon wedges | At serving time, heat the oil in a large skillet over medium heat. Add the spinach and toss until wilted. Sprinkle with the salt. Serve with the lemon wedges.

Dinner (450 calories and 48 grams of total carbohydrate):

- **All-American Portobello "Cheeseburgers"** (page 140)
- Side salad (serves 4): 1 (5-ounce) package fresh baby arugula + 3 tablespoons no-sugar-added vinaigrette of choice + 1/2 cup shelled, roasted, unsalted pistachios (or nuts of choice) | Toss all ingredients together at serving time.

Snack 1 (150 calories and 7 grams of total carbohydrate):

- Tomatoes and cheese plate (serves 4): 1 pint grape tomatoes + 4 pieces string cheese + 1/3 cup shelled, roasted, unsalted pistachios (or nuts of choice) | Arrange all ingredients on a plate.

Snack 2 (140 calories and 17 grams of total carbohydrate):

- Fruit and yogurt (serves 4): 24 ounces plain 0% fat Greek yogurt + 2 cups fresh or thawed frozen cherries

Daily Total (including snacks): 1,520 calories and 152 grams of carbohydrate per serving

MONDAY

Breakfast (410 calories and 31 grams of total carbohydrate):

- No-cook breakfast platter (serves 4): 3 cups low-fat cottage cheese + 4 cups sliced fresh or thawed frozen peaches + 1 1/3 cups shelled, roasted, unsalted pistachios | Arrange all ingredients on a platter.

Lunch (390 calories and 44 grams of total carbohydrate):

- **Asian Peanut Soba Noodles with Slaw** (page 132)
- Chicken (serves 4): Sliced or shredded chicken from 2 pre-cooked (rotisserie) chicken breasts | Toss with the soba noodles and slaw.

Dinner (350 calories and 37 grams of total carbohydrate):

- Veggie burgers (serves 4): 4 frozen veggie burgers (preferably bean-based) + 4 whole-grain English muffins + 3 cups fresh baby salad greens

(mesclun) + 1/4 cup fruit-sweetened or no-sugar-added ketchup + 2 tablespoons mayonnaise | At serving time, prepare the veggie burgers according to package directions. Serve in English muffins with the greens, ketchup, and mayonnaise.

- Avocado (serves 4): 1 Hass avocado, sliced

Snack 1 (210 calories and 16 grams of total carbohydrate):

- Fruit, yogurt, and nuts (serves 4): 1 1/2 cups sliced fresh or thawed frozen peaches + 24 ounces plain 0% fat Greek yogurt + 1/2 cup shelled, roasted, unsalted pistachios

Snack 2 (180 calories and 19 grams of total carbohydrate):

- Veggies and hummus (serves 4): 8 ounces baby carrots + 1 1/2 cups hummus

Daily Total (including snacks): 1,540 calories and 147 grams of carbohydrate per serving

TUESDAY

Breakfast (380 calories and 51 grams of total carbohydrate):

- Bagel breakfast (serves 4): 4 ounces Neufchâtel (light cream cheese) + 2 bakery-style whole-grain "everything" or other whole-grain bagels, halved and toasted + 1/2 English cucumber, sliced | Spread Neufchâtel onto the toasted bagel halves and arrange cucumber slices on top.
- Fruit and seeds (serves 4): 1/2 cup dried, unsulfured apricots or prunes + 1/2 cup roasted, unsalted sunflower seeds

Lunch (380 calories and 40 grams of total carbohydrate):

- Fast Mexican salad (serves 4): 8 ounces fresh baby salad greens (mesclun) + 1 (15-ounce) can unsalted kidney or black beans, drained + 1 Hass avocado, cubed + 2 1/2 ounces Monterey Jack cheese, cubed + 4 ounces tortilla chips + 3/4 cup preservative-free salsa verde | Toss all ingredients together at serving time.

Dinner (420 calories and 40 grams of total carbohydrate):

- **Turkey Meatballs Arrabbiata** (page 206)
- Rolls (serves 4): 4 small (1 1/2-ounce) whole-grain rolls
- Tomato and herb salad (serves 4): 3 large tomatoes, sliced + 1/4 cup packed fresh basil or mint leaves + 2 teaspoons red wine vinegar + 2 teaspoons extra-virgin olive oil | Arrange the tomato slices on a platter. Sprinkle with the basil or mint, vinegar, and olive oil.

Snack 1 (190 calories and 9 grams of total carbohydrate):

- Cottage cheese platter (serves 4): 2 cups low-fat cottage cheese + 1/2 English cucumber, sliced + 1/2 cup whole roasted or smoked almonds

Snack 2 (160 calories and 17 grams of total carbohydrate):

- Fruit and nuts (serves 4): 2 cups red seedless grapes + 1/2 cup whole roasted or smoked almonds

Daily Total (including snacks): 1,530 calories and 157 grams of carbohydrate per serving

WEDNESDAY

Breakfast (410 calories and 31 grams of total carbohydrate):

- No-cook breakfast platter (serves 4): 3 cups low-fat cottage cheese + 4 cups sliced fresh or thawed frozen peaches + 1 1/3 cups shelled, roasted, unsalted pistachios | Arrange all ingredients on a platter.

Lunch (350 calories and 37 grams of total carbohydrate):

- Veggie burgers (serves 4): 4 frozen veggie burgers (preferably bean-based) + 4 whole-grain English muffins + 3 cups fresh baby salad greens (mesclun) + 1/4 cup fruit-sweetened or no-sugar-added ketchup + 2 tablespoons mayonnaise | Prepare veggie burgers according to package directions. Serve in English muffins with the greens, ketchup, and mayonnaise. (Note: Ideally prepare in advance at dinner time on Monday.)
- Avocado (serves 4): 1 Hass avocado, sliced

HINT: IT'S PREP TIME!

Dinner (500 calories and 36 grams of total carbohydrate):

- **Cajun Fish & Roasted Cherry Tomatoes** (page 172)
- Grains (serves 4): 2 cups cooked farro or brown rice
- Side salad (serves 4): 1 (5-ounce) package fresh baby arugula + 1/2 cup shelled, roasted, unsalted pistachios + 3 tablespoons no-sugar-added vinaigrette of choice | Toss all ingredients together at serving time.

Snack 1 (140 calories and 20 grams of total carbohydrate):

- Fruit, cheese, and pita chips (serves 4): 1 1/2 cups red seedless grapes + 2 ounces feta cheese (preferably block) + 2 ounces whole-grain pita chips

Snack 2 (120 calories and 4 grams of total carbohydrate):

- Veggies and dip (serves 4): 1/2 English cucumber, sliced + 1/2 cup natural Caesar or ranch dressing

Daily Total (including snacks): 1,520 calories and 128 grams of carbohydrate per serving

THURSDAY

Breakfast (380 calories and 30 grams of total carbohydrate):

- Hummus toast (serves 4): 4 slices whole-grain bread, toasted + 2 cups hummus + 1 tablespoon extra-virgin olive oil + 1 teaspoon hot pepper sauce | At serving time, top each slice of toast with 1/2 cup hummus. Drizzle each slice with 3/4 teaspoon oil and 1/4 teaspoon hot pepper sauce.
- Eggs (serves 4): 4 hard-boiled eggs

Lunch (380 calories and 40 grams of total carbohydrate):

- Fast Mexican salad (serves 4): 8 ounces fresh baby salad greens (mesclun) + 1 (15-ounce) can unsalted kidney or black beans, drained + 1 Hass avocado, cubed + 2 1/2 ounces Monterey Jack cheese, cubed + 4 ounces tortilla chips + 3/4 cup preservative-free salsa verde | Toss all ingredients together at serving time.

Dinner (520 calories and 57 grams of total carbohydrate):

- **Sheet Pan Zucchini, Red Pepper & Tofu "Stir-Fry"** (page 156)
- Grains (serves 4): 2 cups cooked farro or brown rice + 1/4 cup sesame seeds
- Fruit (serves 4): 4 mandarin oranges or 2 large oranges
- Nuts (serves 4): 1/2 cup roasted, unsalted peanuts (sprinkle onto "stir-fry")

Snack 1 (160 calories and 18 grams of total carbohydrate):

- Fruit and nuts (serves 4): 4 mandarin oranges or 2 large oranges + 1/2 cup roasted, unsalted peanuts

Snack 2 (160 calories and 19 grams of total carbohydrate):

- Chips and salsa (serves 4): 4 ounces tortilla chips + 1/2 cup preservative-free salsa verde

Daily Total (including snacks): 1,600 calories and 164 grams of carbohydrate per serving

FRIDAY

Breakfast (370 calories and 38 grams of total carbohydrate):
- **Savory Tzatziki-Style Yogurt** (page 110)
- Bread (serves 4): 3 large whole-grain pitas, cut into wedges

Lunch (430 calories and 49 grams of total carbohydrate):
- **Sporty Halftime Chili** (page 282)
- Side salad (serves 4): 1 (5-ounce) package fresh baby spinach + 1/3 cup shelled, roasted, unsalted pistachios + 3 tablespoons no-sugar-added vinaigrette of choice | Toss all ingredients together at serving time.
- Cheese (served 4): 3 ounces Monterey Jack cheese, shredded or diced (add onto chili)

Dinner (390 calories and 47 grams of total carbohydrate):
- Pasta marinara with sausage bowls (serves 4): 6 ounces dry whole-wheat penne + 4 (3-ounce) links pre-cooked natural turkey or chicken sausage + 4 teaspoons extra-virgin olive oil + 3/4 cup no-sugar-added, unsalted marinara sauce + 1 (5-ounce) package fresh baby arugula or spinach | Boil the pasta according to package directions; drain. Pan-cook the sausage links in oil according to package directions, then slice into coins. Toss the pasta with the marinara, sausage, and arugula.

Snack 1 (160 calories and 19 grams of total carbohydrate):
- Chips and salsa (serves 4): 4 ounces tortilla chips + 1/2 cup preservative-free salsa verde

Snack 2 (150 calories and 19 grams of total carbohydrate):
- **Buffalo Garbanzo Snackers** (page 70) | Ideally prepare at snack-time.

Daily Total (including snacks): 1,500 calories and 172 grams of carbohydrate per serving

SATURDAY

Breakfast (430 calories and 46 grams of total carbohydrate):

- Yogurt bowl (serves 4): 48 ounces plain 0% fat Greek yogurt + 2 cups thawed frozen raspberries or sliced strawberries + 2 cups no-sugar-added granola + 2 tablespoons roasted, unsalted sunflower seeds | Divide the yogurt evenly among 4 bowls or jars, then top with the berries, granola, and seeds.

Lunch (400 calories and 33 grams of total carbohydrate):

- **Party Pan Chicken Sausage Frittata** (page 114)
  (Note: Recipe makes 8 servings, so it's on Sunday's menu, too.)
- Avocado and egg toast (serves 4): 4 slices whole-grain bread, toasted + 2 Hass avocados + 2 teaspoons lemon juice | On each slice of toast, mash 1/2 avocado, drizzle with 1/2 teaspoon lemon juice. Ideally prepare at breakfast time.
- Fruit (serves 4): 1/2 cup dried, unsulfured apricots or figs

Dinner (360 calories and 23 grams of total carbohydrate):

- **BBQ Chicken Strips** (page 186)
- Side salad (serves 4): 1 (5-ounce) package fresh baby spinach + 3 tablespoons no-sugar-added vinaigrette of choice | Toss all ingredients together at serving time. If desired, serve the BBQ chicken strips on top.
- Fruit (serves 4): 2 cups red seedless grapes

Snack 1 (120 calories and 4 grams of total carbohydrate):

- Veggies and dip (serves 4): 1/2 English cucumber, sliced + 1/2 cup natural Caesar or ranch dressing

Snack 2 (180 calories and 19 grams of total carbohydrate):

- Veggies and hummus (serves 4): 8 ounces baby carrots + 1 1/2 cups hummus

Daily Total (including snacks): 1,490 calories and 125 grams of carbohydrate per serving

TWO WEEKS OF MENUS WHEN COOKING FOR ONE

SUNDAY

Breakfast (470 calories and 60 grams of total carbohydrate):

- **Savory Farmer's Market Oatmeal—** 1 serving (page 120)
  (Note: Recipe makes 2 servings, so it's on Wednesday's menu, too.)
- Fruit, yogurt, and nuts: 1 cup plain 0% fat Greek yogurt + 1/2 cup thawed frozen raspberries or sliced strawberries + 2 tablespoons sliced almonds

Lunch (380 calories and 41 grams of total carbohydrate):

- Avocado and egg toast: 1/2 Hass avocado + 1 slice whole-grain bread, toasted + 1/2 teaspoon lemon juice + 1 large hard-boiled egg, sliced | At serving time, mash the avocado on the toast, drizzle with the lemon juice, and arrange the egg slices on top.

- **Saucy Caribbean Beans**—1 serving (page 246)
  (Note: Recipe makes 4 servings; it's on Friday's and Saturday's menus, too.)
- Veggies: 1 cup grape or cherry tomatoes

HINT: IT'S PREP TIME!

Dinner (470 calories and 46 grams of total carbohydrate):

- **Sheet Pan Eggplant Parmesan with Vine Tomatoes**—1 serving (page 154)
  (Note: Recipe makes 2 servings, so it's on Monday's menu, too.)
- Spaghetti marinara: 1 ounce dry red lentil or other spaghetti + 3 tablespoons no-sugar-added, unsalted marinara sauce + 2 teaspoons pine nuts | Prepare the spaghetti according to package directions. Toss with the marinara and top with the pine nuts.

Snack 1 (130 calories and 14 grams of total carbohydrate):

- Veggies and dip: 1 cup baby carrots + 1 1/2 tablespoons natural Caesar or ranch dressing

Snack 2 (150 calories and 18 grams of total carbohydrate):

- Fruit and nut butter: 1 extra-small apple + 1 tablespoon natural, unsweetened almond or peanut butter.

Daily Total (including snacks): 1,600 calories and 179 grams of carbohydrate

MONDAY

Breakfast (330 calories and 31 grams of total carbohydrate):

- **Just Peachy Yogurt & Granola Jar**—1 serving (page 108) (Note: Recipe makes 2 servings, so it's on Tuesday's menu, too.)
- Egg: 1 hard-boiled egg
- Nuts: 6 whole roasted or smoked almonds

Lunch (390 calories and 43 grams of total carbohydrate):

- PB&J sandwich: 2 slices whole-grain bread + 2 tablespoons natural, unsweetened almond butter + 2 teaspoons fruit-sweetened strawberry fruit spread (jam)
- Veggie: 1 cup broccoli florets, raw or cooked

Dinner (470 calories and 46 grams of total carbohydrate):

- **Sheet Pan Eggplant Parmesan with Vine Tomatoes**—1 serving (page 154)
- Spaghetti marinara: 1 ounce dry red lentil or other spaghetti + 3 tablespoons no-sugar-added, unsalted marinara sauce + 2 teaspoons pine nuts | Prepare the spaghetti according to package directions. Toss with the marinara and top with pine nuts.

Snack 1 (150 calories and 13 grams of total carbohydrate):

- Tomatoes and avocado: 1 cup grape tomatoes + 1/2 avocado, sliced + 1 teaspoon lemon juice

Snack 2 (190 calories and 12 grams of total carbohydrate):

- Munchies: 1/3 cup trail mix

Daily Total (including snacks): 1,530 calories and 145 grams of carbohydrate

TUESDAY

Breakfast (330 calories and 31 grams of total carbohydrate):

- **Just Peachy Yogurt & Granola Jar—** 1 serving (page 108) (Note: Recipe makes 2 servings, so it's on Monday's menu, too.)
- Egg: 1 hard-boiled egg
- Nuts: 6 whole roasted or smoked almonds

Lunch (400 calories and 48 grams of total carbohydrate):

- **Overstuffed Veggie & Hummus Sandwich** (page 136)
- Nuts: 6 whole roasted or smoked almonds

Dinner (380 calories and 40 grams of total carbohydrate):

- **"Love Your Leftovers" BBQ Bowl** (page 100)
- Mini salad: 1 cup packed fresh baby arugula + 2 teaspoons no-sugar-added vinaigrette of choice | Toss all ingredients together at serving time.

Snack 1 (140 calories and 16 grams of total carbohydrate):

- Fruit and nuts: 1/2 Texas red or pink grapefruit + 2 tablespoons roasted, unsalted sunflower seeds

Snack 2 (130 calories and 14 grams of total carbohydrate):

- Veggies and dip: 1 cup baby carrots + 1 1/2 tablespoons natural Caesar or ranch dressing

Daily Total (including snacks): 1,380 calories and 149 grams of carbohydrate

WEDNESDAY

Breakfast (470 calories and 60 grams of total carbohydrate):

- **Savory Farmer's Market Oatmeal—** 1 serving (page 120) (Note: Recipe makes 2 servings, so it's on Sunday's menu, too.)
- Fruit, yogurt, and nuts: 1 cup plain 0% fat Greek yogurt + 1/2 cup thawed frozen raspberries or sliced strawberries + 2 tablespoons sliced almonds

Lunch (390 calories and 42 grams of total carbohydrate):

- PB&J sandwich: 2 slices whole-grain bread + 2 tablespoons natural, unsweetened peanut butter + 2 teaspoons fruit-sweetened strawberry fruit spread (jam)
- Veggie: 1 cup broccoli florets, raw or cooked

HINT: IT'S PREP TIME!

Dinner (510 calories and 32 grams of total carbohydrate):

- **Spice-Rubbed Salmon**—1 serving (page 168)
- Grains: 1/2 cup cooked farro or brown rice
- Veggie: 10 spears asparagus + 2 teaspoons extra-virgin olive oil | Toss the asparagus with the oil. Pan-grill or pan-cook until desired doneness.

Snack 1 & 2 (130 + 130 calories and 18 + 18 grams of total carbohydrate):

- **BBQ Popcorn** (page 72) (Note: Recipe makes 2 servings, so enjoy 1 serving for each snack!)

Daily Total (including snacks): 1,630 calories and 170 grams of carbohydrate

THURSDAY

Breakfast (510 calories and 58 grams of total carbohydrate):

- **Superfood Breakfast Burrito—** 1 serving (page 90) (Note: Recipe makes 2 servings, so it's on Friday's menu, too.)
- Fruit and cottage cheese: 1 cup thawed frozen or fresh peach slices + 1/2 cup low-fat cottage cheese

Lunch (440 calories and 31 grams of total carbohydrate):

- **Mason Jar Sesame Chicken Salad** (page 208)
- Fruit: 1 medium orange
- Nuts: 2 tablespoons roasted, unsalted peanuts (serve on the salad)

Dinner (360 calories and 40 grams of total carbohydrate):

- Pesto pasta with chicken: 1 1/2 ounces dry whole-wheat linguine + 3 ounces deli-prepared chicken breast, thinly sliced + 1 1/2 tablespoons jarred pesto sauce + 1 lemon wedge | Boil the pasta according to package directions. Drain and rinse in cold water (or toss with ice) to cool. Toss the pasta with the pesto and chicken. Serve with the lemon.
- Simple dressed tomatoes: 1 cup cherry or grape tomatoes, halved + 1 teaspoon extra-virgin olive oil + 1 teaspoon red wine vinegar | Toss all ingredients together at serving time.

Snack 1 (150 calories and 17 grams of total carbohydrate):

- Fruit and nuts: 1 extra-small apple + 12 whole roasted or smoked almonds

Snack 2 (130 calories and 14 grams of total carbohydrate):

- Veggies and dip: 1 cup baby carrots + 1 1/2 tablespoons natural Caesar or ranch dressing

Daily Total (including snacks): 1,590 calories and 160 grams of carbohydrate

FRIDAY

Breakfast (510 calories and 58 grams of total carbohydrate):

- **Superfood Breakfast Burrito—** 1 serving (page 90) (Note: Recipe makes 2 servings, so it's on Thursday's menu, too.)
- Fruit and cottage cheese: 1 cup thawed frozen or fresh peach slices + 1/2 cup low-fat cottage cheese

Lunch (360 calories and 40 grams of total carbohydrate):

- Pesto pasta with chicken: 1 1/2 ounces dry whole-wheat linguine + 3 ounces deli-prepared chicken breast, thinly sliced + 1 1/2 tablespoons jarred pesto sauce + 1 lemon wedge | Boil the pasta according to package directions. Drain and rinse in cold water (or toss with ice) to cool. Toss the pasta with the pesto and chicken. Serve with the lemon.

- Simple dressed tomatoes: 1 cup cherry or grape tomatoes, halved + 1 teaspoon extra-virgin olive oil + 1 teaspoon red wine vinegar | Toss all ingredients together at serving time.

Dinner (360 calories and 41 grams of total carbohydrate):

- **Spiced Cauliflower Roast**—1 serving (page 146)
  (Note: Recipe makes 2 servings, so it's on Saturday's menu, too.)
- **Saucy Caribbean Beans**—1 serving (page 246)
  (Note: Recipe makes 4 servings, so it's on Saturday and Sunday's menus, too.)
- Avocado: 1/2 Hass avocado, sliced

Snack 1 (150 calories and 7 grams of total carbohydrate):

- Dressed tomatoes and cheese: 1 cup cherry or grape tomatoes, halved +

1 teaspoon extra-virgin olive oil + 1 teaspoon red wine vinegar + 1 piece string cheese, sliced or diced | Toss all ingredients together at serving time.

Snack 2 (190 calories and 12 grams of total carbohydrate):

- Munchies: 1/3 cup trail mix

Daily Total (including snacks): 1,570 calories and 158 grams of carbohydrate

SATURDAY

Breakfast (430 calories and 46 grams of total carbohydrate):

- Yogurt bowl (serves 4): 12 ounces plain 0% fat Greek yogurt + 1/2 cup thawed frozen raspberries or sliced strawberries + 1/2 cup no-sugar-added granola + 1 1/2 teaspoons roasted, unsalted sunflower seeds | Add the yogurt to a bowl or jar, then top with the berries, granola, and seeds.

Lunch (440 calories and 31 grams of total carbohydrate):

- **Mason Jar Sesame Chicken Salad** (page 208)
- Fruit: 1 medium orange
- Nuts: 2 tablespoons roasted, unsalted peanuts (serve on the salad)

Dinner (360 calories and 41 grams of total carbohydrate):

- **Spiced Cauliflower Roast**—1 serving (page 146)
  (Note: Recipe makes 2 servings, so it's on Friday's menu, too.)
- **Saucy Caribbean Beans**—1 serving (page 246)
  (Note: Recipe makes 4 servings, so it's on Friday and Sunday's menu, too.)
- Avocado: 1/2 Hass avocado, sliced

Snack 1 (150 calories and 7 grams of total carbohydrate):

- Dressed tomatoes and cheese: 1 cup cherry or grape tomatoes, halved + 1 teaspoon extra-virgin olive oil + 1 teaspoon red wine vinegar + 1 piece string cheese, sliced or diced | Toss all ingredients together at serving time.

Snack 2 (170 calories and 21 grams of total carbohydrate):

- **Saucy Caribbean Beans**—1 serving (page 246) + 1/3 Hass avocado, cubed

Daily Total (including snacks): 1,550 calories and 146 grams of carbohydrate

SUNDAY

Breakfast (430 calories and 40 grams of total carbohydrate):

- **Big Chocolate Protein Pancake** (page 124)
- Nuts: 1/4 cup shelled, roasted, unsalted pistachios

Lunch (440 calories and 50 grams of total carbohydrate):

- **Oaxacan Brunch-Style Nachos Skillet**—1 serving (page 92) (Note: Recipe makes 2 servings, so it's on Monday's menu, too.)

HINT: IT'S PREP TIME!

Dinner (370 calories and 41 grams of total carbohydrate):

- **Cacio e Pepe e Spinaci** (page 150) (Note: Recipe makes 2 servings, so it's on Monday's menu, too.)
- Deviled eggs: 1 hard-boiled egg + 1 teaspoon mayonnaise | Halve the egg. Mix the mayonnaise and yolk together in a small bowl and stuff back into the egg-white halves.

Snack 1 (100 calories and 5 grams of total carbohydrate):

- Veggies and dip: 1 cup broccoli florets + 1 1/2 tablespoons natural Caesar or ranch dressing

Snack 2 (200 calories and 15 grams of total carbohydrate):

- Fruit and nuts: 6 strawberries + 1/4 cup shelled, roasted, unsalted pistachios

Daily Total (including snacks): 1,540 calories and 151 grams of carbohydrate

MONDAY

Breakfast (430 calories and 43 grams of total carbohydrate):

- **No-Cook Cocoa-Covered Strawberry Overnight Oatmeal** (page 122)
- Poultry sausage: 4 links natural breakfast chicken sausage | Prepare according to package directions.

Lunch (370 calories and 41 grams of total carbohydrate):

- **Cacio e Pepe e Spinaci** (page 150) (Note: Recipe makes 2 servings, so it's on Sunday's menu, too.)
- Deviled eggs: 1 hard-boiled egg + 1 teaspoon mayonnaise | Halve the egg. Mix the mayonnaise and yolk together in a small bowl and stuff back into the egg-white halves.

Dinner (440 calories and 50 grams of total carbohydrate):

- **Oaxacan Brunch-Style Nachos Skillet**—1 serving (page 92) (Note: Recipe makes 2 servings, so it's on Sunday's menu, too.)

Snack 1 (140 calories and 17 grams of total carbohydrate):

- Fruit and yogurt: 1/2 cup fresh or thawed frozen cherries + 3/4 cup plain 0% fat Greek yogurt

Snack 2 (160 calories and 19 grams of total carbohydrate):

- Chips and salsa: 1 ounce tortilla chips + 2 tablespoons preservative-free salsa verde

Daily Total (including snacks): 1,540 calories and 170 grams of carbohydrate

TUESDAY

Breakfast (430 calories and 35 grams of total carbohydrate):

- Breakfast salad: 1 egg + 2 cups packed fresh baby salad greens (mesclun) + 2 teaspoons extra-virgin olive oil + 2 teaspoons lemon juice | Prepare the egg as desired. Toss the greens, oil, and lemon juice together at serving time, and top with the egg.
- Fruit: 1 cup fresh or thawed frozen cherries
- Nuts: 1/4 cup shelled, roasted, unsalted, pistachios

Lunch (420 calories and 32 grams of total carbohydrate):

- **Stuffed Turkey & Red Grape Salad Pita** (page 202)
- Veggies & cottage cheese: 1 cup sliced English cucumber + 1/2 cup low-fat cottage cheese

Dinner (420 calories and 50 grams of total carbohydrate):

- **Three-Minute Skillet Beans & Greens**—1 serving (page 142) (Note: Recipe makes 2 servings, so it's on Wednesday's menu, too.)
- Sautéed carrots: 8 baby carrots + 2 teaspoons extra-virgin olive oil | Cook the carrots in a medium skillet over medium heat until lightly browned.

Snacks 1 & 2 (130 + 130 calories and 18 + 18 grams of total carbohydrate):

- **BBQ Popcorn** (page 72) (Note: Recipe makes 2 servings, so enjoy 1 serving for each snack!)

Daily Total (including snacks): 1,530 calories and 153 grams of carbohydrate

WEDNESDAY

Breakfast (390 calories and 32 grams of total carbohydrate):

- Breakfast salad: 1 egg + 2 cups packed fresh baby salad greens (mesclun) + 2 teaspoons extra-virgin olive oil + 2 teaspoons lemon juice | Prepare the egg as desired. Toss the greens, oil, and lemon juice together at serving time, and top with the egg.
- Almond butter toast: 1 slice whole-grain bread, toasted + 1 tablespoon natural, unsweetened almond butter
- Fruit: 1/2 Texas red or pink grapefruit

Lunch (420 calories and 50 grams of total carbohydrate):

- **Three-Minute Skillet Beans & Greens**—1 serving (page 142) (Note: Recipe makes 2 servings, so it's on Tuesday's menu, too.)
- Sautéed carrots: 8 baby carrots + 2 teaspoons extra-virgin olive oil | Cook the carrots in a medium skillet over medium heat until lightly browned.

HINT: IT'S PREP TIME!

Dinner (440 calories and 47 grams of total carbohydrate):

- **Ginger, Tempeh & Snow Pea Stir-Fry**—1 serving (page 144) (Note: Recipe makes 2 servings, so it's on Thursday's menu, too.)
- Grains: 1/2 cup cooked farro or brown rice

Snack 1 (160 calories and 21 grams of total carbohydrate):

- Fruit and cheese: 3/4 cup red seedless grapes + 1 string cheese

Snack 2 (160 calories and 19 grams of total carbohydrate):

- Chips and salsa: 1 ounce tortilla chips + 2 tablespoons preservative-free salsa verde

Daily Total (including snacks): 1,570 calories and 169 grams of carbohydrate

THURSDAY

Breakfast (430 calories and 40 grams of total carbohydrate):

- **Big Chocolate Protein Pancake** (page 124)
- Nuts: 1/4 cup shelled, roasted, unsalted pistachios

Lunch (450 calories and 51 grams of total carbohydrate):

- **No-Brainer Bean Burrito Wrap** (page 128)
- Sautéed peppers: 1 cup red or green bell pepper strips + 2 teaspoons avocado oil or sunflower oil | Cook the peppers in a large skillet over medium-high heat until lightly browned.

Dinner (440 calories and 47 grams of total carbohydrate):

- **Ginger, Tempeh & Snow Pea Stir-Fry**—1 serving (page 144) (Note: Recipe makes 2 servings, so it's on Wednesday's menu, too.)
- Grains: 1/2 cup cooked farro or brown rice

Snack 1 (170 calories and 20 grams of total carbohydrate):

- Fruit, yogurt, and nuts: 1/2 medium banana + 1/2 cup plain 0% fat Greek yogurt + 1 tablespoon roasted, unsalted peanuts

Snack 2 (170 calories and 20 grams of total carbohydrate):

- Fruit, yogurt, and nuts: 1/2 medium banana + 1/2 cup plain 0% fat Greek yogurt + 1 tablespoon roasted, unsalted peanuts

Daily Total (including snacks): 1,660 calories and 178 grams of carbohydrate

FRIDAY

Breakfast (360 calories and 43 grams of total carbohydrate):

- Bagel breakfast: 2 tablespoons Neufchâtel (light cream cheese) + 1/2 bakery-style whole-grain "everything" or other whole-grain bagel, halved and toasted + 1/4 cup English cucumber slices | Spread the Neufchâtel onto the toasted bagel half and arrange the cucumber slices on top.
- Munchies: 3 tablespoons trail mix

Lunch (360 calories and 41 grams of total carbohydrate):

- Fast Mexican bean and chicken salad: 2 ounces fresh baby salad greens (mesclun) + 1/2 Hass avocado, cubed + 2 ounces pre-cooked chicken breast, shredded or cubed + 1/2 (15-ounce) can black beans, drained + 3 tablespoons preservative-free salsa or salsa verde | Toss all ingredients together at serving time.

Dinner (290 calories and 25 grams of total carbohydrate):

- **Toasty Rancher Chicken Sandwich** (Page 198)
- Veggies: 1 cup red or green bell pepper pieces, raw or pan-grilled

Snack 1 (150 calories and 18 grams of total carbohydrate):

- Fruit and yogurt: 1/2 cup thawed frozen raspberries or sliced strawberries + 3/4 cup plain 0% fat Greek yogurt

Snack 2 (180 calories and 6 grams of total carbohydrate):

- Side salad with egg: 2 cups packed fresh baby salad greens (mesclun) + 1 tablespoon no-sugar-added vinaigrette of choice + 1 hard-boiled egg, sliced + 1 tablespoon shelled, roasted, unsalted pistachios | Toss all ingredients together at serving time.

Daily Total (including snacks): 1,340 calories and 133 grams of carbohydrate

SATURDAY

Breakfast (360 calories and 43 grams of total carbohydrate):

- Bagel breakfast: 2 tablespoons Neufchâtel (light cream cheese) + 1/2 bakery-style whole-grain "everything" or other whole-grain bagel, halved and toasted + 1/4 cup English cucumber slices | Spread the Neufchâtel onto the toasted bagel half and arrange the cucumber slices on top.
- Munchies: 3 tablespoons trail mix

Lunch (390 calories and 31 grams of total carbohydrate):

- **Mandarin, Greens & Protein Bowl** (page 182)

Dinner (390 calories and 47 grams of total carbohydrate):

- Pasta marinara with sausage bowl: 1 1/2 ounces dry whole-wheat penne + 3 tablespoons no-sugar-added, unsalted marinara sauce + 1 (3-ounce) link pre-cooked natural turkey or chicken sausage + 1 teaspoon extra-virgin olive oil + 2 cups fresh baby arugula | Boil the pasta according to package directions; drain. Pan-cook the sausage link in oil according to package directions, then slice into coins. Toss the pasta with the marinara, sausage, and arugula.

Snack 1 (150 calories and 18 grams of total carbohydrate):

- Fruit and yogurt: 1/2 cup thawed frozen raspberries or sliced strawberries + 3/4 cup plain 0% fat Greek yogurt

Snack 2 (180 calories and 6 grams of total carbohydrate):

- Side salad with egg: 2 cups packed fresh baby arugula or mesclun + 1 tablespoon no-sugar-added vinaigrette of choice + 1 hard-boiled egg, sliced + 1 tablespoon shelled, roasted, unsalted pistachios | Toss all ingredients together at serving time.

Daily Total (including snacks): 1,470 calories and 145 grams of carbohydrate

USING THIS COOKBOOK

Want to get the most out of *The Clean & Simple Diabetes Cookbook*? Follow this helpful advice.

Embracing all of the sections of this cookbook

The Clean & Simple Diabetes Cookbook provides over 100 recipes—and plenty of insightful nutrition advice and clever cooking tips. Take advantage of all that the book has to offer.

- Read all of the opening text. It'll help give you a better grasp of cooking for your diabetes-friendly lifestyle.
- When in a pinch, prepare a tasty, no-recipe-required concept from the "25 of the Easiest-Ever Three-Ingredient Recipe Ideas" section (page 27).
- For a diabetes-friendly meal plan, use the "Meal Prep: Make-Ahead Weekly Menus" section (page 31).
- Select from recipes in all of the following chapters: "Appetizers & Snacks," "One-Dish Meals," all four of the Main Dishes sections ("Breakfasts," "Plant-Based," "Fish & Shellfish," and "Chicken & Turkey"), "Side Salads," "Savory Sides," "Soups & Stews," "Condiments," and "Desserts & Drinks."
- Don't forget to use the sections after the recipes. The "Ingredients of Choice" section (page 323) is a list of ingredient options you can choose from if any of the ingredients in the recipes are unfamiliar to you—or if you'd like to know which brand may work well in a recipe. Of course, for help with finding specific information or recipes—for example, maybe you're looking for a main dish featuring garbanzo beans or chicken—use the Table of Contents and/or the Index (page 327).

Understanding the recipe components

Before you begin cooking, read all of the information associated with the recipe—it'll help make sure preparation goes smoothly.

- Look at the symbols at the top of the recipe. This will help you select recipes based on cooking ease: easy (three spoons), easier (two spoons) and easiest (one spoon)!
- Enjoy the headnote—it's the paragraph under the recipe name. It's a little story about the recipe which may help give you a better understanding of it.
- Do pay attention to servings and serving size. This will guide you when meal planning as well as help you determine if you need to plan for leftovers.
- To determine the total time you'll need to allot for the cooking process—from start to finish—add together the "Prep Time" and "Cooking Time."
- Browse the ingredient list before you start cooking to make sure you have everything you need and in the form that you need it. The ingredients are listed in the order you'll use them.
- Read through the directions before cooking to make sure you have a good understanding of what you'll be doing and when you'll be doing it.
- Check the list of kitchen tools needed for preparation of the recipe and gather them all before starting preparation.
- Don't skip over the "Easy Tip!" and any additional tips for each recipe. They may offer the bonus info you desire or need.

- Utilize the complete nutrition information. It's based on one serving of each recipe. The info can help you determine how to fit a recipe into your meal plan—or if you need to skip a recipe because it doesn't fit into your individualized plan.

Preparing the recipes

Taste is the number one priority for the recipes in this cookbook! But the recipes are also streamlined to make them as easy as possible. Plus, they follow healthful criteria so they can fit into virtually every diabetes meal plan. Following the tips below will help ensure that the recipes stay tasty, easy, and healthy.

- Keep it real(ly) convenient. Ease is a key aspect of this cookbook. So some convenience items are called for in the ingredients lists to keep recipes as easy as possible. Just be sure to keep it real whenever possible by choosing convenient items, such as condiments and sauces, that contain no artificial ingredients and no added sugars.
- Be cost conscious. Please use healthful ingredients that fit into your budget. It's A-OK to pick store brands, generic brands, and other budget-friendly finds. Alternatively, if you're lucky enough to not be on a tight budget, you can aim to buy

100% organic foods. In either case, make sure you actually *like* the taste of the healthful ingredients you've picked.

- Opt for eco-friendliness whenever possible. It's simply a good idea to cook with ingredients that are good for your health *and* good for the health of the planet. When you're able, choose ingredients like low-mercury tuna and no-antibiotic chicken.

- Go seasonal. When a recipe gives you an option for using various vegetables or fruits, aim to select what's in season. If it's available at your local farmer's market, it's seasonal. Browse the seasonality charts available at cuesa.org/eat-seasonally/charts to find out what's at its peak season in your area.

- Aim for non-stickiness. I call for stick-resistant skillets in the recipes in this cookbook. Choose whichever type of stick-resistant skillet you prefer. Personally, I almost always use a cast-iron skillet. The more you use it, the more stick-resistant it becomes. For roasting and baking, use parchment paper (preferably unbleached) when noted. This will not only help prevent food from sticking to pans, but it also makes clean-up a breeze. (By the way, you should bake and roast using the middle oven rack for recipes in this cookbook.)

- Choose the right oil. I recommend using extra-virgin olive oil regularly. However, when a recipe needs a neutral-flavored oil and you'll be cooking at a medium-high or high temperature, I recommend using avocado oil or sunflower oil. If you choose sunflower oil, look for one labeled "high-oleic," which means it has mostly monounsaturated fat—a heart-healthy fat.

- Where's the red meat? In this cookbook, you won't find beef, lamb, pork, or veal—or processed red meats, such as bacon or ham. That was intentional. Current research suggests there may be an association between increased red meat consumption and type 2 diabetes; however, more research is needed to fully understand this link.

- Add "freebies." If you want to add a zero-calorie or very, very low-calorie ingredient to a recipe, do it if you feel it will make the recipe tastier to you. For instance, you can add black pepper, dried herbs and spices, or a splash of vinegar. Unfortunately, even though salt provides zero calories, it doesn't count as a "freebie" since the sodium can have negative health consequences at high levels. Measure out the exact amount of salt listed in these recipes. I suggest sea salt for the best taste experience.

- Add "almost freebies." For extra satisfaction,

it's generally fine to punch up meals by adding nonstarchy veggies, such as peppers, mushrooms, onions, broccoli, leafy salad greens, or fresh herbs. For instance, add grilled peppers to a sandwich or burrito. Just keep in mind that every serving will punch up the total carbohydrate value about 5 grams— as well as give you a boost of good nutrition.

- *Mise en place.* Just a friendly reminder to gather, measure or weigh, and pre-prep all the ingredients you need for a recipe before you begin making a recipe.

You're all set! Happy cooking!

APPETIZERS & SNACKS

nutty energy bites

These bites are definitely nutty! And they'll absolutely give you energy. Keep a stash of these ball-shaped bites on hand in the fridge or freezer. Pop one into your mouth for a quick anytime snack—or for a post-exercise nosh to replenish your body. Enjoy it along with some yogurt for extra nourishment or a refreshing glass of water to quench your thirst, too. (Hint: For an occasional bite-sized dessert, try my trick: Add in 1/4 cup of bittersweet chocolate chips to the recipe!)

1	cup old-fashioned rolled oats
5 1/2	ounces unsulfured dried apricots (about 1 cup)
1/2	cup creamy, natural, unsweetened almond butter (with no added sugars)
2	teaspoons cold water
1 1/2	teaspoons pure vanilla extract
1/4	cup shelled, roasted, lightly salted pistachios

KITCHEN TOOLS

- Dry measuring cups
- Kitchen scale (optional)
- Measuring spoons
- Food processor
- Flexible spoon-shaped spatula or spoon

DIRECTIONS

1. Add all ingredients to a food processor. Cover and pulse several times (about 20–25 times), until the mixture is crumbly yet well combined.

2. With clean hands, form the mixture into 12 extra-firm balls, about 2 tablespoons each.

3. Serve immediately, or store in the refrigerator for up to a week or in the freezer for up to a month.

EASY TIP!

Create playful combinations. Use any nut butter, dried fruit, and nuts you have. Try pitted dried plums (prunes), peanut butter, and pecans. The plumper and juicier the dried fruit, the better.

WHAT ARE DRIED, UNSULFURED APRICOTS?

Dried apricots shouldn't be bright orange! If they are, they've likely been preserved with sulfur dioxide. I encourage cooks to steer clear of synthetic preservatives whenever possible as the healthiest eating approach. So choose dried, unsulfured apricots. They'll look brownish, but still taste scrumptiously sweet.

NUTRITION INFORMATION

Choices/Exchanges:

1/2 starch, 1/2 fruit, 1 1/2 fat

Per Serving:

Calories	130
Calories from fat	60
Total fat	7 g
Saturated fat	0.7 g
Trans fat	0 g
Cholesterol	0 mg
Sodium	10 mg
Potassium	270 mg
Total carbohydrate	15 g
Dietary fiber	3 g
Sugars	7 g
Added sugars	0 g
Protein	4 g
Phosphorus	100 mg

buffalo garbanzo snackers

I've got a crush on garbanzo beans! That can happen when you grow up on hummus pita sandwiches instead of all-American PB&J sandwiches. Now, with the popularity of the garbanzo bean dip, I love spreading my culinary crush on garbanzo beans by sharing the other ways I prepare these favorite pulses. This oven-roasted recipe offers a way to enjoy garbanzos as a snack. You'll love them as salad toppers or meal garnishes. They're surprisingly versatile. And while they don't actually taste like wild buffalo chicken wings, their flavor is inspired by that fun food. Your taste buds will get a kick out of it!

1	(15-ounce) can no-salt-added garbanzo beans (chickpeas), well drained
1	tablespoon extra-virgin olive oil
2	teaspoons hot pepper sauce
2	teaspoons white wine vinegar
1/4	teaspoon sea salt

KITCHEN TOOLS

- Unbleached parchment paper
- Can opener
- Mesh strainer
- Measuring spoons
- Medium bowl
- Large rimmed baking sheet

serves: 4 | **serving size:** 1/3 cup
prep time: 5 minutes | **cooking time:** 25 minutes

DIRECTIONS

1. Preheat oven to 425°F. Line a large rimmed baking sheet with unbleached parchment paper.

2. Add the beans and oil to a medium bowl; toss to combine. Add the hot pepper sauce, white wine vinegar, and salt; toss to combine.

3. Arrange beans in a single layer on the baking sheet. Bake until the beans are crisp on the outside and still creamy in the center, about 25 minutes.

4. Serve while warm or at room temperature. (Hint: They're best when enjoyed immediately.)

EASY TIP!

There's no need to rinse beans when choosing a no-salt-added variety. But if you prefer rinsing them, go for it. To ensure they're well drained, wrap in a clean kitchen towel before using here.

HOT, HOTTER, HOTTEST

Hot pepper sauce, such as Frank's RedHot Original, comes in varying degrees of spiciness, from mild to fiery. Use more or less hot sauce in recipes based on how well you handle "heat." Or pick one just right for your taste buds. There actually is such a thing as taste-testing hot sauces, like at Heatonist—a shop in my Brooklyn neighborhood.

NUTRITION INFORMATION

Choices/Exchanges:
1 starch, 1 lean protein, 1/2 fat

Per Serving:

Calories	150
Calories from fat	45
Total fat	5 g
Saturated fat	0.7 g
Trans fat	0 g
Cholesterol	0 mg
Sodium	240 mg
Potassium	210 mg
Total carbohydrate	19 g
Dietary fiber	5 g
Sugars	3 g
Added sugars	0 g
Protein	6 g
Phosphorus	120 mg

bbq popcorn

In the past, popcorn was considered a "junk food." The movie-friendly munchie was typically served heavily salted and doused in ladles of butter or a strange, butter-like substance. But that was then. Today, popcorn isn't just for the movies, and most of the time it isn't junky. We now embrace popcorn as the whole-grain food that it is—and often prepare it in hipper and healthier fashions. This lightly coated, highly flavored BBQ popcorn is an excellent example of that. Pop a batch for movie night—or any night—soon!

1	tablespoon no-sugar-added barbecue sauce or Fruit-Sweetened BBQ Sauce (page 286)
1/2	teaspoon smoked paprika
1/8	teaspoon sea salt
2	teaspoons avocado oil or sunflower oil
1/4	cup popcorn kernels

KITCHEN TOOLS

- Dry measuring cups
- Measuring spoons
- Small bowl
- Small spoon
- Large saucepan with lid
- Large cooking spoon

serves: 2 | serving size: 2 1/2 cups
prep time: 5 minutes | cooking time: 10 minutes

DIRECTIONS

1. In a small bowl, stir together the barbecue sauce, smoked paprika, and salt; set aside.

2. In a large saucepan over medium heat, fully heat the oil. Add the popcorn kernels, cover with a lid, and periodically shake the saucepan until you hear the popping begin. Let the popcorn pop undisturbed until it stops, about 3 minutes. Carefully remove lid.

3. Immediately pour the barbecue sauce mixture onto popcorn while over medium heat. Stir well until the popcorn is lightly coated and re-crisped, about 2 minutes. Serve.

EASY TIP!

Want to make sure your popcorn is not genetically modified? Simply choose a USDA-certified organic variety; it's always non-GMO.

POPCORN IS "SEE" FOOD

Though they might get stuck in between your teeth, you'll definitely want to appreciate those little popcorn hulls. They're loaded with plant nutrients, including lutein and zeaxanthin. These carotenoids may play a key role in keeping your eyes healthy.

NUTRITION INFORMATION

Choices/Exchanges:
1 starch, 1 fat

Per Serving:

Calories	130
Calories from fat	50
Total fat	6 g
Saturated fat	0.7 g
Trans fat	0 g
Cholesterol	0 mg
Sodium	200 mg
Potassium	100 mg
Total carbohydrate	18 g
Dietary fiber	3 g
Sugars	1 g
Added sugars	0 g
Protein	3 g
Phosphorus	75 mg

diy pita chips

Yes, you can eat chips! But choose chips wisely. When you pick DIY Pita Chips, you'll be getting some whole grains when you munch on them. They're mildly flavored with sesame seeds and thyme and offer a nice crunch. And it only takes 5 minutes of prep time to make this home-baked version. Enjoy these pita chips as is. Better yet, pair them with good-for-you toppings, like you'll do in the Hummus Canapés recipe (page 80). And if you like dipping, dunk them into Grape Tomato Pico de Gallo (page 294) or your favorite bean dip.

2	large, thin, whole-grain pitas
2	teaspoons extra-virgin olive oil
3/4	teaspoon sesame seeds
1/2	teaspoon dried thyme leaves

KITCHEN TOOLS

- Measuring spoons
- Culinary/pastry brush
- Cutting board
- Chef's knife or pizza cutter
- Large rimmed baking sheet
- Cooling rack

serves: 3 | **serving size:** 4 wedges
prep time: 5 minutes | **cooking time:** 15 minutes

DIRECTIONS

1. Preheat oven to 350°F.

2. Lightly brush both sides of the pitas with the oil. Cut into 6 wedges each, like pizza.

3. Arrange the pita wedges on a baking sheet. Sprinkle the top of each with sesame seeds and thyme.

4. Bake until crisp, about 15 minutes. Place the tray on a cooling rack to cool. Serve or store in a sealed container at room temperature for up to a week.

EASY TIP!

The thinner the pita, the crispier the result. But if you do start with fluffier pita, bake up to 3 minutes longer to properly crisp.

PITA CHIP SEASONING SWAPS

Add your own flavor twist to these chips. Try out some of my swaps. Instead of thyme, use 1/2 teaspoon dried tarragon or dill and 1/4 teaspoon garlic powder. Or, instead of both sesame seeds and thyme, use 1 teaspoon of "everything" bagel seasoning. Alternatively, go heavier on sesame seeds and thyme for bigger, bolder flavor.

NUTRITION INFORMATION

Choices/Exchanges:
1 1/2 starch, 1/2 fat

Per Serving:

Calories	140
Calories from fat	35
Total fat	4 g
Saturated fat	0.5 g
Trans fat	0 g
Cholesterol	0 mg
Sodium	230 mg
Potassium	75 mg
Total carbohydrate	24 g
Dietary fiber	3 g
Sugars	1 g
Added sugars	0 g
Protein	4 g
Phosphorus	80 mg

almost hummus

Just as the name implies, this is like traditional hummus, but it's faster to fix and simpler tasting since it's spice-free. That makes it a bit more versatile as a dip or when used within recipes, including Overstuffed Veggie & Hummus Sandwich (page 136) and Caramelized Cauliflower & Herbs on Bed of Hummus (page 148). By the way, for a hint of flavor intrigue, use unsweetened green or herbal tea in place of the cold water in the recipe. Try my favorite: jasmine green tea.

2	garlic cloves, peeled
1	(15-ounce) can no-salt-added garbanzo beans (chickpeas), drained (do not rinse)
3	tablespoons tahini
3	tablespoons bottled lemon juice (not from concentrate)
3	tablespoons cold water or unsweetened green tea
1/4	teaspoon sea salt

KITCHEN TOOLS

- Can opener
- Mesh strainer
- Measuring spoons
- Blender
- Flexible spatula

serves: 8 | **serving size:** 3 tablespoons
prep time: 8 minutes | **cooking time:** 0 minutes

DIRECTIONS

1. Add the garlic, beans, tahini, lemon juice, water, and salt to a blender.

2. Cover and purée on high speed until velvety smooth. (Hint: If mixture is too thick, add more water 1 teaspoon at a time to desired consistency.) Serve.

EASY TIP!

Firmly press on the whole, unpeeled garlic cloves using the unopened can of beans. Then easily peel off the garlic skin.

FINISH WITH FLAIR

Prefer this recipe with extra pizzazz? Add a pinch of an ingredient with a flavor punch, such as grated lemon peel (zest), ground cumin, or paprika. For Mediterranean appeal, drizzle with extra-virgin olive oil or harissa sauce. Try a lovely garnish, such as fresh parsley leaves or edible flowers. Or, if you're a culinary daredevil, try an all-of-the-above approach!

NUTRITION INFORMATION

Choices/Exchanges:
1 starch, 1/2 fat

Per Serving:

Calories	90
Calories from fat	35
Total fat	4 g
Saturated fat	0.5 g
Trans fat	0 g
Cholesterol	0 mg
Sodium	80 mg
Potassium	135 mg
Total carbohydrate	11 g
Dietary fiber	3 g
Sugars	2 g
Added sugars	0 g
Protein	4 g
Phosphorus	100 mg

super green guacamole

It's easy eating green! If you have three simple ingredients on hand—a jar of salsa verde (that's tomatillo salsa), a little bunch of fresh cilantro, and a ripe avocado—you can whip up a batch of this "cheater" guacamole in 5 minutes or less. Just be sure to pick a salsa verde without sodium benzoate or other synthetic preservative to keep it "clean." If you're a freestyle kind of cook, simply toss in whole cilantro leaves—no chopping necessary. And if you're the quirky type who prefers precision, use exactly 24 cilantro leaves rather than measuring them!

1	Hass avocado, peeled and diced
3	tablespoons preservative-free salsa verde
2	tablespoons fresh cilantro leaves, roughly chopped or whole

KITCHEN TOOLS

- Cutting board
- Chef's knife
- Measuring spoons
- Medium bowl
- Fork

serves: 3 | **serving size:** 1/4 cup
prep time: 5 minutes | **cooking time:** 0 minutes

DIRECTIONS

In a medium bowl, stir together all ingredients with a fork until gently smashed. Serve.

EASY TIP!

See page 25 for "How to cut an avocado."

KEEP GUACAMOLE GREEN

When making this in advance or if you have leftovers, spoon the guacamole into a small food-storage container; press with the back of the spoon to release air pockets. Cut a piece of unbleached parchment paper that's the same shape and diameter as the container and press it directly on top of the guacamole. Seal with the lid and chill.

NUTRITION INFORMATION

Choices/Exchanges:
1/2 carbohydrate, 1 1/2 fat

Per Serving:

Calories	90
Calories from fat	60
Total fat	7 g
Saturated fat	1.1 g
Trans fat	0 g
Cholesterol	0 mg
Sodium	70 mg
Potassium	280 mg
Total carbohydrate	5 g
Dietary fiber	4 g
Sugars	1 g
Added sugars	0 g
Protein	1 g
Phosphorus	30 mg

hummus canapés

Here's a fun food! These apps will impress anyone at a festive party or on any given day. Add a special handmade touch by using the simple recipes for pita chips, hummus, and roasted chickpea snacks from this cookbook. Or make quicker canapés using store-bought versions of these ingredients. If you do use packaged hummus, go organic—or read the ingredient list and ideally select one without synthetic preservatives, such as potassium sorbate. These preservatives can make some hummus brands last longer, but your body doesn't need them!

16	whole-grain pita chips or DIY Pita Chips (page 74)
1	cup packaged organic hummus or Almost Hummus (page 76)
16	fresh cilantro leaves
16	crunchy roasted chickpea snacks (plain or flavored) or Buffalo Garbanzo Snackers (page 70)

KITCHEN TOOLS

- Dry measuring cups
- Measuring spoons

serves: 8 | **serving size:** 2 canapés
prep time: 8 minutes | **cooking time:** 0 minutes

DIRECTIONS

1. Top each pita chip with 1 tablespoon hummus.

2. Place a cilantro leaf and roasted chickpea on top of each. Serve.

EASY TIP!

Serving at a soirée? Measure 1 cup of hummus and count out 16 pita chips and roasted chickpea snacks in advance. You'll be able to make this in just a couple of minutes at party time.

APPETIZING VARIATIONS

Go for a personalized touch. If you need kid-friendlier canapés, top with thinly sliced grape tomatoes instead of the cilantro and garbanzo beans (chickpeas). If you prefer to go lower-carb (or your party guests are all veggie radicals!), enjoy sliced English cucumber coins and extra thinly sliced fresh red hot chile pepper instead of the pita chips and chickpea snacks, respectively.

NUTRITION INFORMATION

Choices/Exchanges:
1/2 starch, 1 fat

Per Serving:

Calories	80
Calories from fat	35
Total fat	4 g
Saturated fat	0.6 g
Trans fat	0 g
Cholesterol	0 mg
Sodium	170 mg
Potassium	85 mg
Total carbohydrate	9 g
Dietary fiber	3 g
Sugars	2 g
Added sugars	0 g
Protein	3 g
Phosphorus	65 mg

sonoma chicken & fig bruschetta

Let your favorite local market cook a rotisserie chicken for you. That'll save you significant time here since it's the key ingredient for this anytime appetizer. Or, if you prefer, bring leftover grilled or roasted chicken found in your fridge back to life! This recipe is basically a twist on a chicken salad sandwich served party style. The fig glams up the bruschetta to make it extra special, even if just for a party of one . . . make that six parties for one!

3	slices whole-grain pumpernickel or rye bread
1	cup chopped pre-cooked chicken breast, chilled
2	tablespoons no-sugar-added mayonnaise
1/2	teaspoon dried tarragon leaves or 1 teaspoon chopped fresh tarragon leaves
1	large fresh or dried fig, cut into 6 slices

KITCHEN TOOLS

- Toaster
- Cutting board
- Chef's knife
- Measuring cup
- Measuring spoons
- Small mixing bowl
- Soup spoon

serves: 6 | **serving size:** 1 bruschetta
prep time: 10 minutes | **cooking time:** 5 minutes

DIRECTIONS

1. Toast the bread. While warm, cut each piece diagonally in half.

2. In a small bowl, stir together the chicken, mayonnaise, and tarragon.

3. Top each toast piece with about 3 tablespoons chicken salad and a fig slice. Serve.

EASY TIP!

One cup of chopped cooked chicken breast is about the amount you'll get from one rotisserie chicken breast!

A ROTISSERIE CHICKEN PLAN

If using a whole rotisserie chicken, you'll only need one chicken breast for this recipe, leaving you with another breast, two thighs, drumsticks, and wings. Here's a plan: Serve all the dark meat for dinner while still warm. Slice the remaining chilled breast meat and toss into a leafy salad or grain bowl the next day.

NUTRITION INFORMATION

Choices/Exchanges:
1/2 starch, 1 lean protein, 1/2 fat

Per Serving:

Calories	120
Calories from fat	45
Total fat	5 g
Saturated fat	0.8 g
Trans fat	0 g
Cholesterol	20 mg
Sodium	140 mg
Potassium	120 mg
Total carbohydrate	10 g
Dietary fiber	1 g
Sugars	2 g
Added sugars	0 g
Protein	9 g
Phosphorus	85 mg

ricotta & blackberry jam crostini

Need something fancyish? This crostini recipe will become your go-to hors d'oeuvre pick. It does double duty as a stress-free after-work or after-school snack, too. To make it, you don't actually need an entire footlong baguette here; the recipe works surprisingly well with slices from a standard hoagie or submarine roll—as long as it's not already split. The combination of crisp crostini toasts, creamy ricotta, fruity jam, and touch of sea salt is rather craveable. But, shh . . . don't give away the "secret" to anyone else that this recipe is so simple to fix!

1	(4-ounce) whole-grain hoagie or submarine roll
3/4	cup part-skim ricotta cheese
1/4	cup fruit-sweetened blackberry fruit spread (jam)*
3/4	cup fresh or thawed frozen blackberries
1/8	teaspoon sea salt

*Note: Ideally, choose a fruit spread without added sugars.

KITCHEN TOOLS

- Cutting board
- Bread knife
- Toaster
- Dry measuring cups
- Measuring spoons

serves: 6 | **serving size:** 2 crostini
prep time: 8 minutes | **cooking time:** 5 minutes

DIRECTIONS

1. Using a bread knife, thinly trim off the rounded ends of the roll. Cut the roll into 12 slices, about 1/2-inch thick each. Toast the bread slices in a toaster until golden brown.

2. Top each toast with a 1-tablespoon dollop of the ricotta cheese, then 1 teaspoon jam. Top with the blackberries, then sprinkle with the salt. Serve.

EASY TIP!

Since these bread slices are small, you'll likely be able to toast 2 or 3 slices per bread slot in your toaster.

RECIPE TWISTS

Can't find a hoagie or submarine roll? Use a 6–7-inch portion of a whole-grain baguette. Prefer a different flavor of a no-sugar-added jam? Pick another berry option, like blueberry, strawberry, or raspberry. Want extra flair? Sprinkle with a few small herb leaves, such as thyme, basil, or mint.

NUTRITION INFORMATION

Choices/Exchanges:
1/2 starch, 1/2 fruit, 1/2 fat

Per Serving:

Calories	120
Calories from fat	30
Total fat	3.5 g
Saturated fat	1.7 g
Trans fat	0 g
Cholesterol	10 mg
Sodium	180 mg
Potassium	125 mg
Total carbohydrate	18 g
Dietary fiber	2 g
Sugars	8 g
Added sugars	0 g
Protein	5 g
Phosphorus	100 mg

wild chicken nuggets

If you like watching your favorite sports team over pub grub, you've got to try this. It's inspired by buffalo wings, in a better-for-you style. The chicken nuggets are skinless, baked, and butter-free. Plus, they're ultra-saucy thanks to the cleverly created sauce made with simply creamy hummus and hot pepper sauce. Don't look for a deep red color; the nuggets will be a lovely shade of salmon. They're semi-spicy, but when you drizzle or dunk each nugget into the remaining hot sauce at serving time, they're wild. Use toothpicks to enjoy every bit of chicken messiness, if you like!

1/4	cup packaged organic hummus or Almost Hummus (page 76)
1	tablespoon hot pepper sauce, divided
8	ounces raw boneless, skinless chicken breast (about 1 large breast), cubed

KITCHEN TOOLS

- Cutting board
- Chef's knife
- 9 × 13-inch baking pan
- Unbleached parchment paper
- Dry measuring cups
- Measuring spoons
- Large and medium mixing bowls
- Large spoon or flexible spatula
- Instant-read (meat) thermometer (optional)

serves: 3 | **serving size:** about 5 nuggets
prep time: 8 minutes | **cooking time:** 15 minutes

DIRECTIONS

1. Preheat oven to 425°F. Line a 9 x 13-inch baking pan with unbleached parchment paper

2. In a large bowl, stir together the hummus and 1 1/2 teaspoons hot pepper sauce. Transfer 2 tablespoons sauce to a medium bowl; set aside.

3. Add the chicken cubes to the large bowl and stir to coat. One at a time, transfer the cubes onto the baking pan. Roast until a slight crust forms on top and well done (minimum internal temperature of at least 165°F), about 15 minutes. No flipping or stirring required.

4. Transfer the roasted nuggets to the medium bowl. Toss to coat in the reserved hummus mixture. Serve with the remaining 1 1/2 teaspoons hot pepper sauce.

EASY TIP!

Ideally, cut the raw chicken into about 15 (1-inch) cubes. Or look for chicken that's already cubed (diced) for you in the freezer or meat aisle of your supermarket.

INGREDIENT TIPS

Not sure which brand to buy? Check out page 323 for "Ingredients of Choice." It's my personalized list of select brand suggestions to consider using in recipes, including this one. I've provided it simply as a guide. For instance, if you decide to use packaged hummus for preparing Wild Chicken Nuggets, consider this pick: Tribe Organic Classic Hummus.

NUTRITION INFORMATION

Choices/Exchanges:
2 lean protein, 1/2 fat

Per Serving:

Calories	120
Calories from fat	35
Total fat	4 g
Saturated fat	0.8 g
Trans fat	0 g
Cholesterol	45 mg
Sodium	320 mg
Potassium	180 mg
Total carbohydrate	3 g
Dietary fiber	1 g
Sugars	1 g
Added sugars	0 g
Protein	17 g
Phosphorus	155 mg

ONE-DISH MEALS

superfood breakfast burrito

This burrito is filled with greenness thanks to baby kale and guacamole. The addition of eggs further punches up the nutritional richness, providing high-quality protein, lutein, and choline. In basic terms, this burrito is really tasty and really good for you. And you don't have to worry about overdoing it on carbohydrates. By choosing an 8-inch tortilla rather than a larger tortilla, you won't have excess carbs. In fact, it'll make your superfood burrito feel super-stuffed. Enjoy it at breakfast time—or any time of day.

1	teaspoon extra-virgin olive oil
2	large eggs, lightly beaten with whisk
4	cups packed fresh baby kale
1/8	teaspoon sea salt
2	(8-inch) sprouted whole-grain or whole-wheat tortillas
1/2	cup Super Green Guacamole (page 78) or deli-prepared guacamole

KITCHEN TOOLS

- Measuring spoons
- Dry measuring cups
- Medium bowl
- Whisk or fork
- Large, deep, stick-resistant skillet
- Flexible silicone turner
- Regular dinner spoon

DIRECTIONS

1. Fully heat the oil in a large, deep, stick-resistant skillet over medium-low heat.

2. Add the eggs, kale, and salt, and cook while gently stirring (or folding) the mixture until the eggs are scrambled and the kale is fully wilted, about 4 minutes.

3. Divide the mixture among the tortillas. Top each with 1/4 cup guacamole. Roll up or fold like a taco. Serve.

EASY TIP!

If you have tortillas or wraps that are larger than 8 inches, trim them using kitchen shears/scissors. Save the tortilla scraps to enjoy later in a soup or salad.

SUPERFOOD TORTILLA

Beyond the burrito filling, the tortilla itself can be full of nutrient goodness. Ideally choose a sprouted whole-grain tortilla. Sprouting reduces some of the starch content in grains, which could increase the ratio of other nutrients, including protein.

NUTRITION INFORMATION

Choices/Exchanges:
1 1/2 starch, 3 nonstarchy vegetable, 1 medium-fat protein, 2 fat

Per Serving:

Calories	360
Calories from fat	150
Total fat	17 g
Saturated fat	3.2 g
Trans fat	0 g
Cholesterol	185 mg
Sodium	570 mg
Potassium	970 mg
Total carbohydrate	38 g
Dietary fiber	11 g
Sugars	4 g
Added sugars	0 g
Protein	17 g
Phosphorus	335 mg

oaxacan brunch-style nachos skillet

Like nachos? You'll love this Mexican-inspired recipe bursting with scrumptiousness. It's like nachos with a breakfast-style spin that's served in a skillet. First, you'll scramble eggs with black beans. (Hint: Rinsing the black beans here will help make this recipe look more appealing.) Then you'll stir in baby spinach and tortilla chips. Finally, you'll top with salsa and a touch of cheese. That means it's not only delicious, it's totally nutritious. It's ideal served for a quick weekday dinner or weekend brunch fix. Plan to make it often. (Though you really don't need me to tell you to do that!)

1	teaspoon avocado oil or sunflower oil
2	large eggs or vegan eggs, lightly beaten with whisk
1	(15-ounce) can no-salt-added black beans, rinsed and drained
4	cups packed fresh baby spinach
14	red or blue corn tortilla chips
1/3	cup preservative-free salsa verde or other salsa
1/4	cup shredded Monterey Jack cheese or vegan cheese

KITCHEN TOOLS

- Small bowl
- Small whisk or fork
- Can opener
- Mesh strainer
- Dry measuring cups
- Measuring spoons
- Large cast-iron or other stick-resistant skillet
- Cooking spatula or spoon-shaped spatula

serves: 2 | **serving size:** 2 rounded cups
prep time: 12 minutes | **cooking time:** 6 minutes

DIRECTIONS

1. Fully heat the oil in a large cast-iron or other stick-resistant skillet over medium heat. Add the eggs and beans, and cook while gently stirring until the eggs are softly scrambled yet still moist, about 2 1/2 minutes. Stir in the spinach until just wilted, about 2 minutes. Then stir in the tortilla chips.

2. Sprinkle with the salsa and cheese. (Hint: Ideally, use salsa and cheese that are at room temperature, not cold.) Serve from the skillet.

EASY TIP!

For egg and cheese alternative recommendations, see page 324 for "Ingredients of Choice."

A POP OF COLOR

This skillet recipe is colorful. But when using salsa verde, it may not showcase a vibrant color. If you'd like extra eye-popping appeal in the skillet, sprinkle with extra thinly sliced grape tomatoes or fresh red hot chile pepper to garnish. Or be (superficially!) selective and pick a salsa based on looks, not just taste.

NUTRITION INFORMATION

Choices/Exchanges:
3 starch, 1 nonstarchy vegetable, 2 medium-fat protein, 1/2 fat

Per Serving:

Calories	440
Calories from fat	140
Total fat	16 g
Saturated fat	5 g
Trans fat	0 g
Cholesterol	200 mg
Sodium	440 mg
Potassium	1270 mg
Total carbohydrate	50 g
Dietary fiber	11 g
Sugars	5 g
Added sugars	0 g
Protein	25 g
Phosphorus	465 mg

easy cheesy gemelli & kale bake

A pasta bake—or, in this case, a gemelli pasta bake—isn't actually that much more challenging to make than pasta on the stovetop. That's because it is pasta on the stovetop, then it's transferred to a baking pan to bake for a bit. That's it! I think of it as a nutritionally pumped up recipe because of the baby kale addition. And, of course, I want to make sure it tastes great. It's finished with goat cheese and pine nuts for a just-right touch of decadence. Go ahead, give this recipe a go.

4	cups packed fresh baby kale
2	teaspoons extra-virgin olive oil
8	cups cold water
8	ounces dry whole-wheat gemelli or other pasta shape
1/4	teaspoon sea salt, divided
1	cup no-sugar-added marinara sauce, divided
3 1/2	ounces soft goat cheese or soft vegan cheese, crumbled
1	tablespoon pine nuts

KITCHEN TOOLS

- Measuring spoons
- Liquid measuring cup
- Medium bowl
- Large saucepan
- Large cooking spoon
- Large strainer
- 2-quart baking dish (such as 8 × 12 inches)
- Dry measuring cups

serves: 5 | serving size: about 1 1/2 cups
prep time: 12 minutes | cooking time: 15 minutes

DIRECTIONS

1. Preheat oven to 400°F. In a medium bowl, toss together the kale and oil. Set aside.

2. Add water to a large saucepan. Bring to a boil over high heat. Stir in the pasta and cook according to package directions, about 9 minutes. Drain the pasta using a large strainer.

3. In a 2-quart baking dish, arrange in even layers half the pasta and half the kale; sprinkle with 1/8 teaspoon salt; and drizzle with 1/2 cup marinara sauce. Then evenly top with the remaining pasta, kale, salt, and sauce. Bake until the kale is fully wilted and sauce is steamy, about 6 minutes.

4. Sprinkle with the goat cheese and pine nuts. Serve.

EASY TIP!

If you can't find gemelli, use any whole-wheat pasta shape you can find, such as cavatappi or penne. Save up to 1 cup of pasta cooking liquid if you need to moisten the pasta after baking.

PASTA ALTERNATIVES

Beyond regular and whole-wheat varieties, today there are so many types of pasta finding their way to supermarkets. Many are made with pulses, like red or green lentils, garbanzo beans, and black beans. You can generally swap them one-for-one in recipes in place of traditional pasta. They often provide more protein and fiber than their traditional counterparts. Try garbanzo bean pasta in this recipe!

NUTRITION INFORMATION

Choices/Exchanges:
2 1/2 starch, 1 nonstarchy vegetable, 1 lean protein, 1 fat

Per Serving:

Calories	300
Calories from fat	100
Total fat	11 g
Saturated fat	3.8 g
Trans fat	0 g
Cholesterol	10 mg
Sodium	390 mg
Potassium	570 mg
Total carbohydrate	42 g
Dietary fiber	6 g
Sugars	2 g
Added sugars	0 g
Protein	13 g
Phosphorus	270 mg

tuna & avocado power bowl

When I hear the word tuna, I think of tuna salad. But tuna doesn't have to be laden with mayo and slapped between two pieces of bread. It can be paired with avocado for creaminess—no mayo needed! It can be served attractively in a bowl for a nourishing lunch with worldly appeal. And your bowl can provide a vehicle for getting more nonstarchy vegetables. Plan ahead so you have leftover grilled, roasted, or steamed veggies to use in the recipe. Otherwise, go ahead and quickly prepare a favorite frozen vegetable for it. Enjoy your power bowl warm or cool.

1/3	cup water
1/3	cup dry whole-wheat couscous
2	cups pre-cooked nonstarchy vegetables of choice (such as steamed Brussels sprouts)
2	(3-ounce) pouches no-salt-added tuna
1	Hass avocado, peeled and sliced
1	tablespoon reduced-sodium tamari (soy sauce)
2	teaspoons toasted sesame oil
1/4	teaspoon crushed red pepper flakes

KITCHEN TOOLS

- Dry measuring cups
- Cutting board
- Chef's knife
- Small saucepan with lid
- Cooking spoon
- Measuring spoons
- 2 dinner bowls

serves: 2 | serving size: 1 bowl (2 1/2 cups)
prep time: 10 minutes | cooking time: 2 minutes
(plus standing time)

NUTRITION INFORMATION

Choices/Exchanges:
1 1/2 starch, 1/2 fruit,
2 nonstarchy vegetable,
4 lean protein, 2 fat

Per Serving:

Calories	450
Calories from fat	180
Total fat	20 g
Saturated fat	3.4 g
Trans Fat	0 g
Cholesterol	25 mg
Sodium	330 mg
Potassium	1130 mg
Total carbohydrate	40 g
Dietary fiber	12 g
Sugars	4 g
Added sugars	0 g
Protein	31 g
Phosphorus	370 mg

DIRECTIONS

1. In a small saucepan, bring water to a boil over high heat. Stir in the couscous, cover, and remove from heat. Let stand 5 minutes to complete the cooking process. Or prepare according to package directions. Evenly divide the couscous among two bowls.

2. In each bowl, arrange 1 cup vegetables, 1 pouch tuna, and half the avocado slices.

3. Sprinkle each with 1 1/2 teaspoons tamari, 1 teaspoon sesame oil, and 1/8 teaspoon crushed red pepper flakes. Serve.

EASY TIP!

See page 25 for "How to cut an avocado."

BUILD-A-BOWL

Vary ingredients here as you wish. Choose any grain, like brown rice, quinoa, or farro. Select any veggie, such as steamed or roasted Brussels sprouts, sautéed cherry tomatoes, grilled zucchini, or a mixture of colorful nonstarchy veggies, like a trio of grilled bell peppers. And pick any protein, like grilled fish, shellfish, chicken, or tofu. The options are practically endless!

salsa, chicken, sweet potatoes & black beans

Looking for a complete meal in one recipe? I highly recommend you look no further! This is the total package, culinarily speaking. This roasted chicken, sweet potato, spinach, black bean, and salsa meal has comforting, stew-like goodness that even those with persnickety palates will find appealing. Everything is so succulent and tender; it tastes like it's been slow cooked all day. The combination of savory and naturally sweet flavors is memorable. To serve, transfer everything into four large flat-rimmed bowls using a large spatula/turner, then drizzle with the pan juices. Plan to include it in your meal repertoire!

1	pound sweet potato, unpeeled, scrubbed, cut into 1/2-inch-thick rounds (about 1 large sweet potato)
1	(5-ounce) package fresh baby spinach
1	pound boneless, skinless chicken thighs, about 4 (4-ounce) thighs
1	(15-ounce) can low-sodium black beans, rinsed and drained
3/4	cup preservative-free salsa verde
1/8	teaspoon sea salt

KITCHEN TOOLS

- Cutting board
- Chef's knife
- Can opener
- Mesh strainer
- Liquid (or dry) measuring cup
- Measuring spoons
- 9 × 13-inch baking pan or 2-quart baking dish
- Aluminum foil
- Instant-read (meat) thermometer (optional)

serves: 4 | **serving size:** about 1 thigh and 1 1/2 cups vegetable mixture | **prep time:** 10 minutes | **cooking time:** 1 hour 15 minutes

DIRECTIONS

1. Preheat oven to 325°F.

2. In a 9 × 13-inch baking pan, layer in order the sweet potatoes, spinach, chicken (flatten it out), black beans, and salsa. Cover and seal well with foil.

3. Bake until the chicken is well done (internal temperature of at least 165°F), about 1 hour 15 minutes.

4. Carefully remove the foil (the contents of the pan will be steamy). Sprinkle with the salt. Serve.

EASY TIP!

Weigh the sweet potato on the scale in the produce section of your market—or have them weigh it at the farmer's market—so you have an appropriate amount at recipe time.

GARNISH (IF DESIRED)

If you want to keep recipes as easy as possible, garnishes aren't required. But if you've got an extra minute and you've got a garnishing ingredient on hand, add it for extra appeal. Make sure it's an edible ingredient, not something just for show! Ideal garnishes for this dish include fresh cilantro leaves and roasted pumpkin seeds (pepitas).

NUTRITION INFORMATION

Choices/Exchanges:

2 1/2 starch, 3 lean protein

Per Serving:

Calories	330
Calories from fat	60
Total fat	7 g
Saturated fat	1.8 g
Trans fat	0 g
Cholesterol	105 mg
Sodium	400 mg
Potassium	1250 mg
Total carbohydrate	40 g
Dietary fiber	8 g
Sugars	9 g
Added sugars	0 g
Protein	27 g
Phosphorus	350 mg

"love your leftovers" bbq bowl

In America, about 40% of our food is wasted. Yikes! But it's absolutely possible to have great taste without waste. This bowl of yum offers a fantastic way to do that . . . by creatively using leftovers. Make it 100% plant-based by using grilled or sautéed tofu, bell peppers, and brown rice. After a holiday gathering, try it with roasted turkey, green beans, and whole-wheat couscous. Or post-cookout, go for grilled chicken, zucchini, and quinoa. Generally, the more mild tasting the ingredients the better, so they'll work well together. Plus, you'll finish the bowl with a tangy BBQ sauce, cilantro, and lime.

1 1/2	cups packed fresh baby spinach
3	ounces large, bite-sized pieces pre-cooked lean protein (such as roasted chicken breast), chilled
1 1/2	cups large, bite-sized pieces pre-cooked nonstarchy veggies (such as steamed broccoli), chilled
1/3	cup pre-cooked whole grains (such as quinoa), chilled
1 1/2	tablespoons no-sugar-added barbecue sauce or Fruit-Sweetened BBQ Sauce (page 286)
2	tablespoons packed fresh cilantro leaves
1 or 2	lime wedges

KITCHEN TOOLS

- Cutting board
- Chef's knife
- Dry measuring cups
- Kitchen scale
- Measuring spoons
- Microwave-safe dinner bowl

serves: 1 │ **serving size:** 1 bowl (about 3 cups)
prep time: 10 minutes │ **cooking time:** 1 minute 15 seconds
(if using pre-cooked protein, veggies, and grains)

DIRECTIONS

1. Add the spinach to a microwave-safe bowl. Arrange the lean protein, veggies, and whole grains on top. Drizzle with the barbecue sauce.

2. Heat in the microwave on high for 1 minute 15 seconds, or until hot. Adjust seasoning.

3. Sprinkle with the cilantro and serve with the lime wedge(s).

EASY TIP!

For a take-to-work (or take-to-school) lunch, make your bowl and seal it tight at night. Grab and go in the morning and stash in the office fridge until ready for zapping. Others will be envious!

MIX-N-MATCH BOWLS

This bowl works well with a Texan, Mexican, or Asian vibe. Pre-cooked protein? Try chicken breast, turkey breast, or tofu. Pre-cooked nonstarchy veggies? Try broccoli, zucchini, or bell peppers. Pre-cooked whole grains? Try farro, brown rice, or sorghum. Sauce other than BBQ? Try salsa, Asian peanut sauce, or a little bit of hot sauce. There are endless possibilities!

NUTRITION INFORMATION

Choices/Exchanges:

1 starch, 4 nonstarchy vegetable, 4 lean protein

Per Serving:

Calories	340
Calories from fat	50
Total fat	6 g
Saturated fat	1.3 g
Trans fat	0 g
Cholesterol	70 mg
Sodium	420 mg
Potassium	1500 mg
Total carbohydrate	38 g
Dietary fiber	11 g
Sugars	8 g
Added sugars	0 g
Protein	37 g
Phosphorus	485 mg

turkey jambalaya

A warm, comforting bowl of yum for four awaits. Or if you're not a sharer, a bowl of jambalaya awaits you—and only you—for your next four meals of choice! You'll appreciate that ground turkey acts as the "sausage," and the natural fat within the ground turkey, along with chicken broth, acts as the "oil" here, so it stays lean. The Cajun seasoning ensures that you won't miss out on flavor while providing a "Fat Tuesday" vibe. Enjoy with a leafy salad, steamed greens, or a side of roasted carrots.

10	ounces raw ground turkey, about 93% lean (1 1/4 cups)
1	large green bell pepper, cut into 1-inch-square pieces
1/2	cup chicken broth, divided
1	tablespoon no-salt-added Cajun seasoning or DIY Salt-Free Cajun Seasoning (page 173), divided
1 3/4	cups pre-cooked brown rice or other whole grain, warm or cool
1	(15-ounce) can no-salt-added red kidney beans, drained
1	(14.5-ounce) can fire-roasted diced tomatoes (do not drain)

KITCHEN TOOLS

- Cutting board
- Chef's knife
- Can opener
- Mesh strainer
- Large, deep, cast-iron or other stick-resistant skillet
- Dry measuring cups
- Liquid measuring cup
- Measuring spoons
- Cooking spoon

serves: 4 | serving size: about 1 1/2 cups
prep time: 10 minutes | cooking time: 8 minutes
(if using pre-cooked brown rice)

DIRECTIONS

1. Preheat a large, deep, cast-iron or other stick-resistant skillet over medium-high heat.

2. Add the turkey, bell pepper, 1/4 cup broth, and 1 1/2 teaspoons Cajun seasoning, and cook while stirring until the turkey is crumbled and well done, about 5 minutes.

3. Stir in the rice, beans, tomatoes (with liquid), and remaining 1/4 cup broth and 1 1/2 teaspoons Cajun seasoning, and cook while stirring until the rice is hot and no excess liquids remain, about 3 minutes. Serve.

EASY TIP!

See page 173 for a tip on making DIY Salt-Free Cajun Seasoning.

A PRE-COOKED WHOLE-GRAIN PLAN

For speed, try a heat-n-eat pouch of pre-cooked brown rice or other whole grains. Alternatively, pick up Chinese takeout steamed brown rice. But ideally, you can plan ahead and make a big batch of brown rice or another whole grain, like farro, sorghum, or bulgur, in advance to use for several recipes throughout the week, including this jambalaya.

NUTRITION INFORMATION

Choices/Exchanges:
2 1/2 starch, 2 nonstarchy vegetable, 2 lean protein

Per Serving:

Calories	340
Calories from fat	60
Total fat	7 g
Saturated fat	1.9 g
Trans fat	0.1 g
Cholesterol	55 mg
Sodium	440 mg
Potassium	830 mg
Total carbohydrate	45 g
Dietary fiber	9 g
Sugars	6 g
Added sugars	0 g
Protein	23 g
Phosphorus	355 mg

MAIN DISHES: BREAKFASTS

homemade fruit-sweetened granola

When I was growing up in the 70s, I always thought of granola as something only grownups ate. It was nothing like the "kid" cereal I preferred (hello, Cap'n Crunch!). And then when I did decide that I was a full-fledged grownup, I discovered granola that I thought was healthy, but it was overloaded with sugar. Luckily, I became a dietitian and soon thereafter a chef, and realized that there was a tasty way to get the plant-based benefits of granola without all of that added sugar. This is one way to do it . . . make it yourself!

1 1/2	cups old-fashioned rolled oats
1/2	cup slivered almonds
1	teaspoon ground cinnamon
1/2	cup unsweetened applesauce
1/2	teaspoon pure vanilla extract

KITCHEN TOOLS

- Large rimmed baking sheet
- Unbleached parchment paper
- Measuring cups
- Measuring spoons
- Medium mixing bowl
- Cooking spoon
- Cooling rack

DIRECTIONS

1. Preheat oven to 300°F. Line a baking sheet with unbleached parchment paper.

2. In a medium bowl, stir together all ingredients. Spread in an even layer on the baking sheet.

3. Bake in the oven until toasted, about 35 minutes. No stirring required. Cool on the tray on a cooling rack. Serve or store in a sealed jar or container for up to a week.

EASY TIP!

Combine the oats, almonds, and cinnamon in a jar, label it "Homemade Granola Mix," and store in the pantry for up to a month. Actually, make several jars of it. It'll be ready to make; just add applesauce and vanilla, and bake!

BEYOND BREAKFAST

Pair granola with fruit and yogurt, like in the Just Peachy Yogurt & Granola Jar recipe (page 108). It's tasty! But you can also use granola as a crunchy coating for baked chicken. Sprinkle it onto salads as a crouton swap. And try it as a "crumble" topping or crust-style ingredient in Single-Serve Peach Cobbler with Pecans (page 300) or No-Bake Cheesecake-in-a-Glass (page 302).

NUTRITION INFORMATION

Choices/Exchanges:
1 starch, 1/2 fat

Per Serving:

Calories	110
Calories from fat	45
Total fat	5 g
Saturated fat	0.5 g
Trans fat	0 g
Cholesterol	0 mg
Sodium	0 mg
Potassium	120 mg
Total carbohydrate	14 g
Dietary fiber	3 g
Sugars	2 g
Added sugars	0 g
Protein	4 g
Phosphorus	95 mg

just peachy yogurt & granola jar

You can't go wrong with the classic combination of fruit, yogurt, and granola. But here it gets a fresh spin; you'll enjoy it straight from a jar. You'll combine plain Greek yogurt, fruit-sweetened peach fruit spread, and pure vanilla extract to make a lovely, fruity yogurt.

You can make these jars in advance so they're instantly ready for breakfast—just seal the filled jars and chill overnight. If you do make them in advance, as well as use frozen rather than fresh peaches, skip the thawing step; the peaches will thaw naturally overnight in the fridge. What a delight!

1 1/3	cups plain 0% fat Greek yogurt
1 1/2	tablespoons fruit-sweetened peach or apricot fruit spread (jam)*
1/4	teaspoon pure vanilla extract
1	cup thawed frozen or fresh peach slices
1/3	cup Homemade Fruit-Sweetened Granola (page 106) or no-sugar-added granola

*Note: Ideally, choose a fruit spread without added sugars.

KITCHEN TOOLS

- 1 (2-cup-capacity) liquid measuring cup
- Dry measuring cups
- Measuring spoons
- Spoon
- 2 (12-ounce-capacity) jars with lids

serves: 2 | serving size: 1 jar
prep time: 8 minutes | cooking time: 0 minutes

DIRECTIONS

1. In a liquid measuring cup, stir together the yogurt, fruit spread, and vanilla.

2. In each of two jars, layer the peaches, yogurt mixture, and granola. Serve.

EASY TIP!

For a fruit spread recommendation, see page 324 for "Ingredients of Choice."

SEMI-HOMEMADE FRUITY YOGURT

Most fruit-flavored Greek yogurts on the market generally contain both fruit purée and added sugar. They're overly sugary. I suggest making your own so that the fruit provides all of the sweetness naturally and in a nutrient-rich manner. That's exactly what you're creating here. You can also just mix any fruit into plain 0% fat Greek yogurt. That's it!

NUTRITION INFORMATION

Choices/Exchanges:
1/2 starch, 1 fruit, 1/2 fat-free milk, 1 lean protein

Per Serving:

Calories	210
Calories from fat	25
Total fat	3 g
Saturated fat	0.4 g
Trans fat	0 g
Cholesterol	10 mg
Sodium	60 mg
Potassium	450 mg
Total carbohydrate	29 g
Dietary fiber	3 g
Sugars	19 g
Added sugars	0 g
Protein	18 g
Phosphorus	265 mg

savory tzatziki-style yogurt

If this sounds Greek to you, it is! Or at least it's Greek inspired. The recipe is an easy yet artsy twist on tzatziki—a traditional Greek yogurt-based sauce—that's then transformed into a protein-powered entrée. It's a scrumptious way to enjoy the thick and tangy yogurt. If you're someone who enjoys playing with your food, you won't want to pass up the opportunity to create this bowl of savory goodness. Skip the spoon and enjoy scooping it up with fresh whole-grain pita wedges or pita chips, like DIY Pita Chips (page 74).

1	(3-inch) piece English cucumber, unpeeled (3 1/2 ounces)
3/4	cup plain 0% fat Greek yogurt
1	tablespoon extra-virgin olive oil
1/8	teaspoon sea salt
16	small fresh mint leaves

KITCHEN TOOLS

- Cutting board
- Chef's knife
- Dry measuring cups
- Measuring spoons
- Luncheon-sized rimmed plate or flat bowl
- Spoon

serves: 1 | **serving size:** 1 rounded cup
prep time: 7 minutes | **cooking time:** 0 minutes

DIRECTIONS

1. Slice the 3-inch-long piece of cucumber into quarters lengthwise. Then slice the four (3-inch-long) pieces into thin slices crosswise.

2. Scatter half the cucumber pieces onto a luncheon-sized rimmed plate or flat bowl. Dollop the yogurt onto the cucumbers. Spread it with the back of a spoon. Attractively arrange the remaining cucumber on the yogurt.

3. Drizzle with the oil. Sprinkle with the salt and mint leaves. Serve.

EASY TIP!

Don't have a ruler handy? A 3-inch piece of English cucumber is basically 1/4 of the whole cucumber, which is usually about 12 inches long.

THE POWER OF PROBIOTICS

Greek yogurt is a source of live active cultures, which are called probiotics. They're actually "good" bacteria. Research suggests that regularly consuming probiotics may improve glucose metabolism. In addition, they have positive gut health benefits.

NUTRITION INFORMATION

Choices/Exchanges:
1/2 fat-free milk, 1 nonstarchy vegetable, 2 lean protein, 2 fat

Per Serving:

Calories	240
Calories from fat	130
Total fat	14 g
Saturated fat	2.1 g
Trans fat	0 g
Cholesterol	10 mg
Sodium	350 mg
Potassium	470 mg
Total carbohydrate	12 g
Dietary fiber	2 g
Sugars	7 g
Added sugars	0 g
Protein	19 g
Phosphorus	265 mg

fried egg taco with pico de gallo

A taco for breakfast? Sure! It's more taste-bud intriguing than plain eggs and toast. And this taco is ready in only 8 minutes from start to finish. That's less time than one cycle of your snooze alarm. After rolling out of bed, just fry an egg and add it to a fresh, soft tortilla. For pizzazz, top it with pico de gallo, which you can make the night before. Or just use 3 tablespoons of deli-prepared pico de gallo for an even faster fix. Create an eye-opening meal by pairing your taco with a simple side salad or yogurt—or both.

1/2	teaspoon avocado oil or sunflower oil
1	large egg
1	(5 1/2-inch) soft blue or yellow corn tortilla
1/4	cup Grape Tomato Pico de Gallo (page 294), drained of excess liquid

KITCHEN TOOLS

- Small mesh strainer
- Small stick-resistant skillet
- Measuring spoons
- Measuring cup
- Cooking spatula/turner

all-american portobello "cheeseburgers"
page 140

bbq popcorn

page 72

herbs de provence roasted chicken breasts with easy middle eastern green beans
pages 190 and 262

hummus canapés
page 80

cajun fish & roasted
cherry tomatoes
page 172

asian peanut soba
noodles with slaw
page 132

herbed soft scrambled
eggs on toast
page 118

"love your leftovers" bbq bowl
page 100

serves: 1 │ **serving size:** 1 taco
prep time: 5 minutes │ **cooking time:** 3 minutes

DIRECTIONS

1. In a small stick-resistant skillet over medium-high heat, fully heat the oil. Carefully crack the egg into the hot skillet and fry to desired doneness. (Note: Consumption of undercooked eggs may increase the risk of foodborne illness.)

2. Transfer the egg onto the tortilla. Top with the pico de gallo. Serve.

EASY TIP!

See page 25 for "How to fry eggs."

EAT BREAKFAST, THEN EXERCISE

Some studies suggest having a morning meal may be associated with better carbohydrate metabolism for certain people. For those with diabetes who workout in the morning, it's usually a good idea to eat a carbohydrate-containing meal beforehand—and ideally monitor blood glucose levels during and after exercising.

NUTRITION INFORMATION

Choices/Exchanges:
1 starch, 1 medium-fat protein, 1/2 fat

Per Serving:

Calories	160
Calories from fat	70
Total fat	8 g
Saturated fat	1.9 g
Trans fat	0 g
Cholesterol	185 mg
Sodium	140 mg
Potassium	210 mg
Total carbohydrate	14 g
Dietary fiber	2 g
Sugars	2 g
Added sugars	0 g
Protein	8 g
Phosphorus	190 mg

party pan chicken sausage frittata

Need a brunch dish for a bunch? You'll flip for this foolproof baked frittata recipe. It's packed with colorful peppers, and chicken sausage gives it just-right savory richness. When shopping for the ingredients, look for a natural or organic brand of chicken sausage to ensure that potentially heart-unfriendly preservatives, such as sodium nitrite, aren't sneaking into the recipe. If you find a mild sausage, you can add a minced jalapeño to the frittata mixture for extra kick, if you like. Pair it with whole-grain toast and a salad. Happy brunching!

3	large red or green bell peppers (or a mixture), thinly sliced
2	(3-ounce) links pre-cooked natural or organic chicken sausage, thinly sliced into 1/4-inch-thick coins
10	large eggs
1/3	cup fat-free milk
1/4	teaspoon sea salt
1/2	cup shredded part-skim mozzarella cheese

KITCHEN TOOLS

- Cutting board
- Chef's knife
- 9 × 13-inch baking (cake) pan
- Unbleached parchment paper
- Large mixing bowl
- Liquid measuring cup
- Measuring spoons
- Whisk
- Dry measuring cups

serves: 8 | **serving size:** 1 piece
prep time: 15 minutes | **cooking time:** 40 minutes

DIRECTIONS

1. Preheat oven to 350°F. If not stick-resistant, line the bottom of a 9 × 13-inch baking pan with unbleached parchment paper.

2. Evenly arrange the bell peppers onto the baking pan. Sprinkle with the sausage coins.

3. Crack the eggs into a large bowl. Add the milk and salt, and whisk until well combined. Pour the egg mixture over the peppers and sausage. Sprinkle with the cheese.

4. Bake until the egg mixture is firm, about 40 minutes. Cut into 8 pieces and serve.

EASY TIP!

See page 23 for "How to slice a bell pepper." For a sausage recommendation, see page 326 for "Ingredients of Choice."

ONE EGG A DAY

Some research suggests that eating an egg a day may help prevent diabetes. This may occur because of bioactive compounds in whole eggs. That means going the "egg-white-only" route may be the wrong direction for eating right.

NUTRITION INFORMATION

Choices/Exchanges:
1 nonstarchy vegetable,
2 medium-fat protein

Per Serving:

Calories	170
Calories from fat	80
Total fat	9 g
Saturated fat	3.1 g
Trans fat	0 g
Cholesterol	255 mg
Sodium	400 mg
Potassium	270 mg
Total carbohydrate	4 g
Dietary fiber	1 g
Sugars	3 g
Added sugars	0 g
Protein	14 g
Phosphorus	220 mg

parmesan turkey & egg scramble skillet

Savor the flavors of Italy at breakfast. All you need to do is head on over to your kitchen—no extra travel time required! In addition to the memorable flavors, you'll be pleased to know this skillet recipe for two provides plenty of protein from the combination of eggs and turkey. Plus there's a perfect pop of color from the addition of tomatoes and spinach—which also makes the dish extra satisfying. Make your egg scramble a complete meal by enjoying it with fiber-rich whole-grain toast or a dish of berries.

1	teaspoon extra-virgin olive oil
4	ounces raw ground turkey, about 93% lean (1/2 cup)
1	cup grape tomatoes (6 ounces)
2	large eggs, lightly beaten with whisk
1	(5-ounce) package fresh baby spinach
1/4	teaspoon sea salt
2	teaspoons grated Parmesan cheese

KITCHEN TOOLS

- Measuring spoons
- Dry measuring cups
- Medium mixing bowl
- Small whisk or fork
- Large, deep, stick-resistant skillet
- Flexible silicone spatula or turner

serves: 2 | **serving size:** 1 1/2 cups
prep time: 10 minutes | **cooking time:** 8 minutes

DIRECTIONS

1. In a large, deep, stick-resistant skillet over medium heat, fully heat the oil. Add the turkey and tomatoes, and cook while stirring until the turkey is well done and crumbled, about 5 minutes.

2. Add the eggs and cook while gently stirring the mixture until the eggs are no longer runny, yet are still moist, about 1 minute. Add the spinach and salt, and cook while stirring until the spinach is slightly wilted, about 1 minute.

3. Remove skillet from heat. Stir until the spinach is fully wilted, about 1 minute.

4. Sprinkle with the Parmesan cheese. Serve from the skillet.

EASY TIP!

Ground turkey usually comes in a 1-pound package. You can save the rest in the fridge for up to a week, or in the freezer for up to a month. Or you can pick up ground turkey from the meat counter at the store and request exactly 4 ounces of fresh ground turkey. (Hint: Pre-formed turkey burger patties are often 4 ounces, too.)

ITALIAN ENTICEMENT

For an extra-vivid flavor experience from this morning-time egg entrée, add a pinch of fennel seeds or crushed red pepper flakes or both. The fennel seeds give the turkey a sausage-like taste. Serve with lemon wedges for bonus brightness. And then create the right ambiance—play some classic Italian music for the full experience.

NUTRITION INFORMATION

Choices/Exchanges:
1 nonstarchy vegetable, 3 lean protein, 1 1/2 fat

Per Serving:

Calories	220
Calories from fat	110
Total fat	12 g
Saturated fat	3.4 g
Trans fat	0.1 g
Cholesterol	230 mg
Sodium	460 mg
Potassium	790 mg
Total carbohydrate	6 g
Dietary fiber	3 g
Sugars	3 g
Added sugars	0 g
Protein	20 g
Phosphorus	270 mg

herbed soft scrambled eggs on toast

Avocado toast is an American obsession thanks to its popularity on Instagram. But what if you don't want or don't have an avocado? Do egg toast! The addition of one ingredient—fresh herbs—makes it delightful. Just stir the fresh herbs into the eggs at the end of the cooking process. Use whatever herbs you have on hand, or try any of these dynamic duos: parsley and mint, dill and chives, parsley and tarragon, or mint and basil. Pair it with Pan-Roasted Sweet Bell Peppers (page 256) or serve with an arugula salad and seasonal fruit for a lovely meal.

2	slices sprouted whole-grain or whole-wheat bread, toasted
1	teaspoon extra-virgin olive oil
2	large eggs, lightly beaten with whisk
1/8	teaspoon sea salt
1/4	cup loosely packed fresh herb leaves

KITCHEN TOOLS

- Toaster
- Measuring spoons
- Medium bowl
- Whisk or fork
- Medium stick-resistant skillet
- Flexible silicone spatula
- Dry measuring cups

serves: 2 | serving size: 1 piece topped toast
prep time: 7 minutes | cooking time: 5 minutes

DIRECTIONS

1. Toast the bread in a toaster or toaster oven to desired doneness.

2. While the bread is toasting, prepare the eggs: fully heat the oil in a medium stick-resistant skillet over medium-low heat. Pour the eggs into the hot skillet and cook while gently stirring (or folding) the mixture until the eggs are no longer runny, yet are still moist, about 1 1/2–2 minutes. Remove the skillet from the heat, sprinkle with the salt, and gently stir (or fold) in the herbs.

3. Transfer the toasts to plates. Top each toast with half the herbed eggs. If desired, sprinkle with freshly ground black pepper to taste. Serve.

EASY TIP!

The night before you plan to enjoy this (or any breakfast dish), set out all of the kitchen tools you'll need, so it's a faster fix on a busy morning.

THE EGG-FOLDING TECHNIQUE

For the fluffiest scrambled eggs, try gently folding rather than continuously stirring them. All you'll do is slowly scrape up beaten eggs as they cook using a flexible silicone spatula, one row at a time, while folding (gently flopping!) the cooked egg portion on top of the runnier portion. Continue just until there's no more runniness.

NUTRITION INFORMATION

Choices/Exchanges:
1 starch, 1 medium-fat protein, 1/2 fat

Per Serving:

Calories	170
Calories from fat	70
Total fat	8 g
Saturated fat	1.9 g
Trans fat	0 g
Cholesterol	185 mg
Sodium	290 mg
Potassium	190 mg
Total carbohydrate	16 g
Dietary fiber	3 g
Sugars	0 g
Added sugars	0 g
Protein	11 g
Phosphorus	165 mg

savory farmer's market oatmeal

When I was younger, I turned my nose up at oatmeal, even after learning of the health benefits of oats' soluble fiber. Luckily, about 10 years ago, I began appreciating it in the culinary sense. It's because of this recipe concept. If you've only eaten plain, fruity, or sugary oatmeal, you're in for a real treat—a savory one. Think of this veggie version of oatmeal like risotto (or ris-oat-o!), just higher in fiber, which makes it more satiating. It's an awesome way to kickstart your veggie intake for the day. Enjoy a bowl of it any time. I do!

2 1/2	cups low-sodium vegetable broth or water
1/8	teaspoon sea salt
1	cup old-fashioned rolled oats
1	cup grape tomatoes (6 ounces)
3	cups packed fresh baby spinach
2	tablespoons crumbled feta cheese or soft goat cheese
2	lemon wedges

KITCHEN TOOLS

- Small cutting board
- Chef's knife
- Large liquid measuring cup
- Measuring spoons
- Medium saucepan
- Large cooking spoon
- Dry measuring cups

serves: 2 | serving size: 2 cups
prep time: 8 minutes | cooking time: 10 minutes

DIRECTIONS

1. In a medium saucepan over high heat, bring the broth and salt to a boil.

2. Reduce heat to medium, add the oats and grape tomatoes, and cook while stirring occasionally until the oats are cooked through, about 5 minutes.

3. Stir in the spinach until wilted, about 30 seconds.

4. Divide the oatmeal evenly between 2 bowls. Sprinkle with the cheese. Serve with the lemon wedges.

EASY TIP!

Measure everything out in advance, such as the night before. Stash the broth, spinach, cheese, and lemon in the fridge; keep the salt, oats, and tomatoes on the kitchen counter.

FARMER'S MARKET OPTIONS

Go for a change of taste. Savor this oatmeal with seasonal swaps. Instead of tomatoes, try bell peppers, mushrooms, zucchini, or leftover cooked nonstarchy veggies of choice. Instead of baby spinach, try other leafy greens, like baby kale, shredded chard, or a mixture of spinach and fresh herbs. Top with a farm-fresh cooked egg for a protein boost.

NUTRITION INFORMATION

Choices/Exchanges:
2 starch, 2 nonstarchy vegetable, 1/2 fat

Per Serving:

Calories	230
Calories from fat	40
Total fat	4.5 g
Saturated fat	1.4 g
Trans fat	0.1 g
Cholesterol	5 mg
Sodium	460 mg
Potassium	1000 mg
Total carbohydrate	38 g
Dietary fiber	8 g
Sugars	6 g
Added sugars	0 g
Protein	10 g
Phosphorus	350 mg

no-cook cocoa-covered strawberry overnight oatmeal

Not many people can enjoy the luxury of a slow-paced breakfast Monday through Friday. So here's a fiber-packed overnight oatmeal to the rescue. It's got "sweet treat" appeal, but in a good-for-you way, of course. The Greek yogurt makes it extra creamy. The combination of strawberry fruit spread and sliced strawberries makes the fruitiness pop. The finishing cocoa powder provides "chocolate-covered strawberry" appeal. Prepare it in the evening (or even a couple days in advance), then in the morning . . . just eat it!

1/3	cup old-fashioned rolled oats
1/3	cup unsweetened vanilla almond milk
1/3	cup plain 0% fat Greek yogurt
1	tablespoon fruit-sweetened strawberry fruit spread (jam)*
7	fresh or thawed frozen strawberries, stems removed and thinly sliced
1	teaspoon unsweetened cocoa powder

*Note: Ideally, choose a fruit spread without added sugars.

KITCHEN TOOLS

- Dry measuring cups
- Liquid measuring cup
- 1 (12-ounce or 1 1/2-cup-capacity) jar with lid
- Regular spoon
- Measuring spoons
- Cutting board
- Chef's knife

serves: 1 | **serving size:** 1 jar
prep time: 8 minutes (plus overnight chilling)
cooking time: 0 minutes

DIRECTIONS

1. Add the oats, almond milk, and yogurt to a 1 1/2-cup-capacity jar or sealable container. Stir well.

2. Top the oat mixture with the fruit spread, sliced strawberries, and cocoa.

3. Seal the jar with a lid. Chill in the refrigerator overnight, at least 6 hours. Serve.

EASY TIP!

Make a few jars in advance for a grab-and-go breakfast throughout the week. This oatmeal can be stored in the fridge for up to 4 days.

ALMOND MILK ALTERNATIVES

If preferred, use fat-free milk or another plant-based milk in this recipe. There are so many plant-based options, including flax, oat, almond, brown rice, and peanut milk. Do choose an unsweetened one for this recipe. If you can't find an unsweetened variety that's vanilla flavored, add 1/4 teaspoon pure vanilla extract to the 1/3 cup plain milk of choice used here.

NUTRITION INFORMATION

Choices/Exchanges:
1 starch, 1 fruit, 1/2 carbohydrate, 1 lean protein

Per Serving:

Calories	230
Calories from fat	30
Total fat	3.5 g
Saturated fat	0.6 g
Trans fat	0 g
Cholesterol	4 mg
Sodium	95 mg
Potassium	440 mg
Total carbohydrate	39 g
Dietary fiber	6 g
Sugars	15 g
Added sugars	0 g
Protein	12 g
Phosphorus	255 mg

big chocolate protein pancake

Who eats a chocolate pancake for breakfast? I do. You can, too! So go get the ingredients. You're minutes away from a delicious, almost dessert-like, flourless pancake . . . a big one! The raspberry topping is the perfect pairing. But if your berry of choice happens to be strawberries, chop up four of them, then smash until jam-like, and swap them in place of the raspberries. Either way, this pancake can also be served as an occasional treat for two topped with a little dollop of whipped cream instead of yogurt. Yum!

1/3	cup fresh or thawed frozen raspberries
1	small, fully ripened banana, peeled and broken into 4 pieces
1	large egg
2	teaspoons unsweetened cocoa powder
1/8	teaspoon sea salt
1 1/2	teaspoons avocado oil or sunflower oil
1	tablespoon plain 0% fat Greek yogurt or unsweetened vanilla dairy-free yogurt

KITCHEN TOOLS

- Small bowl
- Dinner fork
- Medium bowl
- Dry measuring cups
- Measuring spoons
- Large (at least 8-inch) stick-resistant skillet
- Large pancake turner/spatula

serves: 1 | **serving size:** 1 large (7-inch) pancake
prep time: 8 minutes | **cooking time:** 8 minutes

DIRECTIONS

1. In a small bowl, mash the raspberries with a fork until jam-like. Set aside.

2. In a medium bowl, mash the banana until jam-like. Crack the egg into the mashed banana. Stir with the fork until combined. Add the cocoa powder and salt, and stir until well combined.

3. In a large stick-resistant skillet over medium heat, fully heat the oil. Pour the banana batter into the center of the skillet. Cook until the pancake is lightly browned on the bottom and no longer sticks to the skillet, about 5 minutes; flip over with a pancake turner (spatula) and cook on the flip slide until cooked through, about 2–3 minutes.

4. Serve while warm topped with the mashed raspberries and yogurt.

EASY TIP!

Buy a few small bananas in advance. When ripe, peel, break each into four pieces, and freeze. That way you won't need to wait for a newly purchased banana to ripen. Thaw overnight in the fridge.

HEART-HEALTHY OIL "CHEAT SHEET"

For a multipurpose oil, use avocado oil or high-oleic sunflower oil for their high smoke points and neutral flavors. For cooking on medium heat or lower, or for use on fresh dishes or to finish hot dishes, use extra-virgin olive oil for robust flavor. And when desiring their unique flavor profiles, use nut or seed oils, like toasted sesame oil.

NUTRITION INFORMATION

Choices/Exchanges:
2 fruit, 1 medium-fat protein, 1 1/2 fat

Per Serving:

Calories	260
Calories from fat	120
Total fat	13 g
Saturated fat	2.8 g
Trans fat	0 g
Cholesterol	185 mg
Sodium	360 mg
Potassium	570 mg
Total carbohydrate	31 g
Dietary fiber	6 g
Sugars	15 g
Added sugars	0 g
Protein	10 g
Phosphorus	180 mg

MAIN DISHES: PLANT-BASED

no-brainer bean burrito wrap

Are you a fan of pre-prepped ingredients? If so, you're in luck. I intentionally created this Mexican-inspired wrap for use with convenient yet nutrient-rich supermarket finds. It's an ideal fast fix for one! When using convenience-style foods, be sure to read any available ingredient lists and aim to keep all of your picks free of artificial ingredients, added sugars, and excess sodium. Keep deliciousness in mind, too. For an added kick, try topping this burrito with a little hot sauce. And for bonus fun, name this stuffed taco-style burrito recipe what my friend Brian calls it . . . a burraco!

1	(8-inch) sprouted whole-grain or whole-wheat tortilla
1/4	cup canned lower-sodium vegetarian refried beans
1/3	cup Super Green Guacamole (page 78) or deli-prepared guacamole
1/2	cup packed fresh mixed salad greens
1/4	cup Grape Tomato Pico de Gallo (page 294) or deli-prepared pico de gallo, drained of excess liquid

KITCHEN TOOLS

- Can opener
- Dry measuring cups
- Mesh strainer
- 8-inch or larger microwave-safe plate
- Small flexible spatula
- Spoon

serves: 1 | **serving size:** 1 wrap
prep time: 5 minutes | **cooking time:** <1 minute

DIRECTIONS

1. Place the tortilla on a microwave-safe plate. Using a spatula, spread the beans onto the tortilla, leaving about a 1-inch rim.

2. Heat in the microwave on high for 20 seconds, or until warm.

3. While still warm, top with the guacamole, salad greens, and pico de gallo. Roll up or fold the tortilla over the fillings and serve.

EASY TIP!

Got leftover roasted or grilled veggies, like peppers or zucchini? Add them here in place of the salad greens— or, for an overstuffed wrap, in addition to the greens.

GOT SATIETY?

One complaint about healthy eating is that it may not seem satisfying. That can happen when calories are too low, or an eating plan isn't well planned. But professionally and personally, I find a key to boosting satiety (the feeling of fullness) is to aim for a notable amount of this trio: protein, dietary fiber, and healthy fat. You'll get that here!

NUTRITION INFORMATION

Choices/Exchanges:
2 1/2 starch, 1 nonstarchy vegetable, 1 lean protein, 2 fat

Per Serving:

Calories	340
Calories from fat	140
Total fat	15 g
Saturated fat	3 g
Trans fat	0 g
Cholesterol	0 mg
Sodium	410 mg
Potassium	1010 mg
Total carbohydrate	45 g
Dietary fiber	12 g
Sugars	4 g
Added sugars	0 g
Protein	11 g
Phosphorus	250 mg

spinach & feta quesadilla

When is a quesadilla good for you? When you make this recipe! The quesadilla uses a sprouted-grain tortilla. It has just-right cheesiness—and you can swap both of the cheeses for 100% plant-based cheeses, if you prefer. No added salt or goopy toppings are required. Plus it's filled with baby spinach for plant-based goodness. Spinach contains a significant amount of lutein and zeaxanthin; these carotenoids are considered eye-friendly nutrients and may play a protective role in diabetic retinopathy, though more research is needed to confirm a direct link. That makes this quesadilla a savory treat for both your palate and your eyes.

2	(8-inch) sprouted whole-grain or whole-wheat tortillas
1	teaspoon extra-virgin olive oil
2 1/2	tablespoons crumbled feta cheese or soft vegan cheese
2	cups packed fresh baby spinach
1/2	cup shredded part-skim mozzarella cheese or vegan cheese
2	lemon wedges

KITCHEN TOOLS

- Measuring spoons
- Cutting board
- Culinary/pastry brush
- Dry measuring cups
- Large skillet
- Pancake turner/spatula
- Chef's knife

serves: 2 | serving size: 2 wedges
prep time: 8 minutes | cooking time: 8 minutes

DIRECTIONS

1. Working on a cutting board, lightly brush one side of each tortilla with the oil. Flip over one tortilla and top the entire surface with the feta cheese, spinach, mozzarella cheese and, if desired, 1/8 teaspoon crushed red pepper flakes. Place the other tortilla on top, oiled side up.

2. Fully heat a large skillet over medium heat. Slide the quesadilla into the skillet. Press down on the quesadilla with a pancake turner to compact. Cook until the quesadilla is browned and cheeses are melted, about 4 minutes on the first side and 3 minutes on the flip side.

3. Slide the quesadilla onto the cutting board, cut into 4 wedges, and serve with the lemon.

EASY TIP!

If you don't have a culinary/pastry brush, use the best "cooking tool" you have—your first three fingers. Rub the oil onto the tortillas. Then wash your hands, of course.

FLIPPING A QUESADILLA

If having messy difficulties flipping over a quesadilla in a skillet, try this. After cooking it on its first side, slide the quesadilla out onto a plate with the help of a pancake turner/spatula. Then place another plate on top of that and flip over. Then slide the quesadilla back into the skillet to cook the remaining side.

NUTRITION INFORMATION

Choices/Exchanges:
1 1/2 starch, 2 medium-fat protein

Per Serving:

Calories	250
Calories from fat	100
Total fat	11 g
Saturated fat	4.5 g
Trans fat	0.1 g
Cholesterol	25 mg
Sodium	550 mg
Potassium	380 mg
Total carbohydrate	26 g
Dietary fiber	5 g
Sugars	2 g
Added sugars	0 g
Protein	15 g
Phosphorus	290 mg

asian peanut soba noodles with slaw

Here's one of my go-to recipes for a quick lunch. It's based on 100% buckwheat soba noodles, which only take about 8 minutes (or less!) to cook. By the way, buckwheat isn't related to wheat; it's a wild plant crop that's a good source of protein and contains the antioxidants rutin and quercetin. And that's good news for your health. As for the taste of the finished noodle dish . . . it's really saucy and downright craveable! You'll love that you can just toss in pre-made coleslaw mix to further punch up the nutrition and crunch in this cool, Asian-inspired fix.

8	cups cold water
1/4	cup creamy, natural, unsweetened peanut butter
1/4	cup no-sugar-added applesauce
1/4	cup rice vinegar
2	tablespoons reduced-sodium tamari (soy sauce)
6	ounces dry 100% buckwheat soba noodles or dry whole-wheat spaghetti
4	cups fresh coleslaw mix (about 10 ounces)
1/4	cup packed fresh cilantro leaves

KITCHEN TOOLS

- Liquid measuring cup
- Large saucepan
- Dry measuring cups
- Measuring spoons
- Kitchen scale (optional)
- Large mixing bowl
- Whisk
- Long-handled tongs
- Large mesh strainer

serves: 4 | **serving size:** 1 1/2 cups
prep time: 8 minutes | **cooking time:** 8 minutes

DIRECTIONS

1. Add water to a large saucepan and bring to a boil over high heat.

2. While the water is coming to a boil, whisk together the peanut butter, applesauce, vinegar, and soy sauce until smooth in a large mixing bowl. Set aside.

3. Using tongs, stir the noodles into the boiling water and cook according to package directions, about 8 minutes. Drain the noodles using a strainer. Rinse noodles with cold water to cool; drain again.

4. Transfer the noodles to the large bowl with the peanut butter sauce. Toss with tongs to combine. Add the coleslaw mix and cilantro, and toss with tongs to combine. If desired, garnish with a little additional cilantro and squeeze a lime wedge over top. Serve.

EASY TIP!

Look for buckwheat soba noodles in the Asian section of major grocery stores or natural food markets. If you can't find them, use whole-wheat spaghetti and cook according to package directions.

GO CONFETTI STYLE

Instead of slaw mix based on green cabbage, choose a tri-color blend. Or go DIY by tossing together 2 cups of shredded green cabbage, 1 1/2 cups of shredded purple cabbage, and 1/2 cup of shredded carrot. For an herbal twist, occasionally finish with mint or basil leaves rather than cilantro. And to transform into a protein-packed pick, toss in grilled chicken, shrimp, or peanuts!

NUTRITION INFORMATION

Choices/Exchanges:

2 1/2 starch, 1 nonstarchy vegetable, 1 1/2 fat

Per Serving:

Calories	290
Calories from fat	90
Total fat	10 g
Saturated fat	1.4 g
Trans fat	0 g
Cholesterol	0 mg
Sodium	270 mg
Potassium	480 mg
Total carbohydrate	44 g
Dietary fiber	6 g
Sugars	5 g
Added sugars	0 g
Protein	9 g
Phosphorus	245 mg

veggie lo mein

These noodles are downright sassy! They have a just-right sweet/salty balance. The natural sweetness is from unsweetened applesauce, not added sugars of any type. For saltiness, you don't actually need to add salt; reduced-sodium tamari (soy sauce) provides plenty of saltiness. After making the noodles, you'll basically stir-fry all the ingredients together. That includes red bell peppers or other favorite nonstarchy vegetables, like a colorful mixture of peppers, carrots, and broccoli. To enjoy, pair the lo mein with a protein-rich side. Or check your fridge for leftovers and toss in any leftover cooked chicken or shrimp.

8	cups cold water
6	ounces dry whole-wheat spaghetti or linguine
1	tablespoon toasted sesame oil
2	large red bell peppers, thinly sliced, or 3 cups sliced nonstarchy vegetable mixture
4	scallions, thinly sliced, green and white parts divided
1/4	cup unsweetened applesauce
2	tablespoons reduced-sodium tamari (soy sauce)

KITCHEN TOOLS

- Kitchen scale (optional)
- Cutting board
- Chef's knife
- Large saucepan
- Strainer
- Wok or large, deep skillet
- Measuring spoons
- Liquid or dry measuring cup
- Long-handled tongs

serves: 4 | serving size: 1 1/3 cups
prep time: 12 minutes | cooking time: 15 minutes

DIRECTIONS

1. Boil the water in a large saucepan. Cook the spaghetti according to package directions, about 8 minutes.

2. Drain the spaghetti in a strainer, quickly rinse with cold water to stop the cooking process, and set aside.

3. In a wok or large, deep skillet over medium-high heat, heat the oil. Add the bell peppers and white part of the scallions, and cook while stirring with tongs until peppers are crisp-tender, about 5 minutes. Stir in the applesauce and soy sauce, then add the drained spaghetti and cook while tossing until the noodles absorb the sauce, about 1 minute. Stir in the green part of the scallions. Serve.

EASY TIP!

See page 23 for "How to slice a bell pepper."

NONSTARCHY VEGGIES

Plan a farmer's market outing. Then make this lo mein with whatever nonstarchy veggies are seasonal. Mix-n-match as you wish. Here are several vegetables from which to choose: broccoli, cauliflower, cabbage, bok choy, snow peas, carrots, and mushrooms. (Hint: For the easiest fix, purchase 3 cups of cut vegetables from your super-market's pre-prepped produce section or a salad bar.)

NUTRITION INFORMATION

Choices/Exchanges:
2 starch, 2 nonstarchy vegetable, 1/2 fat

Per Serving:

Calories	230
Calories from fat	45
Total fat	5 g
Saturated fat	0.7 g
Trans fat	0 g
Cholesterol	0 mg
Sodium	250 mg
Potassium	450 mg
Total carbohydrate	40 g
Dietary fiber	7 g
Sugars	7 g
Added sugars	0 g
Protein	8 g
Phosphorus	190 mg

overstuffed veggie & hummus sandwich

One highlight of nonstarchy vegetables is that they can transform an ordinary sandwich into an extraordinary one . . . even an overstuffed one! And don't worry, if you find it too challenging to eat this overstuffed sandwich, serve some tomato and cucumber on the side instead. Beyond the generous veggie helping, there's another ingredient that may surprise you . . . raw shelled hemp seeds (also called hemp hearts). The seeds, which are stirred into the hummus, are low in carbs and provide heart-healthy fats. They'll give the sandwich an extra punch of protein. I enjoy hemp hearts straight from the spoon!

1/4	cup packaged organic hummus or Almost Hummus (page 76)
1	tablespoon raw shelled hemp seeds or flaxseeds
2	thin slices sprouted whole-grain or whole-wheat bread
1	large, thin slice red onion, separated into rings
1	small plum tomato, thinly sliced
1	(3-inch) piece English cucumber, unpeeled, thinly sliced into coins

KITCHEN TOOLS

- Dry measuring cups
- Measuring spoons
- Cutting board
- Chef's knife
- Small bowl
- Small spoon
- Spreader or butter knife

serves: 1 | **serving size:** 1 sandwich
prep time: 10 minutes | **cooking time:** 0 minutes

DIRECTIONS

1. In a small bowl, stir together the hummus and hemp seeds.

2. Spread the hummus mixture onto both bread slices. Top one bread slice with the onion, tomato, and cucumber. Top with the other bread slice, hummus side down.

3. Serve whole or sliced diagonally in half.

EASY TIP!

Look for hemp seeds in your market's bulk bin section. For a packaged option, try Manitoba Harvest Hemp Hearts—which you can also buy online. If you need to, swap them for sesame seeds.

WHICH HUMMUS TO BUY

If you choose to purchase hummus rather than prepare homemade hummus, just keep it real! If you see ingredients that your body doesn't need, like the preservative potassium sorbate or the thickener guar gum, ideally pick a different brand. Check out "Ingredients of Choice" on page 324 for brand ideas.

NUTRITION INFORMATION

Choices/Exchanges:
2 1/2 starch, 2 nonstarchy vegetable, 1 lean protein, 1 1/2 fat

Per Serving:

Calories	350
Calories from fat	110
Total fat	12 g
Saturated fat	1.4 g
Trans fat	0 g
Cholesterol	0 mg
Sodium	390 mg
Potassium	710 mg
Total carbohydrate	47 g
Dietary fiber	12 g
Sugars	8 g
Added sugars	0 g
Protein	18 g
Phosphorus	425 mg

zucchini "pizza"

Zucchini isn't just a side-dish vegetable. This recipe reveals it can absolutely be an entrée-worthy star of the plate. Zucchini is the base for this crustless pizza–style inspiration. Of course, the recipe won't look like traditional pizza; these are basically pizza boats. The zucchini shows off its comforting side, and you'll still get the scrumptiousness of pizza thanks to the marinara sauce, basil, and cheese toppings. Goat cheese makes it memorable. The recipe proves that you're allowed to have fun when cooking and eating right. Pair with a bean salad for a filling meal with a big dash of fun.

4	large (10-ounce) zucchinis, stem removed, cut in half lengthwise
1	cup no-sugar-added marinara sauce
1	(4-ounce) log soft goat cheese or soft vegan cheese, crumbled
24	small fresh basil leaves

KITCHEN TOOLS

- Cutting board
- Chef's knife
- Liquid or dry measuring cup
- Large rimmed baking sheet
- Unbleached parchment paper
- Spoon

serves: 4 | serving size: 2 zucchini "pizzas"
prep time: 8 minutes | cooking time: 35 minutes

DIRECTIONS

1. Preheat oven to 425°F. Line a large rimmed baking sheet with unbleached parchment paper.

2. Arrange the eight long zucchini halves, cut side up, on the baking sheet. Using a spoon, spread each with the marinara sauce.

3. Bake the zucchini "pizzas" until the zucchini is cooked through, about 35 minutes.

4. Sprinkle with the goat cheese and whole basil leaves. Serve.

EASY TIP!

For marinara sauce and cheese alternative recommendations, see pages 324 and 325 for "Ingredients of Choice."

CHEESY ALTERNATIVES

These "pizzas" can easily be transformed to please plant-based or cheese-free folks by using a vegan cheese alternative in place of the goat cheese. Top with a soft, French-style cashew or other treenut cheese, especially one that has Italian flair, like an herb-garlic flavor. Or if you prefer a more traditional pizza cheese alternative, sprinkle with a shredded mozzarella-style vegan cheese.

NUTRITION INFORMATION

Choices/Exchanges:
3 nonstarchy vegetable,
1 medium-fat protein, 1 fat

Per Serving:

Calories	170
Calories from fat	90
Total fat	10 g
Saturated fat	4.8 g
Trans fat	0 g
Cholesterol	15 mg
Sodium	360 mg
Potassium	930 mg
Total carbohydrate	14 g
Dietary fiber	3 g
Sugars	7 g
Added sugars	0 g
Protein	10 g
Phosphorus	200 mg

all-american portobello "cheeseburgers"

At your next cookout (or cook-in!), grill these cheeseburgers. But rather than meat, you'll get "meatiness" from grilled portobello mushroom caps. It's one way to serve a plant-based option while still having 100% of that burger-style satisfaction. That means both vegetarians and nonvegetarians will enjoy sinking their teeth into one. While simply delicious as is, you can occasionally switch up ingredients for intrigue. Instead of salad greens, try microgreens. In lieu of ketchup, spread with guacamole. Rather than cheddar, top with a plant-based cheddar-style cheese alternative. And for extra smokiness, grill the buns, not just the portobellos.

4	large (5-inch) portobello mushrooms, stems removed
2	teaspoons extra-virgin olive oil
4	thin slices sharp cheddar cheese or vegan cheese (3/4 ounce each)
4	sprouted whole-grain or whole-wheat hamburger buns, split
1/2	medium red onion, thinly sliced
2	cups packed fresh spring mix or other salad greens
1/4	cup fruit-sweetened or no-sugar-added ketchup

KITCHEN TOOLS

- Cutting board
- Chef's knife
- Dry measuring cups
- Grill or grill pan
- Long-handled grilling spatula
- Cooling rack (optional)
- Measuring spoons

serves: 4 | **serving size:** 1 "burger"
prep time: 10 minutes | **cooking time:** 8 minutes

DIRECTIONS

1. Preheat a grill or grill pan over medium-high heat. (Hint: If using a grill pan, grill in batches.)

2. Rub the rounded side of mushrooms with the oil. Do not remove mushroom gills.

3. Grill the mushrooms, rounded side down, until grill marks form, about 4 minutes. Flip over the mushrooms, top with the cheese, and grill until softened, about 4 minutes. If desired, transfer cooked mushrooms to a cooling rack and allow excess liquids to drip off for 2 minutes.

4. Place cheesy portobellos on the bottom bun portions. Top each with the sliced onion, 1/2 cup salad greens, and the bun tops. Or stuff the buns in any order you prefer. Serve with the ketchup on the side.

EASY TIP!

For bun and ketchup recommendations, see pages 323 and 325 for "Ingredients of Choice."

THE "SUNSHINE" VITAMIN

You'll appreciate knowing that portobello mushrooms provide vitamin D—"the sunshine vitamin." In fact, they're the only natural source of the vitamin found in the produce section! Vitamin D may play a beneficial role in overcoming insulin resistance. That's especially helpful when your body isn't getting its daily dose of the vitamin naturally from the sun!

NUTRITION INFORMATION

Choices/Exchanges:
2 starch, 2 nonstarchy vegetable, 1 lean protein, 1 1/2 fat

Per Serving:

Calories	310
Calories from fat	100
Total fat	11 g
Saturated fat	4.8 g
Trans fat	0.2 g
Cholesterol	20 mg
Sodium	420 mg
Potassium	590 mg
Total carbohydrate	41 g
Dietary fiber	7 g
Sugars	3 g
Added sugars	0 g
Protein	17 g
Phosphorus	325 mg

three-minute skillet beans & greens

If you're a fan of quick fixes and highly flavored dishes, you've absolutely come to the right recipe. You'll wonder what took you so long to discover this delicious plant-based dinner for two. The double whammy of fiber and protein make it quite satisfying. And the mixture of spices takes it over the top flavor-wise. You're definitely going to want to stock up on garbanzo beans now that you've discovered the recipe!

1	tablespoon extra-virgin olive oil
1	(15-ounce) can no-salt-added garbanzo beans (chickpeas), drained (do not rinse)
1	teaspoon curry powder
1/2	teaspoon ground ginger
1/4	teaspoon freshly ground black pepper
1	(5-ounce) package fresh baby spinach
1/4	teaspoon sea salt

KITCHEN TOOLS

- Can opener
- Mesh strainer
- Measuring spoons
- Large skillet
- Large cooking spoon

serves: 2 | **serving size:** about 1 1/2 cups
prep time: 6 minutes | **cooking time:** 3 minutes

DIRECTIONS

1. In a large skillet, heat the oil over medium heat.

2. Add the garbanzo beans, curry powder, ginger, and pepper, and stir to coat.

3. Add the spinach and salt, and cook while gently stirring until the beans are heated through and the spinach is just wilted, about 2 1/2 minutes. Serve.

EASY TIP!

Like sauciness? Reserve the liquid from the canned garbanzo beans and stir a desired amount into the skillet along with the spinach. Prefer decadence? Splash with a little coconut milk.

A SPICE WITH BENEFITS

Curcumin is a natural compound in turmeric. And turmeric is a spice found in curry powder. The compound provides a distinctive golden-yellow color and has shown potential for lowering blood glucose levels. So keep curry powder or turmeric near your salt and pepper shakers to remember to sprinkle it onto dishes more regularly.

NUTRITION INFORMATION

Choices/Exchanges:
2 1/2 starch, 1 nonstarchy vegetable, 1 lean protein, 1 1/2 fat

Per Serving:

Calories	310
Calories from fat	100
Total fat	11 g
Saturated fat	1.4 g
Trans fat	0 g
Cholesterol	0 mg
Sodium	340 mg
Potassium	830 mg
Total carbohydrate	42 g
Dietary fiber	13 g
Sugars	7 g
Added sugars	0 g
Protein	15 g
Phosphorus	275 mg

ginger, tempeh & snow pea stir-fry

Tempeh is a fermented soybean cake . . . a savory cake! Its delightfully "meaty" texture works great in stir-fries. Look for tempeh in the refrigerated section of your supermarket, often near tofu or other vegetarian items. Though homemade stir-fries often involve complicated, overly salty sauces, this one features a simple yet highly flavored sauce made from just three ingredients—unsweetened applesauce, reduced-sodium tamari, and fresh gingerroot. You'll also use a cooking technique that's basically a "dry" stir-fry, so no excess sauce or oil is required. Serve with steamed brown rice or other whole grains. Or enjoy with Vegan Farrotto (page 250).

2	teaspoons toasted sesame oil
8	ounces tempeh, halved lengthwise, then cut crosswise into thin (1/3-inch-wide) strips
2	cups fresh snow peas, ends trimmed (5 ounces)
3	scallions, green and white parts, cut into 1 1/2-inch pieces
1/3	cup unsweetened applesauce
1	tablespoon plus 1 teaspoon reduced-sodium tamari (soy sauce)
1 1/2	teaspoons grated fresh gingerroot

KITCHEN TOOLS

- Measuring spoons
- Cutting board
- Chef's knife
- Dry measuring cups
- Spoon or peeler (for peeling ginger)
- Microplane zester/grater
- Wok or large, deep skillet
- Cooking spoon/spatula

serves: 2 | **serving size:** 2 cups
prep time: 15 minutes | **cooking time:** 8 minutes

DIRECTIONS

1. Heat the oil in a wok or large, deep skillet over medium-high heat. Add the tempeh and cook while stirring occasionally until the tempeh is golden brown, about 4 minutes. Add the snow peas and scallions, and cook while stirring until they begin to brown, about 3 minutes.

2. Stir in the applesauce, tamari, and ginger; remove from heat, and serve.

EASY TIP!

See page 23 for "How to grate fresh gingerroot."

CULINARY SWAPS

No snow peas? You can make this stir-fry with any nonstarchy vegetable that you have on hand, like green beans, sliced bell peppers, chopped asparagus, or broccoli florets. Got calories to spare? Top with dry-roasted peanuts for crunch or toasted sesame seeds for intrigue. Want bonus flavor dazzle? Sprinkle with fresh cilantro leaves or hot sauce.

NUTRITION INFORMATION

Choices/Exchanges:
1/2 starch, 1/2 carbohydrate,
1 nonstarchy vegetable,
3 medium-fat protein

Per Serving:

Calories	320
Calories from fat	150
Total fat	17 g
Saturated fat	3.6 g
Trans fat	0 g
Cholesterol	0 mg
Sodium	340 mg
Potassium	730 mg
Total carbohydrate	21 g
Dietary fiber	3 g
Sugars	15 g
Added sugars	0 g
Protein	26 g
Phosphorus	365 mg

spiced cauliflower roast

It's spiced, not spicy. So there's truly no sweat involved with this wow-worthy, 100% plant-based entrée. You can make the cauliflower roast (yes, that's the whole head!) for a special occasion and serve half of it as the main dish for anyone that takes a pass on turkey, chicken, or beef roast. Otherwise, just make it anytime for anyone (yes, that includes you!). Change up the spices from time to time to keep your palate enticed. And serve it with a protein-rich side, like black beans or my Four-Ingredient Bean Salad (page 236), to make it a substantial meal.

1	large (2 1/2-pound) head cauliflower
1	tablespoon extra-virgin olive oil
1	teaspoon curry powder
3/4	teaspoon ground ginger
1/2	teaspoon freshly ground black pepper
1/4	teaspoon sea salt

KITCHEN TOOLS

- Cutting board
- Chef's knife
- Cast-iron skillet or baking pan
- Measuring spoons
- Culinary/pastry brush
- Small mixing bowl
- Small spoon
- Aluminum foil

serves: 2 | **serving size:** 1/2 cauliflower head
prep time: 8 minutes | **cooking time:** 1 hour 40 minutes

DIRECTIONS

1. Preheat oven to 375°F.

2. Cut off enough of the cauliflower stem so that the head can stand upright. Then cut or snap off the outer leaves. Place the whole cauliflower onto a cast-iron skillet or a baking pan. Brush or rub the entire head with the oil.

3. In a small bowl, stir together the curry powder, ginger, black pepper, and salt. Sprinkle or rub the cauliflower head with the spice mixture.

4. Cover the cauliflower well—including the pan—with foil. Roast for 1 hour. Remove foil and roast uncovered until cooked through and well caramelized, about 35–40 minutes more.

5. Cut in half or slice into "steaks." Serve.

EASY TIP!

If you don't have a culinary/pastry brush, use the best "cooking tool" you have—your first three fingers. Rub the oil onto the cauliflower. Then wash your hands, of course.

SPICE SWAPS

Though cauliflower has a mild taste, it pairs well with a variety of not-so-mild herbs and spices. For a change of taste, consider other global cuisine–inspired options in place of the curry powder and ginger. Try ground cumin and ground cinnamon for a Lebanese spin or dried tarragon and garlic powder for French flair.

NUTRITION INFORMATION

Choices/Exchanges:
3 nonstarchy vegetable, 1 1/2 fat

Per Serving:

Calories	150
Calories from fat	70
Total fat	8 g
Saturated fat	1.4 g
Trans fat	0 g
Cholesterol	0 mg
Sodium	370 mg
Potassium	1050 mg
Total carbohydrate	18 g
Dietary fiber	7 g
Sugars	7 g
Added sugars	0 g
Protein	7 g
Phosphorus	155 mg

caramelized cauliflower & herbs on bed of hummus

This recipe transforms the popular snack of hummus and veggies into a warm and comforting entrée featuring sautéed cauliflower. To make it quick, buy pre-cut cauliflower florets. Alternatively, you can buy a 2-pound cauliflower head and chop it up. The cuisine magic then comes from the toppings, which include a sprinkling of hot pepper sauce, fresh herb sprigs (no chopping required!), and pine nuts. When you can find it, use purple or golden cauliflower for bonus enticement. You can use packaged organic hummus for ease. Complete the meal with whole-grain pita and a simple side salad. It's a surprising delight!

1 1/4	cups packaged organic classic hummus or Almost Hummus (page 76)
1	tablespoon extra-virgin olive oil
1 1/2	pounds cauliflower florets (7 cups)
1/8	teaspoon sea salt
1 1/2	teaspoons hot pepper sauce, or to taste
1/2	cup small fresh parsley, mint, or cilantro sprigs
2	tablespoons pine nuts

KITCHEN TOOLS

- Dry measuring cups
- Measuring spoons
- Spreader or bread knife
- 4 luncheon-sized plates
- Large, deep cast-iron or other stick-resistant skillet
- Cooking spoon or spatula

serves: 4 | **serving size:** 2 cups
prep time: 12 minutes | **cooking time:** 18 minutes

DIRECTIONS

1. Thinly spread 5 tablespoons (that's basically a rounded 1/4 cup) hummus onto each of 4 luncheon-sized plates.

2. Fully heat the oil in a large, deep cast-iron or other stick-resistant skillet over medium heat. Add the cauliflower florets and cook while stirring occasionally until cooked through and golden brown, about 18 minutes. Sprinkle with the salt.

3. Divide the cauliflower evenly among the 4 plates and arrange on top of the hummus. Drizzle each plate with the hot pepper sauce. Sprinkle each with 1 tablespoon parsley sprigs and 1/2 tablespoon pine nuts. Serve.

EASY TIP!

For hummus and hot pepper sauce recommendations, see page 324 for "Ingredients of Choice."

PAN-TOASTING PINE NUTS

For extra-nutty taste, toast the pine nuts. The easiest way to do that is to heat a skillet over medium-high heat. No oil is needed. Add the pine nuts and cook while stirring constantly until lightly browned, about 3 minutes. Immediately transfer the pine nuts to a heatproof bowl.

NUTRITION INFORMATION

Choices/Exchanges:
1/2 starch, 2 nonstarchy vegetable, 1 medium-fat protein, 1 1/2 fat

Per Serving:

Calories	230
Calories from fat	130
Total fat	14 g
Saturated fat	2 g
Trans fat	0 g
Cholesterol	0 mg
Sodium	480 mg
Potassium	760 mg
Total carbohydrate	21 g
Dietary fiber	9 g
Sugars	8 g
Added sugars	0 g
Protein	10 g
Phosphorus	240 mg

cacio e pepe e spinaci

This pasta dish has so much Italian-inspired goodness, its name deserves to remain Italian! *Cacio e pepe* is a popular Roman pasta dish. It basically means "cheese and pepper." It's simple, yet so tasty. The pepper isn't an afterthought; it's a key ingredient. This version is a twist on the classic with the addition of baby spinach . . . lots of baby spinach! While traditionally you'll find *cacio e pepe* made with regular bucatini, spaghetti, or tagliolini, this version is based on fun-shaped, better-for-you pasta for added interest. For a punch of protein, choose red lentil rotini or other pulse-based pastas. The flavorful recipe is a welcome change of taste from regular spaghetti marinara.

8	cups cold water
3 1/2	ounces dry whole-wheat or red lentil rotini
1	(5-ounce) package fresh baby spinach
2	teaspoons extra-virgin olive oil
1	teaspoon freshly ground black pepper
1/8	teaspoon sea salt
1/4	cup grated Parmesan cheese or aged vegan cheese

KITCHEN TOOLS

- Kitchen scale
- Liquid measuring cup
- Large saucepan
- Strainer
- Large slotted spoon
- Dry measuring cups
- Measuring spoons

serves: 2 | serving size: 1 1/2 cups
prep time: 6 minutes | cooking time: 10 minutes

DIRECTIONS

1. Add water to a large saucepan. Bring to a boil over high heat. Stir in the rotini and cook according to package directions, about 8 minutes. Drain the pasta using a strainer. Set aside.

2. Add the spinach to the dry saucepan. Place over medium heat. Cook while stirring until the spinach is slightly wilted, about 1 minute. Add the drained pasta, oil, pepper, and salt, and cook while stirring until the spinach is fully wilted, about 1 minute. Stir in the cheese. Serve.

EASY TIP!

For pasta recommendations, see page 325 for "Ingredients of Choice."

BLACK PEPPER BENEFITS

Even when a recipe doesn't specifically call for black pepper, you can absolutely add it. Besides offering its distinctive kick in the palate, black pepper provides polyphenols, which are antioxidants, and a compound called piperine, which may play a role in diabetes treatment. For the biggest flavor, get a pepper mill so you can grind pepper as needed rather than using pre-ground pepper.

Choices/Exchanges:

2 1/2 starch, 1 nonstarchy vegetable, 1 lean protein

Per Serving:

Calories	270
Calories from fat	80
Total fat	9 g
Saturated fat	2.4 g
Trans fat	0 g
Cholesterol	5 mg
Sodium	320 mg
Potassium	640 mg
Total carbohydrate	40 g
Dietary fiber	6 g
Sugars	2 g
Added sugars	0 g
Protein	12 g
Phosphorus	270 mg

"steak" fajitas

The "steak" here is beef-free thanks to meaty portobello mushroom caps. That makes it an ideal pick for a Meatless Monday fix—or any other day that you'd like to go meatless. To arrange your "steak" fajitas, try this: In order, spread each tortilla with the refried beans; top with the vegetable mixture and salsa; then add a dollop of guacamole. For a complete meal with Mexican appeal and extra protein power, serve your fajitas with extra beans on the side. Or, if you're a shellfish fan, pair it with a spicy shrimp appetizer. This recipe can easily be doubled to feed a family of four—or you and three close friends!

1	teaspoon avocado oil or peanut oil
2	large portobello mushrooms, stems removed, cut into 1/3-inch-wide slices
1	large green or red bell pepper (or half of each), cut into 1/3-inch-wide slices
1/4	cup canned lower-sodium vegetarian refried beans
4	(5-inch) soft whole-wheat flour tortillas (about 1 ounce each)
1/4	cup chunky preservative-free salsa or salsa verde
1/4	cup Super Green Guacamole (page 78) or deli-prepared guacamole

KITCHEN TOOLS

- Measuring spoons
- Cutting board
- Chef's knife
- Large cast-iron or other stick-resistant skillet
- Cooking tongs
- Can opener
- Dry measuring cups
- Small microwave-safe bowl
- Small spoon or spoon-shaped spatula

DIRECTIONS

1. Heat the oil in a large cast-iron or other stick-resistant skillet over medium-high heat. Add the mushroom and bell pepper slices, and cook while tossing with tongs occasionally until the mushrooms are wilted and peppers are browned, about 8 minutes.

2. Meanwhile, add the refried beans to a small microwave-safe bowl. Heat in the microwave on high until hot, about 30 seconds.

3. Serve the vegetables (from the skillet), refried beans, tortillas, salsa, and guacamole separately so each person can assemble their own fajitas. Use 1 tablespoon refried beans, 1/4 of the vegetable mixture, 1 tablespoon salsa, and 1 tablespoon guacamole per fajita.

EASY TIP!

You don't need to remove the portobello mushroom gills; they're 100% edible! But if you're weirded out by them, you can choose to scrape them out of the caps with a spoon.

PORTOBELLO MUSHROOM STEM PREP

If your portobello mushrooms have stems, snap them off by hand. Compost the stems. Or better yet, cook and savor them. Thinly slice the stems into extra-thin coins, sauté in a little oil, and serve as a scrambled egg topper. Or season the slices with a pinch of smoked paprika, garlic powder, and sea salt, then enjoy as "pepperoni" for pizza!

NUTRITION INFORMATION

Choices/Exchanges:
2 starch, 2 nonstarchy vegetable, 2 1/2 fat

Per Serving:

Calories	320
Calories from fat	120
Total fat	13 g
Saturated fat	3.5 g
Trans fat	0 g
Cholesterol	0 mg
Sodium	500 mg
Potassium	940 mg
Total carbohydrate	43 g
Dietary fiber	11 g
Sugars	7 g
Added sugars	0 g
Protein	10 g
Phosphorus	340 mg

sheet pan eggplant parmesan with vine tomatoes

Eggplant Parmesan is a classic Italian comfort food. It can traditionally take as much as 45 minutes of prep time alone. Luckily, this is an easy-prep way to make it . . . and all on one sheet pan. It can be quite nutritious, especially when it's heavy on the vegetables and not-so-heavy on the cheese. This is a perfect example of that. You'll get all of the comfort without an excessive amount of calories or saturated fat! You can even serve this eggplant parmesan with a side of spaghetti marinara for extra comfort if your meal plan allows.

1	large (1 1/3-pound) eggplant, cut into 8 rounds
2	tablespoons extra-virgin olive oil
1/8	teaspoon sea salt
2	medium vine-ripened tomatoes, each cut into 4 rounds
3	tablespoons grated Parmesan cheese or aged vegan cheese
1/2	cup shredded part-skim mozzarella cheese or vegan cheese
1/3	cup packed fresh basil leaves

KITCHEN TOOLS

- Cutting board
- Chef's knife
- Large rimmed baking sheet
- Unbleached parchment paper
- Culinary/pastry brush
- Measuring spoons
- Dry measuring cups

serves: 2 | serving size: 4 eggplant rounds
prep time: 12 minutes | cooking time: 40–45 minutes

DIRECTIONS

1. Preheat oven to 400°F. Line a large rimmed baking sheet with unbleached parchment paper.

2. Arrange the 8 eggplant rounds on the baking sheet. Lightly brush the top of each with the oil. Sprinkle with the salt. Top each eggplant round with a tomato slice. Sprinkle with the Parmesan cheese.

3. Bake for 25 minutes. Remove from oven. Sprinkle each round with the mozzarella cheese. Return to the oven and bake until the eggplant is cooked through and mozzarella cheese is golden brown, about 15–20 minutes more.

4. Sprinkle with the whole basil leaves and serve.

EASY TIP!

While firmly holding onto the eggplant towards the stem end of the eggplant, carefully cut it crosswise into 8 thick, round slices. Then compost (or discard) the stem end.

DON'T PEEL THE EGGPLANT

Eat the cooked eggplant skin! It's got fiber and antioxidants as well as a nutritional standout: nasunin. Nasunin is an anthocyanin phytonutrient; research suggests it is a powerful antioxidant that can potentially protect your cells from damage. That's an especially good thing when you have diabetes!

NUTRITION INFORMATION

Choices/Exchanges:
5 nonstarchy vegetable,
1 medium-fat protein, 2 1/2 fat

Per Serving:

Calories	310
Calories from fat	180
Total fat	20 g
Saturated fat	5.5 g
Trans fat	0 g
Cholesterol	20 mg
Sodium	380 mg
Potassium	1100 mg
Total carbohydrate	24 g
Dietary fiber	11 g
Sugars	15 g
Added sugars	0 g
Protein	13 g
Phosphorus	270 mg

sheet pan zucchini, red pepper & tofu "stir-fry"

No wok required here. That means this recipe is technically not a stir-fry. But it looks, tastes, and acts like one; so I've dubbed it "stir-fry"—in quotes, of course! This is the easiest-ever way to make a stir-fry-style recipe . . . simply roast everything on a sheet pan! Then savor as is. Or, if you wish, accessorize it. Sprinkle with peanuts for crunch. Drizzle with hot sauce for pow. Add fresh cilantro for herbal flair. To make it a full meal, serve over steamed brown rice or other whole grains. Grab your chopsticks!

1	(14-ounce; drained weight) package organic extra-firm or super-firm tofu
1	tablespoon grated fresh gingerroot
2	tablespoons plus 2 teaspoons reduced-sodium tamari (soy sauce)
1 1/2	tablespoons rice vinegar
1 1/2	tablespoons toasted sesame oil
2	medium zucchinis, cut into 1/2-inch-thick rounds
2	medium red bell peppers, cut into 1-inch strips

KITCHEN TOOLS

- Spoon or peeler (for peeling ginger)
- Microplane zester/grater
- Cutting board
- Chef's knife
- Large rimmed baking sheet
- Unbleached parchment paper
- Measuring spoons
- Whisk or fork
- Large mixing bowl

serves: 4 | serving size: 1 1/2 cups
prep time: 15 minutes | cooking time: 30 minutes

DIRECTIONS

1. Preheat oven to 450°F. Line a large rimmed baking sheet with unbleached parchment paper.

2. Pat or squeeze the tofu of excess liquid, if necessary. Cut the tofu into (3/4-inch) cubes.

3. In a large bowl, whisk together the ginger, tamari, vinegar, and oil. Add the zucchini and bell pepper pieces to the sauce mixture; toss by hand to coat. Arrange the zucchinis and peppers in a single layer on the baking sheet (fill 2/3 of the sheet), letting excess sauce drip back into the bowl. Add the tofu to the bowl with the remaining sauce mixture; toss to coat. Arrange the tofu in a single layer on the baking sheet (fill the rest of the sheet). Drizzle tofu with any remaining sauce.

4. Roast until the tofu and vegetables are browned, about 30 minutes; no stirring needed. Serve.

EASY TIP!

See page 23 for "How to grate fresh gingerroot" and "How to slice a bell pepper."

TRY SPROUTED SUPER-FIRM TOFU

Just like any tofu, sprouted tofu is made with whole soybeans. But in this case, the soybeans are partially sprouted before being used to make tofu. It's similar to mung bean sprouts or alfalfa sprouts, but those are fully sprouted. Sprouted beans may be associated with better digestion and nutrient absorption.

NUTRITION INFORMATION

Choices/Exchanges:
2 nonstarchy vegetable,
1 medium-fat protein, 1 1/2 fat

Per Serving:

Calories	180
Calories from fat	100
Total fat	11 g
Saturated fat	1.4 g
Trans fat	0 g
Cholesterol	0 mg
Sodium	350 mg
Potassium	580 mg
Total carbohydrate	10 g
Dietary fiber	3 g
Sugars	6 g
Added sugars	0 g
Protein	12 g
Phosphorus	205 mg

italian rotini pasta salad

When can a pasta salad be an entrée? When you toss this together! It's got a notable amount of protein and fiber thanks to the use of pulse pasta instead of regular pasta. In this case, that means red lentil rotini—though if you can't find the red lentil version, simply use whole-grain pasta and serve this recipe as a side. Either way, it's full of Italian flair, and it's a fun way to get some veggies. In this pasta salad, the combination of artichoke hearts, broccoli florets, and sundried tomatoes provides an ideal trio of tastes, textures, and color.

8	cups cold water
7	ounces dry red lentil rotini
1	(13.75-ounce) can quartered artichoke hearts, drained
1 1/2	cups fresh bite-sized broccoli florets
1/4	cup packed sundried tomatoes (not packed in oil), thinly sliced
1/4	cup Simple Italian Vinaigrette (page 292) or natural Italian vinaigrette dressing, divided

KITCHEN TOOLS

- Kitchen scale
- Can opener
- Large strainer
- Cutting board
- Chef's knife
- Large saucepan
- Cooking spoon
- Dry measuring cups
- Liquid measuring cup
- Large mixing bowl

serves: 4 | serving size: 1 1/2 cups
prep time: 8 minutes | cooking time: 12 minutes
(plus cooling time)

DIRECTIONS

1. Fill a large saucepan 3/4 full of water (about 8 cups) and bring to a boil. Stir in the rotini and cook according to package directions until al dente (cooked through yet firm), about 8 minutes. Drain the rotini using the strainer.

2. Add the artichoke hearts, broccoli, sundried tomatoes, and hot, drained rotini to a large bowl. Drizzle with 2 tablespoons dressing. Stir to combine. Set aside to cool for 15 minutes. Stir, then chill in the refrigerator.

3. Stir in the remaining 2 tablespoons dressing just before serving.

EASY TIP!

For a bottled natural Italian vinaigrette recommendation, see page 325 for "Ingredients of Choice."

PAIR WITH PROTEIN

Since this pasta salad is designed to be an entrée, pair it with a protein-rich side dish that you normally might serve as an entrée. For instance, Spice-Rubbed Salmon (page 168), Pesto Grilled Shrimp (page 176), or a quick grilled chicken thigh deliciously complete this meal. Alternatively, go for a fun side, like deviled eggs, a piece of string cheese, or a scoop of cottage cheese.

NUTRITION INFORMATION

Choices/Exchanges:
2 starch, 2 nonstarchy vegetable, 1 lean protein, 1 fat

Per Serving:

Calories	290
Calories from fat	70
Total fat	8 g
Saturated fat	1.1 g
Trans fat	0 g
Cholesterol	0 mg
Sodium	230 mg
Potassium	710 mg
Total carbohydrate	42 g
Dietary fiber	11 g
Sugars	3 g
Added sugars	0 g
Protein	16 g
Phosphorus	215 mg

MAIN DISHES: FISH & SHELLFISH

coastal tuna salad lettuce wraps

Here's a refreshing take on tuna salad with pops of natural sweetness from seedless red grapes. Nature provides the wrap since the creamy salad is served in lovely lettuce leaves for carb-friendliness. And you'll still get protein-packed satisfaction and heart-healthful omega 3 fatty acids. I kept the recipe no-fuss; but if you'd like to accessorize your tuna salad, try poppyseeds and fresh tarragon. Pair the wraps with a fiber-rich side, such as a bean salad or Southern Black-Eyed Peas (page 244), to complete the meal.

1	(3-ounce) pouch no-salt-added tuna or chicken
1	tablespoon no-sugar-added mayonnaise
1	teaspoon bottled lemon juice (not from concentrate)
1	scallion, green part only, thinly sliced
4	large seedless red grapes, thinly sliced
2	Boston or Bibb lettuce leaves

KITCHEN TOOLS

- Cutting board
- Chef's knife
- Medium bowl
- Fork
- Measuring spoons

serves: 1 | **serving size:** 2 wraps
(made with 1/2 cup tuna salad per wrap)
prep time: 8 minutes | **cooking time:** 0 minutes

DIRECTIONS

1. Add the tuna to a medium bowl, and flake it using a fork. Add the mayonnaise, lemon juice (and salt, if desired), and stir well to combine. Stir in the scallion and grapes.

2. Add 1/2 cup tuna salad down the center of each lettuce leaf. Fold or roll up to enjoy as a wrap.

EASY TIP!

For tuna recommendations, see page 324 for "Ingredients of Choice."

ECO-FRIENDLY TUNA

Choose fish responsibly. Look for tuna that's sustainably caught, such as 100% pole-and-line caught, from healthy oceans. Pick a "low-mercury" brand. And buy tuna that's packaged or canned without added fillers or preservatives. For more guidance on tuna selection, see the Environmental Defense Fund's Seafood Selector at seafood.edf.org.

NUTRITION INFORMATION

Choices/Exchanges:

1/2 carbohydrate, 3 lean protein, 1 1/2 fat

Per Serving:

Calories	230
Calories from fat	130
Total fat	14 g
Saturated fat	2.6 g
Trans fat	0 g
Cholesterol	30 mg
Sodium	135 mg
Potassium	320 mg
Total carbohydrate	6 g
Dietary fiber	1 g
Sugars	4 g
Added sugars	0 g
Protein	22 g
Phosphorus	205 mg

california avocado toast with salmon

Count me as a groupie of delicious recipes that require no more than 2 minutes of cooking. That includes this recipe! And the only actual "cooking" is done in your toaster. Avocado toast is a deliciously simple dish. But it's not a notable protein source as is. So add a protein-rich ingredient. One of the tastiest toppers has got to be smoked salmon. That's why I included it here. Arrange it on top of your toast for big flavor in a small amount. Plus, it boosts total protein to make the bodacious avocado toast a more balanced bite.

2	slices sprouted whole-grain or whole-wheat bread, toasted
1	Hass avocado, peeled and thinly sliced
1	teaspoon bottled lemon juice (not from concentrate)
1 1/4	ounces extra thinly sliced smoked salmon
1	teaspoon chopped fresh dill fronds (feathery leaves)

KITCHEN TOOLS

- Toaster
- Cutting board
- Chef's knife
- Kitchen scale
- Soup spoon
- Measuring spoons

serves: 2 | **serving size:** 1 piece topped toast
prep time: 8 minutes | **cooking time:** 2 minutes

DIRECTIONS

1. Top each piece of toast with half the avocado slices. Sprinkle with the lemon juice.

2. Divide the salmon evenly between the two toasts. Sprinkle with the dill. Serve.

EASY TIP!

See page 25 for "How to cut an avocado."

TOPPER SWAPS

If you want a change of taste from time to time, swap out the smoked salmon for other ingredients that also provide a punch of protein and good nutrition. Try boiled or fried eggs, roasted garbanzo beans, shelled edamame, or pistachios.

NUTRITION INFORMATION

Choices/Exchanges:
1 starch, 1/2 fruit, 1 lean protein, 2 fat

Per Serving:

Calories	220
Calories from fat	110
Total fat	12 g
Saturated fat	1.8 g
Trans fat	0 g
Cholesterol	12 mg
Sodium	200 mg
Potassium	480 mg
Total carbohydrate	22 g
Dietary fiber	8 g
Sugars	1 g
Added sugars	0 g
Protein	9 g
Phosphorus	130 mg

smoked salmon open-face sandwich

Sometimes people shy away from smoked salmon because it contains a significant amount of sodium. The healthful trick is to enjoy it as a flavor accent, not in New York deli–sized portions. Since it has bodacious taste, you truly don't need much to find taste-bud bliss. This recipe has another trick. Serving the sandwich open faced using just one slice of bread helps keep total carbohydrate in check. Plus you're showing off the appealing and colorful sandwich contents. All this, and you'll have extra cucumber "chips and dip" to serve alongside.

2	tablespoons Neufchâtel (light cream cheese)
2	tablespoons plain 0% fat Greek yogurt
1	thin slice whole-grain rye bread
1	ounce thinly sliced smoked salmon
1	large, thin slice red onion, separated into rings
1	(3-inch) piece English cucumber, unpeeled, thinly sliced into coins
1	sprig fresh dill, finely chopped

KITCHEN TOOLS

- Cutting board
- Chef's knife
- Measuring spoons
- Small spoon
- Small bowl
- Luncheon-sized plate
- Spreader or butter knife

serves: 1 | **serving size:** 1 sandwich
prep time: 10 minutes | **cooking time:** 0 minutes

DIRECTIONS

1. In a small bowl, stir together the Neufchâtel and yogurt.

2. On a luncheon-sized plate, spread the bread with half the Neufchâtel mixture. Top with the salmon, onion, and half the cucumber slices.

3. Serve the remaining cucumber slices and remaining Neufchâtel mixture on the side.

4. Sprinkle everything with the dill. Enjoy with a fork and knife.

EASY TIP!

Let the Neufchâtel stand at room temperature for 15 minutes before recipe prep. It'll be easier to stir together with the yogurt.

WHAT IS NEUFCHÂTEL?

It's basically reduced-fat cream cheese, kind of like the 2% version of whole milk. You can use American-style Neufchâtel just like regular cream cheese. You'll save calories and saturated fat! Here's the gist: 1 ounce (that's 2 tablespoons) of Neufchâtel provides 70 calories and 4 grams of saturated fat; regular cream cheese provides 110 calories and 6 grams of saturated fat.

NUTRITION INFORMATION

Choices/Exchanges:
1 starch, 1 nonstarchy vegetable, 1 lean protein, 1 1/2 fat

Per Serving:

Calories	210
Calories from fat	80
Total fat	9 g
Saturated fat	4.2 g
Trans fat	0 g
Cholesterol	30 mg
Sodium	470 mg
Potassium	340 mg
Total carbohydrate	19 g
Dietary fiber	2 g
Sugars	5 g
Added sugars	0 g
Protein	13 g
Phosphorus	180 mg

spice-rubbed salmon

Salmon is considered a "superfood" thanks mainly to its heart-healthful omega 3 fatty acids. Lucky for you, the popular fish is tasty, too, especially in this easy grilled preparation—whether grilled indoors or outdoors. The ground coriander and cumin that you'll massage into the fillets provide earthy spiciness and global cuisine–inspired flair. In fact, it's such a pleasing and easy recipe that I occasionally make it with boneless, skinless chicken thighs in place of fresh salmon. Just grill the chicken until well done, about 15 minutes total. Either way, it's splendid when paired with Orange-Pistachio Couscous (page 252) and leafy greens.

24	ounces center-cut salmon fillet with skin, divided into 4 (6-ounce) fillets
2	teaspoons avocado oil or sunflower oil
1	teaspoon ground coriander
1/2	teaspoon ground cumin
1/2	teaspoon sea salt

KITCHEN TOOLS

- Grill or grill pan
- Measuring spoons
- Large plate
- Culinary/pastry brush
- Long-handled tongs
- Instant-read (meat) thermometer (optional)

DIRECTIONS

1. Preheat a grill or a grill pan over medium heat.

2. On a large plate, lightly brush all sides of the salmon with the oil. Skin side down, sprinkle just the flesh side of the salmon with the coriander, cumin, and salt, then rub (massage) the spices into the flesh using your fingers.

3. Grill the salmon, flesh side down first, until grill marks form, about 5 minutes. Flip and grill about 4–5 minutes longer for medium doneness (internal temperature of at least 145°F). Serve.

EASY TIP!

Ask the fishmonger for center-cut salmon so it'll be an even thickness. That way it'll cook evenly, and you won't have overcooked ends.

TOP WITH INTRIGUE

This salmon is flavorful as is. But if serving with basic sides, top with nectarine or mango pico de gallo for culinary excitement. Make a fruity pico de gallo by following the Grape Tomato Pico de Gallo recipe (page 294) and simply using fresh diced fruit in place of the grape tomatoes. Its sweetness is a lovely contrast to the earthy spices on the salmon.

NUTRITION INFORMATION

Choices/Exchanges:
5 lean protein, 1 fat

Per Serving:

Calories	280
Calories from fat	140
Total fat	15 g
Saturated fat	3 g
Trans fat	0 g
Cholesterol	90 mg
Sodium	380 mg
Potassium	610 mg
Total carbohydrate	0 g
Dietary fiber	0 g
Sugars	0 g
Added sugars	0 g
Protein	33 g
Phosphorus	440 mg

korean bbq–inspired baked salmon

My mouth waters whenever I hear the term "Korean barbecue." Unfortunately, that term is not always associated with healthy cuisine. Fortunately, it is here! The Korean BBQ–inspired sauce on this salmon has that ideal balance of sweet, salty, tangy, and spicy. The sweetness comes naturally from fruit, not added sugars. Slather the sauce over fresh or thawed frozen salmon fillets before baking. And, perhaps another time, slather it over 24 ounces of boneless, skinless chicken thighs; bake the chicken without the sauce for 15 minutes, then brush with the sauce and bake until well done, about 15 minutes more.

24	ounces center-cut salmon with skin, divided into 4 (6-ounce) fillets
2	tablespoons fruit-sweetened or no-sugar-added ketchup
1	tablespoon fruit-sweetened apricot fruit spread (jam)*
1	tablespoon reduced-sodium tamari (soy sauce)
2	teaspoons rice vinegar
1/4	teaspoon hot pepper sauce
1	teaspoon sesame seeds

*Note: Ideally, choose a fruit spread without added sugars.

KITCHEN TOOLS

- Large rimmed baking sheet
- Unbleached parchment paper
- Measuring spoons
- Small bowl
- Spoon
- Instant-read (meat) thermometer (optional)

serves: 4 | serving size: 1 fillet
prep time: 8 minutes | cooking time: 16 minutes

DIRECTIONS

1. Preheat oven to 400°F. Line a large rimmed baking sheet with unbleached parchment paper.

2. Place the salmon, skin side down, on the baking sheet.

3. In a small bowl, stir together the ketchup, fruit spread, tamari, vinegar, and hot pepper sauce. Lightly spread the mixture onto the top of each fillet using the back of the spoon. Sprinkle with the sesame seeds.

4. Bake until the salmon is flaky and cooked through (internal temperature of at least 145°F), about 16 minutes. Serve.

EASY TIP!

Ask the fishmonger for center-cut salmon so it'll be an even thickness. That way it'll cook evenly, and you won't have overcooked ends.

ENVIRONMENTALLY FRIENDLY SALMON

All salmon has heart-friendly omega 3 fatty acids, but not all salmon is good for the environment. Before buying salmon, check the Environmental Defense Fund's Seafood Selector to find the type that's best for you and the ocean. Wild Alaskan salmon is a top pick; it's eco-friendly, low in mercury, and high in omega 3s. Go to seafood.edf.org/salmon.

NUTRITION INFORMATION

Choices/Exchanges:
5 lean protein, 1 fat

Per Serving:

Calories	280
Calories from fat	120
Total fat	13 g
Saturated fat	2.8 g
Trans fat	0 g
Cholesterol	95 mg
Sodium	300 mg
Potassium	640 mg
Total carbohydrate	4 g
Dietary fiber	0 g
Sugars	3 g
Added sugars	0 g
Protein	34 g
Phosphorus	450 mg

cajun fish & roasted cherry tomatoes

Fan of flavor? Then you've gotta try this! If you have a palate that prefers simple flavors, though, you can make it with less Cajun seasoning and gradually work up to the full-flavored amount. Fan of poultry? Make this same exact recipe using 24 ounces of boneless, skinless chicken thighs—and just bake about 5 minutes longer. Either way, enjoy your protein along with whole grains and greens. And drizzle any extra pan liquids over your meal for bonus succulence.

24	ounces barramundi, divided into 4 (6-ounce) fillets
1	pint cherry tomatoes or large grape tomatoes
1	tablespoon extra-virgin olive oil
1	tablespoon no-salt-added Cajun seasoning or DIY Salt-Free Cajun Seasoning (see tip on page 173)
1/4	teaspoon sea salt

KITCHEN TOOLS

- Large rimmed baking sheet
- Unbleached parchment paper
- Measuring spoons

serves: 4 | serving size: 1 fillet with 1/2 cup tomatoes
prep time: 6 minutes | cooking time: 13–15 minutes

DIRECTIONS

1. Preheat oven to 450°F. Line a large rimmed baking sheet with unbleached parchment paper.

2. Place the fish fillets on the baking sheet. Arrange the cherry tomatoes around the fillets. Sprinkle the top of the fish and tomatoes with the oil, Cajun seasoning, and salt.

3. Bake until the fish is flaky and cooked through, about 13–15 minutes; no stirring or flipping required. Serve.

EASY TIP!

Look for frozen barramundi, such as Australis All-Natural Barramundi, in the freezer section of your supermarket's fish department. It's already cut into 6-ounce portions.

MAKE DIY SALT-FREE CAJUN SEASONING

If you can't find no-salt-added Cajun seasoning, make this version of it. In a jar, combine 1 tablespoon each of dried thyme, dried oregano, garlic powder, onion powder, sweet paprika, cayenne pepper, and freshly ground black pepper. Use just 1 tablespoon for this recipe. Savor it in other recipes for a distinctive Cajun flavor accent, too.

NUTRITION INFORMATION

Choices/Exchanges:
5 lean protein

Per Serving:

Calories	230
Calories from fat	80
Total fat	9 g
Saturated fat	2.5 g
Trans fat	0 g
Cholesterol	35 mg
Sodium	190 mg
Potassium	630 mg
Total carbohydrate	4 g
Dietary fiber	1 g
Sugars	2 g
Added sugars	0 g
Protein	35 g
Phosphorus	350 mg

seasonal baked whitefish pouch

Pick up California halibut or Alaskan cod fillets from your favorite fish department, then make this recipe while the fish is fresh. It's a fun recipe—everything is baked in personal foil pouches. By sealing the edges of the pouches, you'll seal in all of the moistness. The result—lots of savory sauciness in the pouch after cooking. So serve the steamy fish and vegetables over farro or brown rice. Or sop up this flavorful sauce with a whole-grain roll. Complete your meal with a crisp side salad, too.

4	cups bite-sized pieces seasonal nonstarchy vegetables (such as zucchini)
2	tablespoons extra-virgin olive oil
1/2	teaspoon sea salt, divided
16	ounces halibut or cod, divided into 4 (4-ounce) fillets
1	large shallot, finely chopped (1/4 cup chopped)
1	teaspoon dried herbs (such as crushed rosemary)
1	tablespoon plus 1 teaspoon bottled lemon juice (not from concentrate)

KITCHEN TOOLS

- Cutting board
- Chef's knife
- Large rimmed baking sheet
- Aluminum foil
- Dry measuring cups
- Measuring spoons

serves: 4 | **serving size:** 1 fillet with 3/4 cup cooked vegetables
prep time: 12 minutes | **cooking time:** 18 minutes

DIRECTIONS

1. Preheat oven to 425°F. Cut foil into 4 (12-inch) square pieces.

2. In order, top the right half of each foil square with 1 cup vegetables, 1 1/2 teaspoons oil, dash (1/16 teaspoon) salt, 1 fish fillet, 1 tablespoon shallot, 1/4 teaspoon herbs, and dash (1/16 teaspoon) of remaining salt.

3. Fold the left side of each pouch over the ingredients. Seal the edges well. Place on a baking sheet. Bake until the fish is flaky and cooked through (internal temperature of at least 145°F) and vegetables are tender, about 18 minutes.

4. Let stand about 5 minutes, carefully open pouches, drizzle with the lemon juice, and serve.

EASY TIP!

Pick up bite-sized seasonal veggies from your supermarket's pre-prepped produce section or a salad bar. Or keep a vegetable scrap bowl in the fridge for use in recipes like this.

MAKE IT YOUR WAY

Enjoy your fish pouch using various herb and vegetable combinations. Try these: rosemary with zucchini and/or yellow summer squash; tarragon with asparagus and/or fennel; and thyme with bell peppers and/or mushrooms. And, of course, explore your own personalized combos.

NUTRITION INFORMATION

Choices/Exchanges:
1 nonstarchy vegetable,
3 lean protein, 1 fat

Per Serving:

Calories	210
Calories from fat	90
Total fat	10 g
Saturated fat	1.1 g
Trans fat	0 g
Cholesterol	35 mg
Sodium	350 mg
Potassium	860 mg
Total carbohydrate	6 g
Dietary fiber	2 g
Sugars	3 g
Added sugars	0 g
Protein	25 g
Phosphorus	305 mg

pesto grilled shrimp

Grab some skewers and get your grill on. Of course, first check to make sure you've got olive oil, pesto, and shrimp. Purchase shrimp in a recipe-ready form—so it's less work for you. For this three-ingredient recipe, ideally ask your fishmonger for deveined shrimp with tails and adjoining first segment attached. Once you have the shrimp you need, this party-style entrée is so simple—just thread shrimp onto skewers, brush with olive oil, grill or pan-grill, then top with pesto sauce. For some reason, everything seems to taste better when served on skewers!

1	pound peeled jumbo shrimp* with tails (about 24 shrimp)
2	teaspoons extra-virgin olive oil
2	tablespoons jarred pesto sauce or Cheese-Free Pesto (page 288)

*Note: If possible, use fresh (never frozen) shrimp or shrimp that are free of preservatives (for example, shrimp that have not been treated with salt or STPP [sodium tripolyphosphate]).

KITCHEN TOOLS

- Measuring spoons
- Grill or grill pan
- 8 (7-inch or longer) reusable skewers
- Culinary/pastry brush
- Long-handled tongs
- Spoon

serves: 4 | **serving size:** 2 skewers (about 6 shrimp)
prep time: 8 minutes | **cooking time:** 8 minutes

DIRECTIONS

1. Prepare a grill or grill pan.

2. Thread the shrimp onto eight (7-inch or longer) reusable skewers—about 3 shrimp per skewer, piercing through the tail and head of each shrimp, to allow it to lie flat on the grill. Lightly brush both sides of the shrimp with the oil.

3. Grill shrimp skewers (in batches, if necessary) over direct medium-high heat, turning only as needed, until the shrimp is just cooked through, pink on the outside, and grill marks form, about 3 minutes per side.

4. Transfer the shrimp skewers to a platter. Spoon the pesto on top of the shrimp and spread it on with the back of the spoon. Serve.

EASY TIP!

If using bamboo skewers, soak them in water for 15 minutes before inserting into the shrimp; it'll help prevent burning during grilling.

PROTEIN SWAPS

These skewers are quite versatile. You can swap the shrimp for chicken breast strips or firm tofu cubes. If using chicken, grill until well done, about 4 minutes per side. And whichever protein you pick, consider serving the skewers on a bed of Lemony Freekeh Protein Pilaf (page 248).

NUTRITION INFORMATION

Choices/Exchanges:
3 lean protein

Per Serving:

Calories	140
Calories from fat	40
Total fat	4.5 g
Saturated fat	0.7 g
Trans fat	0 g
Cholesterol	190 mg
Sodium	200 mg
Potassium	260 mg
Total carbohydrate	0 g
Dietary fiber	0 g
Sugars	0 g
Added sugars	0 g
Protein	24 g
Phosphorus	235 mg

sheet pan chile-lime shrimp & peppers

Pick red, orange, and yellow bell peppers, and this easy fajita-like recipe will be super colorful. It's also super moist, so don't try to keep cooking it until you see charring. It's really versatile, too! Enjoy this roast-n-serve mixture as a power bowl by pairing it with brown rice. Make it the main feature of whole-grain burritos, tacos, or fajitas along with some guacamole. Or perhaps showcase it as a Mexican salad on a bed of leafy greens with a drizzling of salsa verde. (Hint: Alternatively, you can make this recipe with bite-sized strips of chicken breasts or thighs.)

3	scallions, thinly sliced, green and white parts separated
3	medium bell peppers (various colors), thinly sliced
1	pound large shrimp,* peeled, deveined, and tail removed
2	tablespoons avocado oil or peanut oil
1 1/2	teaspoons chili powder
1/2	teaspoon sea salt
2	tablespoons bottled lime juice (not from concentrate)

*Note: If possible, use fresh (never frozen) shrimp or shrimp that are free of preservatives (for example, shrimp that have not been treated with salt or STPP [sodium tripolyphosphate]).

KITCHEN TOOLS

- Cutting board
- Chef's knife
- Large rimmed baking sheet
- Unbleached parchment paper
- Measuring spoons
- Large mixing bowl
- Tongs

DIRECTIONS

1. Preheat oven to 450°F. Line a large rimmed baking sheet with unbleached parchment paper.

2. In a large bowl, toss together with tongs (or by hand!) the white parts of the scallions, the bell peppers, shrimp, oil, chili powder, and salt. In a single layer, arrange the mixture onto the baking sheet.

3. Bake until the shrimp is cooked through and pink on the outside, about 12 minutes; no stirring required.

4. Sprinkle with the green parts of the scallions, drizzle with the lime juice, and serve.

EASY TIP!

See page 23 for "How to slice a bell pepper."

IS SHRIMP DIABETES-FRIENDLY?

Yes! But like any food, prepare shrimp wisely and don't overindulge. Consider eating a serving a few times per month. A 3 1/2-ounce cooked serving provides about 95 calories, 21 grams of protein, 0 grams of total carbohydrate, 1 gram of total fat, and 190 milligrams of cholesterol.

NUTRITION INFORMATION

Choices/Exchanges:
2 nonstarchy vegetable,
3 lean protein, 1/2 fat

Per Serving:

Calories	200
Calories from fat	70
Total fat	8 g
Saturated fat	0.9 g
Trans fat	0 g
Cholesterol	190 mg
Sodium	410 mg
Potassium	550 mg
Total carbohydrate	9 g
Dietary fiber	2 g
Sugars	4 g
Added sugars	0 g
Protein	25 g
Phosphorus	275 mg

pan-seared tilapia, black beans & mango salad

When is salad an entire meal? When you make this! The base of the salad is leafy greens and black beans dressed in a simple, fresh lime vinaigrette. You'll use regular instead of low-sodium beans to provide a perfect touch of saltiness in every bite. This cool salad is then topped with pan-seared tilapia fillets—which take just 5 minutes to cook. And for a refreshing and fragrant finish, you'll top the steamy fillets with fresh diced mango and cilantro. It's a wow! (Hint: If you'd also like a pow, sprinkle with hot sauce or minced hot chile pepper.)

2	tablespoons bottled lime juice (not from concentrate)
1	tablespoon avocado oil or peanut oil, divided
1	(15-ounce) can black beans, rinsed and drained
3	cups packed fresh mixed baby salad greens
2	(4-ounce) tilapia fillets
1/3	cup diced fresh or thawed frozen mango or peach
2	tablespoons fresh cilantro leaves

KITCHEN TOOLS

- Can opener
- Mesh strainer
- Large mixing bowl
- Measuring spoons
- Dry measuring cups
- Whisk
- Tongs
- Large stick-resistant skillet
- Spatula/turner

serves: 2 | **serving size:** 2 cups salad and 1 fillet
prep time: 10 minutes | **cooking time:** 6 minutes

DIRECTIONS

1. In a large bowl, whisk together the lime juice and 1 1/2 teaspoons oil. Add the beans and stir to combine. Add the salad greens and gently toss with tongs to combine. Arrange the salad on individual plates.

2. Heat a large stick-resistant skillet over medium-high heat. Rub the fillets with remaining 1 1/2 teaspoons oil. Cook the fillets in the dry skillet until well browned on the first side, and cooked though on the flip side, about 5 minutes total.

3. Top each salad with a tilapia fillet. Evenly sprinkle with mango and whole cilantro leaves. Serve.

EASY TIP!

Buy mango that's already cubed from your supermarket's pre-prepped produce section or salad bar.

BEFRIEND FIBER

Fiber can help manage blood glucose. And research suggests that a higher fiber intake may reduce your risk of cardiovascular disease. To get more fiber, simply eat more plant foods, like black beans, mixed baby salad greens, mango, and cilantro leaves! Ideally, aim for 25 grams of fiber per day for women; 38 grams per day for men—or roughly 14 grams of fiber per 1,000 calories.

NUTRITION INFORMATION

Choices/Exchanges:
2 starch, 1 nonstarchy vegetable, 4 lean protein, 1/2 fat

Per Serving:

Calories	370
Calories from fat	90
Total fat	10 g
Saturated fat	1.8 g
Trans fat	0 g
Cholesterol	50 mg
Sodium	230 mg
Potassium	1020 mg
Total carbohydrate	37 g
Dietary fiber	13 g
Sugars	8 g
Added sugars	0 g
Protein	34 g
Phosphorus	370 mg

mandarin, greens & protein bowl

Here's a fresh and lovely entrée salad with Asian inspiration that's sure to perk up your day. The zingy, citrusy dressing is made by blending together cider vinegar and sesame oil with grated fresh gingerroot and mandarin oranges. Since you'll use orange pieces and not just the juice, you'll get more fiber. That's drizzled onto a bed of fresh baby spinach, shrimp (or other lean protein of choice), and still more mandarin orange pieces. It's a refreshing balance of savory and sweet. And don't forget to top it with peanuts to complete your salad with nutty crunch!

3	ounces pre-cooked lean protein of choice (such as steamed shrimp; leftovers work great!)
2	mandarin oranges or 1 naval orange, peeled and separated into pieces
1	teaspoon grated fresh gingerroot
1	tablespoon apple cider vinegar
2	teaspoons toasted sesame oil
2	cups packed fresh baby spinach
2	tablespoons roasted, salted peanuts

KITCHEN TOOLS

- Kitchen scale
- Spoon or peeler (for peeling ginger)
- Microplane zester/grater
- Cutting board
- Chef's knife
- Blender
- Measuring spoons
- Dry measuring cups

serves: 1 | **serving size:** 3 cups
prep time: 15 minutes | **cooking time:** 0 minutes
(if using pre-cooked protein)

DIRECTIONS

1. Cut the protein of choice into small, bite-sized cubes, if necessary. Set aside.

2. Place half the orange pieces into a blender with the grated ginger, vinegar, and oil (set the other orange pieces aside for later). Cover and purée.

3. Arrange the spinach, protein, and reserved orange pieces in a bowl. Drizzle with the orange-sesame dressing. Sprinkle with peanuts. Serve.

EASY TIP!

See page 23 for "How to grate fresh gingerroot."

PICK A PROTEIN

For the protein in this salad, pick up cooked shrimp (like for shrimp cocktail) or sesame-ginger baked organic tofu from your local market. Or use this recipe as an opportunity to enjoy any leftover (or "planned-over") protein, like a lonely grilled chicken breast remaining from last night's dinner, so it doesn't go to waste.

NUTRITION INFORMATION

Choices/Exchanges:

1 1/2 fruit, 1 nonstarchy vegetable, 4 lean protein, 2 1/2 fat

Per Serving:

Calories	390
Calories from fat	170
Total fat	19 g
Saturated fat	2.7 g
Trans fat	0 g
Cholesterol	160 mg
Sodium	310 mg
Potassium	1120 mg
Total carbohydrate	31 g
Dietary fiber	7 g
Sugars	20 g
Added sugars	0 g
Protein	29 g
Phosphorus	345 mg

MAIN DISHES: CHICKEN & TURKEY

bbq chicken strips

Even if you're cooking for one or two, make this entire super-simple recipe and save the leftovers for lunch. In other words, make "planned-overs." The protein-packed chicken "fingers" remain moist today, tomorrow, and the next day. That's partly because they're scrumptiously slathered with barbecue sauce. It's also because they're made with dark meat chicken instead of white meat. The richer flavor of the thigh pairs better with the rich, tangy taste of the sauce, too.

24	ounces boneless, skinless chicken thighs, about 8 (3-ounce) thighs
2	teaspoons extra-virgin olive oil or peanut oil
1/2	cup no-sugar-added barbecue sauce or Fruit-Sweetened BBQ Sauce (page 286)
1/4	cup loosely packed fresh cilantro or parsley leaves

KITCHEN TOOLS

- Large rimmed baking sheet
- Unbleached parchment paper
- Cutting board
- Fillet knife or chef's knife
- Medium mixing bowl
- Measuring spoons
- Tongs
- Liquid measuring cup
- Dry measuring cups
- Instant-read (meat) thermometer (optional)

serves: 4 | **serving size:** 4 strips
prep time: 8 minutes | **cooking time:** 15 minutes

DIRECTIONS

1. Preheat oven to 450°F. Line a large rimmed baking sheet with unbleached parchment paper.

2. Cut each chicken thigh into 2 long strips, to make about 16 total strips. Add the chicken strips to a medium bowl. Drizzle with the oil and, using tongs, gently toss the chicken in the oil until all strips are fully coated. Add the barbecue sauce and gently toss again until fully coated. Arrange the chicken strips in a single layer on the baking sheet.

3. Roast until the chicken is well done (internal temperature of at least 165°F), about 15 minutes. Sprinkle with the whole cilantro leaves to serve. Enjoy warm or cool.

EASY TIP!

You don't need to flip over these chicken strips during roasting!

SERVING TIPS FOR STRIPS

Toss them onto a lunchtime leafy salad with some beans or corn, red onion, a few tortilla chips, and a drizzle of ranch dressing. Serve them in a whole-grain bun along with a little coleslaw. Thread onto skewers and serve as a party app. Or enjoy them as a simple entrée paired with seasonal veggies and whole grains.

NUTRITION INFORMATION

Choices/Exchanges:
1/2 carbohydrate,
4 lean protein, 1 fat

Per Serving:

Calories	260
Calories from fat	110
Total fat	12 g
Saturated fat	2.9 g
Trans fat	0.1 g
Cholesterol	155 mg
Sodium	360 mg
Potassium	420 mg
Total carbohydrate	7 g
Dietary fiber	0 g
Sugars	4 g
Added sugars	0 g
Protein	28 g
Phosphorus	255 mg

pecan-crusted chicken breasts

For a fine dining–style entrée, you don't need to make a reservation or get dressed up. Go get comfy and head on over to your kitchen. This chicken dish takes just 8 minutes of prep time, 20 minutes in the oven, and voila! The result is actually impressive enough to serve for a special occasion but comforting enough to pair with your comfy clothes. You'll enjoy the homestyle crunchiness from the pecans along with a hint of natural sweetness and spiciness. Serve it with a big salad and a smile.

1/2	cup pecan pieces
24	ounces boneless, skinless chicken breasts, about 4 (6-ounce) breasts
3	tablespoons unsweetened applesauce
1	tablespoon spicy brown mustard
1/4	teaspoon sea salt

KITCHEN TOOLS

- Large rimmed baking sheet
- Unbleached parchment paper
- Dry measuring cups
- Measuring spoons
- Food processor
- Rimmed plate
- Small bowl
- Spoon
- Instant-read (meat) thermometer (optional)

serves: 4 | **serving size:** 1 breast
prep time: 8 minutes | **cooking time:** 20 minutes

DIRECTIONS

1. Preheat oven to 425°F. Line a large rimmed baking sheet with unbleached parchment paper.

2. Add the pecans to a food processor; pulse until they look like breadcrumbs. Transfer the pecans to a rimmed plate.

3. Place the chicken onto the baking sheet. In a small bowl, stir together the applesauce and mustard. Spoon the applesauce-mustard onto the top of each piece of chicken; evenly spread it on with the back of the spoon. Firmly dip the applesauce-mustard-coated side of each chicken breast into the pecans; place back onto the baking sheet, pecan-crusted side up. Sprinkle any remaining pecans onto the chicken; press to adhere. Sprinkle with salt.

4. Bake until the chicken is well done (internal temperature of at least 165°F), about 20 minutes. Serve.

EASY TIP!

Don't have a food processor or don't want to set it up? Finely chop pecan pieces on a cutting board using a chef's knife.

PECAN HALVES VS. PECAN PIECES

When a recipe calls for pecans that you're going to chop, you don't have to start with perfect pecan halves. Instead, use pecan pieces which are basically broken or "semi chopped" halves. You'll potentially save money since pieces may cost less than the halves. And it'll take less time to prep pecans when they're already partially chopped.

NUTRITION INFORMATION

Choices/Exchanges:
5 lean protein, 1 1/2 fat

Per Serving:

Calories	300
Calories from fat	140
Total fat	15 g
Saturated fat	2 g
Trans fat	0 g
Cholesterol	95 mg
Sodium	270 mg
Potassium	370 mg
Total carbohydrate	3 g
Dietary fiber	2 g
Sugars	2 g
Added sugars	0 g
Protein	37 g
Phosphorus	305 mg

herbs de provence roasted chicken breasts

If you're in a need of an entrée for a very special occasion, make this. This roasted chicken has restaurant-quality, south-of-France deliciousness. Plus, you'll get to indulge a bit by savoring the herbed, crisped chicken skin. The herbs de Provence (also known as herbes de Provence) offer an aromatic and rather luxurious appeal. But perhaps the best part is that the recipe only takes 5 minutes of prep time—even if you decide to double or triple it for a larger dinner gathering!

2	(10-ounce) bone-in, skin-on organic chicken breasts
1	teaspoon extra-virgin olive oil
1 1/2	teaspoons dried herbs de Provence or crushed rosemary
1/4	teaspoon sea salt

KITCHEN TOOLS

- Baking pan (about 9 × 13 inches)
- Measuring spoons
- Culinary/pastry brush
- Instant-read (meat) thermometer (optional)

serves: 2 | serving size: 1 breast
prep time: 5 minutes | cooking time: 40–45 minutes
(plus standing time)

NUTRITION INFORMATION

Choices/Exchanges:
6 lean protein, 1 fat

Per Serving:

Calories	330
Calories from fat	140
Total fat	15 g
Saturated fat	3.8 g
Trans fat	0 g
Cholesterol	130 mg
Sodium	380 mg
Potassium	390 mg
Total carbohydrate	0 g
Dietary fiber	0 g
Sugars	0 g
Added sugars	0 g
Protein	47 g
Phosphorus	335 mg

DIRECTIONS

1. Preheat oven to 425°F.

2. Place the chicken in a baking pan. Brush the chicken skin with the oil. Sprinkle with the herbs de Provence and salt.

3. Roast until the chicken is well done (internal temperature of at least 165°F) and skin is crisped and browned, about 40–45 minutes.

4. Let stand for at least 5 minutes. If desired, drizzle the chicken with any pan juices. Serve.

EASY TIP!

If you don't have a culinary/pastry brush, use the best "cooking tool" you have—your first three fingers. Rub the oil onto the chicken skin. Then wash your hands, of course.

WHAT'S IN HERBS DE PROVENCE?

It's often a mixture of thyme, rosemary, marjoram or oregano, savory, and lavender. Can't find it? Make this simplified version: 2 teaspoons of crushed dried rosemary, 2 teaspoons of dried thyme, 1 1/2 teaspoons of dried oregano, and 1/2 teaspoon of dried lavender (if you can't find lavender, use another 1/2 teaspoon of rosemary). Use 1 1/2 teaspoons of your herb mixture for this recipe. Save some for later.

pan-grilled curry-in-a-hurry chicken thighs

Think beyond just chicken breasts! Chicken thighs are healthful—plus they're a bit juicier and more forgiving than chicken breasts if they're accidentally overcooked. If you're big on taste, you'll adore this highly flavored entrée, especially when served on top of a bed of greens, like sautéed or steamed spinach. It's also delicious served cold the next day. Thinly slice the chicken and enjoy in a wrap with slaw, as a topper for avocado toast, or on a salad made with baby spinach and red grapes.

24	ounces boneless, skinless chicken thighs, about 8 (3-ounce) thighs
2	teaspoons avocado oil or sunflower oil
1	teaspoon curry powder
1/2	teaspoon sea salt
1/4	teaspoon freshly ground black pepper
1/4	cup fresh cilantro leaves

KITCHEN TOOLS

- Large cast-iron or other stick-resistant grill pan or skillet
- Measuring spoons
- Dinner plate
- Culinary/pastry brush
- Long-handled tongs
- Instant-read (meat) thermometer (optional)

serves: 4 | **serving size:** 2 thighs
prep time: 5 minutes | **cooking time:** 15 minutes

DIRECTIONS

1. Heat a large cast-iron or other stick-resistant grill pan or skillet over medium-high heat.

2. On a dinner plate, brush the chicken with the oil. Sprinkle the chicken with the curry powder, salt, and pepper.

3. Using tongs, place chicken onto the hot grill pan. Cook on all sides until browned and well done (internal temperature of at least 165°F), about 15 minutes total. Clean tongs as needed.

4. Transfer the cooked chicken to a clean plate or serving platter, sprinkle with the cilantro leaves, and serve.

EASY TIP!

If you don't have a culinary/pastry brush, use the best "cooking tool" you have—your first three fingers. Rub the oil onto the chicken thighs. Then wash your hands, of course.

SPICE SYNERGY

Curry powder contains curcumin, a compound with anti-inflammatory properties that may play a favorable role in diabetes prevention and treatment. When adding it to a recipe, also sprinkle on black pepper, which contains piperine and seems to dramatically boost curcumin's availability in your body, potentially by 2,000%!

NUTRITION INFORMATION

Choices/Exchanges:
4 lean protein, 1 fat

Per Serving:

Calories	220
Calories from fat	110
Total fat	12 g
Saturated fat	2.9 g
Trans fat	0 g
Cholesterol	155 mg
Sodium	370 mg
Potassium	340 mg
Total carbohydrate	0 g
Dietary fiber	0 g
Sugars	0 g
Added sugars	0 g
Protein	27 g
Phosphorus	250 mg

french tarragon-dijon baked chicken

This isn't your ordinary baked chicken. It's fragrant, flavorful, and quite French! It's especially lovely when finished with fresh tarragon. Try growing tarragon in a small clay pot on your windowsill so it's on hand for this recipe—or whenever you need it. The herb is delicious with chicken, fish, eggs, asparagus, and mushrooms. But if you don't have any fresh tarragon, use 1 1/2 teaspoons of dried tarragon here; stir it into the lemony mustard mixture—then garnish the finished chicken with minced fresh chives or scallions.

24	ounces boneless, skinless chicken thighs, about 8 (3-ounce) thighs
3	tablespoons Dijon mustard
1	tablespoon bottled lemon juice (not from concentrate)
1	tablespoon extra-virgin olive oil
1/4	teaspoon sea salt
1	tablespoon minced fresh tarragon leaves

KITCHEN TOOLS

- Cutting board
- Chef's knife
- Large rimmed baking sheet
- Unbleached parchment paper
- Measuring spoons
- Small bowl
- Spoon
- Instant-read (meat) thermometer (optional)

serves: 4 | serving size: 2 thighs
prep time: 8 minutes | cooking time: 30 minutes

DIRECTIONS

1. Preheat oven to 400°F. Line a large rimmed baking sheet with unbleached parchment paper.

2. Place the chicken on the baking sheet. In a small bowl, stir together the mustard, lemon juice, oil, and salt, and lightly spread it on top of each chicken thigh using the back of the spoon.

3. Roast until the chicken is well done (internal temperature of at least 165°F), about 30 minutes.

4. Mince the tarragon, sprinkle onto the roasted chicken, and serve.

EASY TIP!

Don't flip over the chicken during roasting.

ARE YOU A FISH AFICIONADA?

Enjoy this same recipe using 4 (6-ounce) wild salmon fillets instead of 8 chicken thighs. Place the salmon skin side down and bake until flaky and cooked through, about 16 minutes. *Magnifique*!

NUTRITION INFORMATION

Choices/Exchanges:
4 lean protein, 1 fat

Per Serving:

Calories	240
Calories from fat	120
Total fat	13 g
Saturated fat	3.1 g
Trans fat	0.1 g
Cholesterol	155 mg
Sodium	490 mg
Potassium	340 mg
Total carbohydrate	2 g
Dietary fiber	0 g
Sugars	1 g
Added sugars	0 g
Protein	28 g
Phosphorus	260 mg

"vintage" vegetable & chicken bake

Got leftovers? Bake this! It's truly simple if you've got extras in the fridge from a cookout—or cook-in. Just layer everything in a baking dish, add a few ladles of soup and a sprinkling of cheese, then heat and eat. I call that "vintage" cuisine—giving new life to "oldie but goodie" foods! Be sure to pick a creamy mushroom or broccoli soup that's ready-to-eat, not a condensed version. You can vary the ingredients to make this your own, too. Generally, the simpler the flavors, the better everything will likely taste when combined. Whichever way you fix this dish, enjoy with a veggie-rich app or side, like Almost Hummus (page 76) with seasonal vegetable sticks or Mesclun Salad with Beans (page 238), for a complete comfort fix.

3	cups pre-cooked cubed chicken breast, chilled (16 ounces)
3 1/2	cups pre-cooked cut asparagus or other nonstarchy vegetable
3/4	cup shredded Gruyére or Manchego cheese
2 1/2	cups pre-cooked farro or brown rice, chilled
1/4	teaspoon sea salt
2 1/2	cups creamy mushroom or broccoli soup (from carton)

KITCHEN TOOLS

- Box grater
- Cutting board
- Chef's knife
- 1 (2-quart-capacity) baking dish (such as 8 × 12 inches)
- Dry measuring cups
- Measuring spoons
- Liquid measuring cup

serves: 8 | serving size: 1 cup
prep time: 10 minutes | cooking time: 30 minutes
(if using pre-cooked chicken and grains)

DIRECTIONS

1. Preheat oven to 375°F.

2. If necessary, cut the chicken and asparagus into large, bite-sized pieces and shred the cheese.

3. In a 2-quart baking dish, evenly layer the rice and then chicken. Sprinkle with the salt. Layer with the asparagus. Slowly and evenly pour the soup on top. Sprinkle with the cheese.

4. Bake uncovered until steaming hot, about 30 minutes, and serve.

EASY TIP!

No leftover veggies? Use a 16-ounce package of frozen veggies, such as cut asparagus or broccoli florets. Just thaw before use in this recipe.

A "VINTAGE" PLAN

When serving a chicken, vegetable, and grain meal, intentionally plan to make extras so you'll have "planned-overs" for making this recipe. Aim for salt-free or low-sodium preparations to keep sodium in check—though if your chicken or vegetables are mildly seasoned with pepper and herbs, like rosemary or thyme, it'll make this bake even tastier.

NUTRITION INFORMATION

Choices/Exchanges:
1 starch, 1 nonstarchy vegetable, 3 lean protein

Per Serving:

Calories	260
Calories from fat	60
Total fat	7 g
Saturated fat	2.7 g
Trans fat	0 g
Cholesterol	60 mg
Sodium	300 mg
Potassium	450 mg
Total carbohydrate	23 g
Dietary fiber	5 g
Sugars	2 g
Added sugars	0 g
Protein	27 g
Phosphorus	340 mg

toasty rancher chicken sandwich

This chicken sandwich has a lot to brag about—whole grains, nonstarchy vegetables, and a generous amount of lean protein. Importantly, if you have a time-crunched schedule, using a rotisserie chicken breast makes it speedy. And notably for your taste buds, this sandwich has a just-right amount of blue cheese dressing to kick up yumminess. Enjoy this not-so-ordinary sandwich alongside some fresh, nonstarchy veggies. Or, if you're a chip fan, look for crispy baked chips, like beet or carrot chips, that are "naked" baked—that means without oil.

2	thin slices whole-grain bread
1	cup packed fresh baby arugula
2	teaspoons natural or organic blue cheese dressing
1/4	teaspoon freshly ground black pepper
3	ounces rotisserie chicken breast, skin and bones removed, thinly sliced (about 1 small breast)

KITCHEN TOOLS

- Cutting board
- Chef's knife
- Toaster
- Measuring spoons
- Dry measuring cups
- Small bowl
- Tongs

serves: 1 | **serving size:** 1 sandwich
prep time: 8 minutes | **cooking time:** 2 minutes

DIRECTIONS

1. Toast the bread.

2. While the bread is toasting, toss together the arugula, dressing, and black pepper in a small bowl until the arugula is well dressed.

3. Top one of the toast slices with half of the arugula salad, all of the chicken, and then the remaining arugula salad. Top with the other toast slice. Serve.

EASY TIP!

Make this recipe right when you get home after picking up a hot rotisserie chicken. Or you can gently warm the sliced chicken in the microwave for 15 seconds. Otherwise, cool chicken is cool, too.

ROTISSERIE CHICKEN RECIPES

Since this recipe only uses some chicken breast meat, you'll obviously have remaining parts when you purchase a whole rotisserie chicken. Over the next day or two, enjoy extra white meat chicken in Mason Jar Sesame Chicken Salad (page 208) or Sonoma Chicken & Fig Bruschetta (page 82); try dark meat in tacos, burritos, and beyond.

NUTRITION INFORMATION

Choices/Exchanges:
1 starch, 4 lean protein

Per Serving:

Calories	260
Calories from fat	80
Total fat	9 g
Saturated fat	1.7 g
Trans fat	0.2 g
Cholesterol	75 mg
Sodium	560 mg
Potassium	490 mg
Total carbohydrate	20 g
Dietary fiber	6 g
Sugars	3 g
Added sugars	0 g
Protein	31 g
Phosphorus	320 mg

turkey sausage flatbread pizza

Yes, you can enjoy pizza! One way is to make it part of your diabetes-friendly meal and not THE meal. Another way to make it more nutritious is to choose a whole-grain crust. That's easy here since you'll use whole-grain flatbread or pocketless pitas. What's more, you can still have a scrumptious sausage topping; simply choose natural turkey or chicken sausage and go light on the cheese. In other words, this is still 100% pizza! Savor the petite pizza slices paired with a big ol' tossed salad with beans, like Mesclun Salad with Beans (page 238), for a boost of satisfying protein and fiber.

2	(3-ounce) whole-grain naan flatbreads or 3 (2-ounce) pocketless pitas
2	small plum tomatoes (or 1 large), cut into extra-thin rounds
1	(3-ounce) link pre-cooked natural or organic Italian chicken or turkey sausage, cut into extra-thin coins
1/2	cup shredded part-skim mozzarella cheese
12	fresh basil leaves

KITCHEN TOOLS

- Cutting board
- Chef's knife
- Large baking sheet
- Dry measuring cups

serves: 4 | **serving size:** 2 pizza slices (3 slices if using pitas)
prep time: 10 minutes | **cooking time:** 10 minutes

DIRECTIONS

1. Preheat oven to 475°F.

2. Place the naan flatbreads onto a large baking sheet. Top the entire surface of each flatbread with the tomato, sausage, and cheese. Bake on the middle rack until the cheese is melted and golden brown and crust is crisped, about 10 minutes.

3. Cut each naan flatbread into 4 slices. Sprinkle with the whole basil leaves. Serve.

EASY TIP!

For extra simplicity, don't worry about cutting perfectly round tomato slices for this pizza. You can cut a tomato in half, place the halves cut side down on a cutting board, then thinly slice.

PIZZA WITH OOMPH

When lightening up your pizza calorie-wise, don't lighten up on taste. Go for spiciness, if you like. Choose spicy chicken sausage or pick mild sausage and sprinkle with crushed red pepper flakes. Alternatively, sprinkle on any Italian-style spice you choose, like garlic powder, dried oregano, or fennel seeds. Or try an all-of-the-above approach, if you dare!

NUTRITION INFORMATION

Choices/Exchanges:
1 1/2 starch, 1 lean protein, 1 1/2 fat

Per Serving:

Calories	220
Calories from fat	80
Total fat	9 g
Saturated fat	3.1 g
Trans fat	0 g
Cholesterol	30 mg
Sodium	520 mg
Potassium	240 mg
Total carbohydrate	22 g
Dietary fiber	3 g
Sugars	3 g
Added sugars	1 g
Protein	11 g
Phosphorus	195 mg

stuffed turkey & red grape salad pita

During my childhood, my mother and I visited a Lebanese bakery nearly every weekend, where I told the baker exactly which hot and fluffy pita loaves to pluck off of the press for me. It's such a lovely (and yummy!) memory. Today, when I don't eat pita as is, I often stuff the pocket with a salad like this. Visit your local market's meat department to pick up pre-cooked turkey or chicken breast for the recipe. Or request one thickly sliced piece of reduced-sodium turkey breast from the deli department. It's delicious any which way you stuff this pita!

2	ounces pre-roasted turkey or chicken breast, cut into bite-sized cubes
4	large red seedless grapes, thinly sliced
12	shelled, roasted, unsalted pistachios
1	tablespoon no-sugar-added mayonnaise
1/2	teaspoon dried tarragon leaves or 1 teaspoon chopped fresh tarragon leaves
1/2	large whole-grain pita
1/2	cup packed fresh baby arugula

KITCHEN TOOLS

- Cutting board
- Chef's knife
- Kitchen scale (optional)
- Measuring spoons
- Dry measuring cups
- Small bowl
- Spoon

serves: 1 | **serving size:** 1 stuffed pita half
prep time: 10 minutes | **cooking time:** 0 minutes
(if using pre-cooked turkey or chicken)

NUTRITION INFORMATION

Choices/Exchanges:
1 starch, 1/2 carbohydrate,
3 lean protein, 2 fat

Per Serving:

Calories	330
Calories from fat	140
Total fat	16 g
Saturated fat	2.4 g
Trans fat	0 g
Cholesterol	50 mg
Sodium	320 mg
Potassium	380 mg
Total carbohydrate	25 g
Dietary fiber	3 g
Sugars	5 g
Added sugars	0 g
Protein	23 g
Phosphorus	245 mg

DIRECTIONS

1. In a small bowl, stir together the turkey, grapes, pistachios, mayonnaise, and tarragon until combined.

2. Stuff the pita half with the arugula and turkey salad mixture. Serve.

EASY TIP!

This is an ideal recipe for using holiday leftovers. If you plan to roast a turkey or chicken for Thanksgiving or another holiday, plan to make this with extras over the next day or two.

THE "PISTACHIO PRINCIPLE"

When snacking on pistachios, pick a variety that still have their shells. Why? The actual time it takes to remove the shell can help slow down your consumption. Plus the leftover shells can provide a visual cue for portions, which can help prevent you from mindlessly overeating.

baja turkey burgers

A turkey burger can sometimes seem rather blasé. Not here!
You'll get flavor intrigue by adding salsa verde to the grilled turkey
burger patty. And the nontraditional add-ons are quite memorable
. . . creamy avocado, a crunchy slaw mix, and more salsa verde.
Whole-grain English muffins generally provide more fiber than
standard burger buns, so they're the "bun" of choice here. Plus,
they're sturdier—which will come in handy, since these burgers are
generously topped. So think bodacious . . . definitely not blasé!

12	ounces raw ground turkey, about 93% lean (1 1/2 cups)
1/2	cup preservative-free salsa verde, divided
4	sprouted whole-grain or whole-wheat English muffins, split
1	Hass avocado, peeled and thinly sliced
1/8	teaspoon sea salt
2	cups coleslaw mix

KITCHEN TOOLS

- Cutting board
- Chef's knife
- Dry measuring cups
- Grill or grill pan
- Large bowl
- Ruler
- Long-handled cooking/grilling spatula
- Instant-read (meat) thermometer (optional)

DIRECTIONS

1. Preheat a grill or grill pan over medium-high heat.

2. In a large bowl, gently combine the turkey and 1/4 cup salsa verde until just combined. Form the turkey mixture by hand into four patties, about 4 1/2 inches diameter.

3. Grill the burgers until well done (at least 165°F internal temperature), about 5 minutes per side. (Hint: If desired, lightly grill the English muffins, too.)

4. Onto the bottom portion of each English muffin, arrange 1/4 of the avocado slices and sprinkle with salt. Top each with a turkey burger patty, 1/2 cup coleslaw mix, remaining 1 tablespoon salsa verde, and an English muffin top. Serve.

EASY TIP!

See page 25 for "How to cut an avocado."

GO FOR COLOR!

Eating is a sensory experience. And when food is colorful, it can lead to a more enjoyable culinary experience. So rather than a plain coleslaw mix, pick a tri-color variety. Or make your own slaw mixture. Try a combination of 1 1/2 cups of shredded red cabbage or purple kale, 1/4 cup of shredded carrot, and 1/4 cup of fresh cilantro leaves.

NUTRITION INFORMATION

Choices/Exchanges:
2 starch, 1 nonstarchy vegetable, 3 lean protein, 1 1/2 fat

Per Serving:

Calories	370
Calories from fat	120
Total fat	13 g
Saturated fat	2.6 g
Trans fat	0.1 g
Cholesterol	65 mg
Sodium	420 mg
Potassium	680 mg
Total carbohydrate	37 g
Dietary fiber	10 g
Sugars	2 g
Added sugars	0 g
Protein	25 g
Phosphorus	330 mg

turkey meatballs arrabbiata

Nope, this isn't a recipe for spaghetti and meatballs. The scrumptiously moist meatballs steal the show here—no spaghetti needed. The duo of arrabbiata and pesto sauces make the meatballs flavorful. As a bonus, they're good for you because they're made with turkey and oats—and baked. Can you serve them with pasta? Sure, arrange the meatballs on a petite bed of whole-wheat or garbanzo bean/chickpea spaghetti. Better yet, try them on an oversized bed of steamed spiralized zucchini (also known as zoodles). Or simply go noodle-free and savor with crusty whole-grain Italian bread alongside a leafy green salad. *Mangia*!

3/4	cup arrabbiata or marinara sauce, divided
2	tablespoons jarred pesto sauce or Cheese-Free Pesto (page 288)
1	large egg
10	ounces raw ground turkey, about 93% lean (1 1/4 cups)
3/4	cup old-fashioned rolled oats
1/4	cup grated Parmesan cheese

KITCHEN TOOLS

- 9 × 13-inch baking pan
- Unbleached parchment paper
- Medium mixing bowl
- Large spoon
- Liquid measuring cup
- Measuring spoons
- Dry measuring cups
- Instant-read (meat) thermometer (optional)

serves: 4 | **serving size:** 3 meatballs plus 2 tablespoons sauce
prep time: 10 minutes | **cooking time:** 20 minutes

DIRECTIONS

1. Preheat oven to 450°F. Line a 9 × 13-inch baking pan with unbleached parchment paper.

2. In a medium bowl, stir together 3 tablespoons arrabbiata sauce, the pesto, and egg until combined. Add the turkey, oats, and Parmesan cheese, and mix by hand until combined.

3. Roll by hand into 12 loosely formed meatballs, about 3 tablespoons mixture each, and place on the baking pan. (Hint: Divide meatball mixture into four equal-sized portions, then make three meatballs from each portion.) Bake for 15 minutes, no flipping of meatballs required.

4. Using a clean spoon, top each meatball with the remaining arrabbiata, about 2 teaspoons sauce per meatball. Bake until sauce is hot and meatballs are well done (internal temperature of at least 165°F), about 5 minutes more. Serve.

EASY TIP!

For arrabbiata or marinara sauce and pesto recommendations, see page 325 for "Ingredients of Choice."

ITALIAN-STYLE MINI MEATLOAF

You can make personal-sized meatloaves instead of meatballs with this recipe. Simply form the mixture into 4 football-shaped loaves, about 4 inches long and 2 1/4 inches wide. Bake for about 10 minutes more, rather than 5 minutes more, in the final step. That means 25 minutes of total baking time.

NUTRITION INFORMATION

Choices/Exchanges:
1 starch, 2 lean protein, 2 fat

Per Serving:

Calories	260
Calories from fat	130
Total fat	14 g
Saturated fat	3.6 g
Trans fat	0.1 g
Cholesterol	105 mg
Sodium	360 mg
Potassium	330 mg
Total carbohydrate	12 g
Dietary fiber	2 g
Sugars	1 g
Added sugars	0 g
Protein	19 g
Phosphorus	265 mg

mason jar sesame chicken salad

Jar salads are so much fun, including this Asian-inspired chicken slaw salad. Hey, you can even burn some calories, depending on how long you shake up the protein-packed salad in the jar. Or just shake for a few seconds and dig in, if you prefer. Either way, you'll find the dressing practically addictive—in a good way. It's made with sesame oil, tamari, rice vinegar, and applesauce to satisfy every taste bud. (Hint: Make this dressing for other recipe uses, too. Try tossing with whole-grain noodles, adding to steamed veggies, or brushing onto grilled kebabs.)

1	teaspoon toasted sesame oil
1	teaspoon reduced-sodium tamari (soy sauce)
1	teaspoon rice vinegar
3	tablespoons unsweetened applesauce
3/4	cup cubed pre-roasted or rotisserie chicken breast meat (4 ounces)
1	cup tri-color coleslaw mix or shredded cabbage

KITCHEN TOOLS

- Cutting board
- Chef's knife
- 1 (2-cup- or 16-ounce-capacity) jar with lid
- Measuring spoons
- Dry measuring cups

serves: 1 | **serving size:** 1 (2-cup) jar
prep time: 5 minutes | **cooking time:** 0 minutes

DIRECTIONS

1. In a 2-cup-capacity jar, add in order the oil, tamari, vinegar, applesauce, chicken, and coleslaw mix. Seal and store in the refrigerator for up to 3 days.

2. When ready to enjoy, vigorously shake the jar to combine the salad ingredients. Eat the salad with a fork or chopsticks directly from the jar.

EASY TIP!

Make this jar salad in advance so it will take just seconds from fridge to fork . . . or chopsticks!

SALAD JAR ADD-INS

This simple Asian-style salad is absolutely tasty as is. But if you're in the mood for extra pizzazz, here are a few ideas. Pick one or more! Add 1/2 teaspoon of grated fresh gingerroot in with the applesauce. Add 2 tablespoons of fresh mint or cilantro leaves in with the slaw mix. Sprinkle with sesame seeds or peanuts before serving.

NUTRITION INFORMATION

Choices/Exchanges:
1/2 carbohydrate, 5 lean protein

Per Serving:

Calories	270
Calories from fat	80
Total fat	9 g
Saturated fat	1.8 g
Trans fat	0 g
Cholesterol	95 mg
Sodium	260 mg
Potassium	480 mg
Total carbohydrate	9 g
Dietary fiber	2 g
Sugars	5 g
Added sugars	0 g
Protein	36 g
Phosphorus	280 mg

SIDE SALADS

tri-color coleslaw

The main ingredient in coleslaw is cabbage, a health protective "superfood." Research suggests that a diet rich in leafy green veggies, including cabbage, is associated with a reduced risk of type 2 diabetes. Unfortunately, coleslaw can be laden with dressing, transforming that "superfood" into an overly rich side with hidden sugar. But you can still have full plant-based enjoyment without undesirable goopiness. This not-so-goopy dressed slaw is brightly flavored. Using tri-color slaw mix makes it brightly colored. And fruit spread provides a desirable hint of sweetness, naturally.

2	tablespoons fruit-sweetened apricot fruit spread (jam)*
2	tablespoons no-sugar-added mayonnaise
2	tablespoons apple cider vinegar
1/4	teaspoon celery salt
4	cups packed tri-color or other coleslaw mix (11 ounces)

*Note: Ideally, choose a fruit spread without added sugars.

KITCHEN TOOLS

- Large mixing bowl
- Measuring spoons
- Dry measuring cups
- Whisk
- Large spoon

serves: 4 | **serving size:** 1 cup
prep time: 8 minutes | **cooking time:** 0 minutes

DIRECTIONS

1. In a large bowl, whisk together the fruit spread, mayonnaise, vinegar, and celery salt until well combined. Add the coleslaw mix and stir to combine.

2. Serve or store covered in the refrigerator for up to a day.

EASY TIP!

If you can't find celery salt, just season with a combination of sea salt and freshly ground black pepper instead.

NOT ALL SLAWS ARE CREATED EQUAL

One cup of "fast food" coleslaw can provide about 275 calories, 17 grams of total fat, 2.5 grams of saturated fat, 360 milligrams of sodium, and 30 grams of total carbohydrate, of which 26 grams are sugar. With those not-so-healthful numbers, it's well worth it to make your own slaw . . . especially when you can do so in minutes.

NUTRITION INFORMATION

Choices/Exchanges:
1/2 fruit, 1 nonstarchy vegetable, 1 fat

Per Serving:

Calories	90
Calories from fat	45
Total fat	5 g
Saturated fat	0.8 g
Trans fat	0 g
Cholesterol	5 mg
Sodium	100 mg
Potassium	210 mg
Total carbohydrate	10 g
Dietary fiber	2 g
Sugars	5 g
Added sugars	0 g
Protein	0 g
Phosphorus	20 mg

trail mix arugula salad

You don't need to eat trail mix just when you're hiking or biking on a trail! The nutrient-rich combo of nuts, seeds, and dried fruits makes a delightful addition to this simple recipe. If you prefer, personalize this leafy side salad and make your own nut and dried fruit mix (see the DIY Trail Mix tip on page 215). For dressing your salad, be sure to select a salad dressing that's free of artificial ingredients and added sugars. That's it. So easy!

2	cups packed fresh baby arugula
1/4	cup trail mix (nuts and dried fruit)
1	tablespoon natural vinaigrette-style salad dressing

KITCHEN TOOLS

- Medium mixing bowl
- Dry measuring cups
- Measuring spoons
- Tongs

serves: 1 | serving size: 2 cups salad
prep time: 5 minutes | cooking time: 0 minutes

DIRECTIONS

In a medium bowl, toss together the arugula, trail mix, and salad dressing using tongs. Serve.

EASY TIP!

If you like, whisk up your own easiest-ever, tangy vinaigrette with just two ingredients: 1 1/2 teaspoons each of extra-virgin olive oil and apple cider vinegar. Or adjust the ratio to taste.

DIY TRAIL MIX

Mix together your favorite nuts, seeds, and dried fruits for a three-ingredient trail mix. Or keep it really easy by choosing just nuts and dried fruits for a two-ingredient trail mix. For this salad, try a mixture of 2 tablespoons each of pistachios and no-sugar-added dried tart cherries or pecans and raisins.

NUTRITION INFORMATION

Choices/Exchanges:
1 fruit, 1/2 carbohydrate, 2 fat

Per Serving:

Calories	210
Calories from fat	90
Total fat	10 g
Saturated fat	1.3 g
Trans fat	0 g
Cholesterol	0 mg
Sodium	170 mg
Potassium	420 mg
Total carbohydrate	24 g
Dietary fiber	3 g
Sugars	17 g
Added sugars	4 g
Protein	5 g
Phosphorus	205 mg

harmony raspberry sunrise salad

What's the first food you think of as a breakfast side dish? You're not alone if hash browns, bacon, sausage, or buttery toast were what came to mind first. Well, meet this refreshing new side to start your day. It's a tangy salad with pops of sweetness from raspberries and crunchiness from almonds. You can even change up the salad topper for every season. Try diced apple and pecans in fall or sliced peach and pistachios in summer. Of course, do enjoy it as a lunch or dinner side salad, too.

2	tablespoons plain 0% fat Greek yogurt
1 1/2	teaspoons apple cider vinegar
1	teaspoon extra-virgin olive oil
2	cups packed fresh baby arugula
1/2	cup fresh or thawed frozen raspberries
2	tablespoons sliced natural almonds

KITCHEN TOOLS

- Medium mixing bowl
- Measuring spoons
- Dry measuring cups
- Whisk
- Tongs

serves: 1 | **serving size:** 2 cups salad
prep time: 8 minutes | **cooking time:** 0 minutes

DIRECTIONS

1. In a medium bowl, whisk together the yogurt, vinegar, and oil until creamy.

2. Add the arugula and toss with tongs to combine.

3. Top with the raspberries and almonds. Serve.

EASY TIP!

Running out of healthy snack ideas? This salad makes a delightful and satisfying snack.

PAN-TOASTING NUTS

Make nuts seem nuttier by toasting them. Pan-toasting them is easy. Heat a skillet over medium-high heat. Add nuts of choice, like sliced almonds. Cook while stirring constantly until the nuts are lightly browned and fragrant, about 3 minutes. Immediately transfer the pan-toasted nuts to a heatproof bowl. If you need to chop the nuts for recipe use, do so after toasting.

NUTRITION INFORMATION

Choices/Exchanges:

1/2 fruit, 1/2 carbohydrate, 1 lean protein, 1 1/2 fat

Per Serving:

Calories	170
Calories from fat	100
Total fat	11 g
Saturated fat	1.2 g
Trans fat	0 g
Cholesterol	0 mg
Sodium	25 mg
Potassium	420 mg
Total carbohydrate	13 g
Dietary fiber	6 g
Sugars	5 g
Added sugars	0 g
Protein	7 g
Phosphorus	135 mg

vegan caesar-style kale salad

A Caesar salad is notable for its simplicity and scrumptiousness! But some don't want the uncooked egg yolk or anchovies that are found in the classic dressing. So here's a 100% plant-based Caesar-style salad. The baby kale provides more flavor and richness than romaine. The nutritional yeast flakes provide that Parmesan cheese–like zing. The chickpea snacks act like croutons. And it's dressed with lemony, peppery goodness for a delightful punch in your palate. Oh . . . and you absolutely don't need to be a vegan to enjoy it!

3	tablespoons bottled lemon juice (not from concentrate)
2	tablespoons extra-virgin olive oil
1	teaspoon freshly ground black pepper
1	(5-ounce) package fresh baby kale
1/4	cup nutritional yeast flakes
1/2	cup roasted, salted chickpea snacks

KITCHEN TOOLS

- Large mixing bowl
- Measuring spoons
- Whisk
- Dry measuring cups
- Tongs

DIRECTIONS

1. In a large bowl, whisk together the lemon juice, oil, and pepper.

2. Add the kale and toss with tongs to combine. Sprinkle with the nutritional yeast flakes and toss to combine.

3. Sprinkle with the chickpea snacks. Serve.

EASY TIP!

For chickpea snacks and lemon juice recommendations, see pages 324 and 325, respectively, for "Ingredients of Choice."

WHAT IS NUTRITIONAL YEAST?

It's powdery, golden flakes of deactivated yeast often found in bulk bins at the market. Nutritional yeast provides a significant amount of protein and B vitamins. It tastes a little bit like Parmesan cheese thanks to its umami (savoriness). Use it just like grated Parmesan cheese, as it's done as an ingredient swap in this salad recipe.

NUTRITION INFORMATION

Choices/Exchanges:
1/2 starch, 1/2 carbohydrate, 1 lean protein, 1 1/2 fat

Per Serving:

Calories	170
Calories from fat	80
Total fat	9 g
Saturated fat	1.3 g
Trans fat	0 g
Cholesterol	0 mg
Sodium	100 mg
Potassium	410 mg
Total carbohydrate	16 g
Dietary fiber	6 g
Sugars	1 g
Added sugars	0 g
Protein	8 g
Phosphorus	135 mg

mesclun with blueberry vinaigrette & goat cheese

This leafy salad is so pretty. It's got a double dose of vibrant purplish-blue from the blueberry vinaigrette and the whole blueberries on top. There's a creamy white contrast from the goat cheese and a perfect amount of crunch from the walnuts, too. It's definitely nutritious thanks to blueberries and mesclun, which are loaded with micronutrients and antioxidants. You can make this salad with other fruits, too, including various berries, grapes, or diced peaches.

1 1/2	cups thawed frozen blueberries, divided
2	tablespoons white wine vinegar
1	tablespoon extra-virgin olive oil
1/8	teaspoon sea salt
1	(5-ounce) package fresh mesclun or other mixed salad greens
1/4	cup chopped walnuts
1/4	cup crumbled soft goat cheese

KITCHEN TOOLS

- Dry measuring cups
- Measuring spoons
- Blender
- Tongs

serves: 4 | **serving size:** 1 1/2 cups salad
prep time: 10 minutes | **cooking time:** 0 minutes

DIRECTIONS

1. Add 3/4 cup blueberries, the vinegar, oil, and salt to a blender. Cover and purée for at least 1 minute on high speed.

2. Arrange the mesclun on a platter or individual plates, drizzle with the blueberry vinaigrette, and top with remaining blueberries, walnuts, and goat cheese. Serve.

EASY TIP!

Need help crumbling soft goat cheese? Use a fork. It crumbles best when it's chilled. It tastes the best when it's at room temperature, though.

GO NUTS FOR YOUR HEART

Regularly eating nuts may play a role in reducing the risk of cardiovascular disease for people with type 2 diabetes. Choose a variety, such as walnuts, almonds, cashews, pistachios, pecans, and pine nuts. Keep them in jars, so you can easily sprinkle a little onto salads or entrées for bonus crunch and enjoyment anytime.

NUTRITION INFORMATION

Choices/Exchanges:
1/2 fruit, 2 fat

Per Serving:

Calories	140
Calories from fat	90
Total fat	10 g
Saturated fat	2 g
Trans fat	0 g
Cholesterol	5 mg
Sodium	105 mg
Potassium	160 mg
Total carbohydrate	10 g
Dietary fiber	3 g
Sugars	6 g
Added sugars	0 g
Protein	3 g
Phosphorus	60 mg

harvest salad with pecans & apple vinaigrette

This salad is a celebration of fall—and will transport you to the season, even if it's winter, spring, or summer! The crunchy pecans and aromatic blue cheese, paired with distinctive apple flair, are a classic and comforting combination. And the three-ingredient vinaigrette is so easy to make. It cleverly includes unsweetened applesauce to provide natural fruity sweetness. I bet you'll fall for it. I certainly have!

1/4	cup unsweetened applesauce
2	tablespoons apple cider vinegar
1	tablespoon extra-virgin olive oil
1	(5-ounce) package fresh mixed salad greens
1/3	cup pecan pieces
1/4	cup crumbled blue cheese

KITCHEN TOOLS

- Large mixing bowl
- Dry measuring cups
- Measuring spoons
- Whisk
- Tongs

DIRECTIONS

1. In a large bowl, whisk together the applesauce, vinegar, and oil. Add the salad greens and toss well with tongs to combine.

2. Sprinkle with the pecans and blue cheese. Serve.

EASY TIP!

To make this salad in advance, toss the salad greens, pecan pieces, and blue cheese together in a large bowl. Keep the apple vinaigrette separate in a small bowl. Chill. Toss the salad and dressing together at serving time.

NUTS AND A1C

People with type 2 diabetes may be able to reduce their A1C levels by enjoying nuts. A key to improving glycemic control may occur when swapping nuts for some carbo-hydrate-rich foods. So topping a salad with nuts instead of croutons or snacking on nuts instead of pretzels may be a very good thing!

NUTRITION INFORMATION

Choices/Exchanges:
3 fat

Per Serving:

Calories	140
Calories from fat	120
Total fat	13 g
Saturated fat	2.6 g
Trans fat	0.1 g
Cholesterol	5 mg
Sodium	125 mg
Potassium	170 mg
Total carbohydrate	4 g
Dietary fiber	2 g
Sugars	2 g
Added sugars	0 g
Protein	3 g
Phosphorus	70 mg

party sorghum salad with arugula & pistachios

Need a salad that's fit for a party as well as for those with food intolerances? This recipe is it! It's vegan and gluten-free. And it's full of culinary intrigue, starting with the desirably chewy sorghum—an ancient grain that's finally getting its day in the spotlight on modern tables. The peppery arugula adds freshness and liveliness to the lemony-dressed grains. Everyone is sure to love the confetti-like pop of color and texture from the pistachios and pomegranate arils, too!

4	cups cold water
1	cup uncooked whole-grain sorghum
3	tablespoons bottled lemon juice (not from concentrate)
2	tablespoons extra-virgin olive oil
1	teaspoon sea salt
4	cups packed fresh baby arugula (4 ounces)
1/2	cup shelled, roasted, unsalted pistachios
1/3	cup pomegranate arils

KITCHEN TOOLS

- Medium saucepan with lid
- Liquid measuring cup
- Dry measuring cups
- Measuring spoons
- Large mixing bowl
- Whisk
- Large spoon

serves: 10 | serving size: 3/4 cup salad
prep time: 15 minutes | cooking time: 60 minutes
(plus cooling time)

DIRECTIONS

1. In a medium saucepan, bring water to a boil over high heat. Add the sorghum and bring back to boil. Cover, reduce heat to medium low, and cook until tender, about 55 minutes or according to package directions. Set aside, covered, for 10 minutes to complete the cooking process.

2. In a large bowl, whisk together the lemon juice, oil, and salt. Stir in the hot sorghum. Set aside to cool for 30 minutes. Stir, then chill.

3. When the sorghum is cool, stir in the arugula, pistachios, and pomegranate arils. Serve.

EASY TIP!

If you don't have bottled lemon juice, know that one whole lemon typically provides about 3 tablespoons of juice.

WHAT ARE POMEGRANATE ARILS?

They're fruity-fleshed pomegranate seeds. To remove arils from a whole pomegranate, cut it into 4 sections. Rub the arils out of the peel while it is submerged in a bowl of cold water. The white, pithy part (skin) floats; the arils sink. For simplicity, recipe-ready arils ("pom-poms") may be available in your market's produce or freezer section.

NUTRITION INFORMATION

Choices/Exchanges:
1 starch, 1 fat

Per Serving:

Calories	140
Calories from fat	50
Total fat	6 g
Saturated fat	0.8 g
Trans fat	0 g
Cholesterol	0 mg
Sodium	220 mg
Potassium	190 mg
Total carbohydrate	19 g
Dietary fiber	4 g
Sugars	2 g
Added sugars	0 g
Protein	4 g
Phosphorus	95 mg

seasonal mediterranean farro salad

You're going to love this grain salad's versatility. In fact, you're going to love it, period. It's got a crave-worthy duo of sweet and salty tastes, along with lots of ingredient intrigue, especially from farro. Farro is an ancient grain that's a type of wheat. It has a pleasurably chewy texture. If forced to choose my favorite grain, farro wins! This salad is fit for a family of four for today and tomorrow—or serve it for a party. Otherwise, if there's just one or two of you, enjoy it meal-prep style over several days. That's how I do it.

1	cup uncooked farro
5	cups cold water
3	tablespoons white balsamic vinegar
2	tablespoons extra-virgin olive oil
1	cup small, bite-sized pieces fresh seasonal fruit (such as blueberries)
3	cups packed fresh baby arugula
1/2	teaspoon sea salt
1/2	cup shelled, roasted, salted pistachios

KITCHEN TOOLS

- Cutting board
- Chef's knife
- Large saucepan with lid
- Dry measuring cups
- Liquid measuring cup
- Mesh strainer
- Large mixing bowl
- Measuring spoons
- Whisk
- Large spoon

serves: 8 | **serving size:** 3/4 cup salad
prep time: 10 minutes | **cooking time:** 35 minutes
(plus cooling time)

DIRECTIONS

1. In a large saucepan, add the farro and water. Bring to a boil over high heat. Reduce heat to medium low, cover, and simmer until tender, about 30 minutes or according to package directions. Drain excess liquid from farro using a strainer.

2. In large bowl, whisk together the vinegar and oil. Add the farro and stir. Set aside to cool for 30 minutes. Stir, then chill.

3. When farro is cool, stir the fruit, arugula, and salt into the farro, sprinkle with the pistachios, and serve.

EASY TIP!

If you can't find farro at your market, use 2 1/2 cups of another favorite cooked whole grain in this recipe, such as bulgur, quinoa, or freekeh. Then begin with step 2 of the recipe.

SEASONAL FRUIT SWAPS

When fruit is in season, it's at its peak of ripeness, nutritional value, color, and flavor. So go ahead and make this salad just right for the season you're in. Instead of blueberries, you can try diced fresh figs in fall, thinly sliced pear in winter, halved cherries in spring, and diced apricots in summer.

NUTRITION INFORMATION

Choices/Exchanges:
1 starch, 1/2 carbohydrate, 1 1/2 fat

Per Serving:

Calories	190
Calories from fat	70
Total fat	8 g
Saturated fat	1 g
Trans fat	0 g
Cholesterol	0 mg
Sodium	150 mg
Potassium	260 mg
Total carbohydrate	27 g
Dietary fiber	4 g
Sugars	5 g
Added sugars	0 g
Protein	6 g
Phosphorus	155 mg

greek quinoa salad

Feta cheese and lemon are two distinct ingredients in Greek cuisine. They're also what make this brightly flavored quinoa salad a culinary joy for your taste buds. When tossed with fresh baby spinach, crisp cucumber, and chewy quinoa, you'll have a salad that's refreshing, filling, and full of texture intrigue. If you like to eat with your eyes, choose tri-color or red quinoa for extra color. And for an extra pop of Greek appeal, pair each serving with a few kalamata olives, if you like.

1/2	cup uncooked, pre-rinsed quinoa
1	cup cold water
1	(4-inch) piece English cucumber, unpeeled, finely diced
2	cups packed fresh baby spinach
1/4	cup crumbled feta cheese
2	tablespoons bottled lemon juice (not from concentrate)
1	tablespoon plus 1 teaspoon extra-virgin olive oil
1/4	teaspoon sea salt

KITCHEN TOOLS

- Cutting board
- Chef's knife
- Medium saucepan with lid
- Dry measuring cups
- Liquid measuring cup
- Medium mixing bowl
- Measuring spoons
- Large spoon
- Small whisk

serves: 4 | **serving size:** 1 1/4 cups salad
prep time: 10 minutes | **cooking time:** 20 minutes
(plus cooling time)

DIRECTIONS

1. In a medium saucepan, add the quinoa and water. Bring to a boil over high heat. Reduce heat to low, cover, and simmer until tender, about 15 minutes or according to package directions. Transfer to a medium bowl and set aside to cool for 30 minutes. Stir, then chill.

2. When quinoa is cool, stir in the cucumber, baby spinach, and feta until evenly combined.

3. Whisk together the lemon juice, oil, and salt in a liquid measuring cup. Drizzle over the quinoa salad. Stir to combine. Serve.

EASY TIP!

No quinoa? No problem! In its place, simply swap 1 1/2 cups of a cooked whole grain of choice, such as bulgur, freekeh, or farro. Then begin with step 2 of the recipe.

WHAT IS QUINOA?

Quinoa is used as a whole grain, but botanically it's a seed. Therefore, it's gluten-free and offers unique nutritional benefits. A highlight is that it contains significant amounts of all essential amino acids. One half cup of cooked quinoa provides about 110 calories, 4 grams of protein, 20 grams of total carbohydrate, and almost 3 grams of fiber.

NUTRITION INFORMATION

Choices/Exchanges:
1 starch, 1 1/2 fat

Per Serving:

Calories	150
Calories from fat	60
Total fat	7 g
Saturated fat	1.7 g
Trans fat	0.1 g
Cholesterol	5 mg
Sodium	240 mg
Potassium	300 mg
Total carbohydrate	17 g
Dietary fiber	2 g
Sugars	3 g
Added sugars	0 g
Protein	5 g
Phosphorus	140 mg

niçoise-inspired salad

The niçoise salad (or *salade niçoise*) was born in France in the city of Nice. It's classically made with niçoise olives, anchovies, tomatoes, hard-boiled eggs, and an olive oil dressing. And while the salad is typically served as an entrée, this simplified version is designed as a glammed up, carb-friendly side salad that's packed with protein. That makes it ideal paired with an entrée that's richer in carbs and lower in protein, like some vegetarian noodle dishes can be. However, if you're looking for a really light lunch main dish, pick this and pair it with a simple, crusty, whole-grain roll.

1	(5-ounce) package fresh baby arugula
1/3	cup Easy Dijon Vinaigrette (page 290) or natural, no-sugar-added vinaigrette, divided
4	large hard-boiled eggs, peeled and quartered lengthwise
1/4	cup canned sliced black olives, drained
1	(5-ounce) can no-salt-added, low-mercury tuna, drained and flaked with a fork
2	cups grape tomatoes (12 ounces)

KITCHEN TOOLS

- Cutting board
- Chef's knife
- Can opener
- Mesh strainer
- Fork
- Large mixing bowl
- Dry measuring cups
- Measuring spoons
- Liquid measuring cup
- Tongs

serves: 4 | serving size: 2 cups salad
prep time: 8 minutes | cooking time: 0 minutes
(if using pre-cooked eggs)

DIRECTIONS

1. In a large bowl, add the arugula and 3 tablespoons vinaigrette, and toss well with tongs to combine. Arrange on a platter or individual plates.

2. Top the salad with the eggs, olives, tuna, and tomatoes. Drizzle with remaining vinaigrette. Serve.

EASY TIP!

Shop for pre-boiled (hard-boiled) eggs at your supermarket. Or make a large batch of hard-boiled eggs in advance, so they're ready when you are. See page 25 for "How to make hard-boiled eggs."

OLIVE MYTH BUSTING

Some people think olives aren't healthful. They're wrong! One serving of California ripe olives provides just 25 calories, 1 gram of total carbohydrate, and 2.5 grams of total fat, which is mostly monounsaturated—the "good" kind. Plan for its 115 milligrams of sodium, though, knowing it's what makes olives so tasty. Olives also contain health-promoting polyphenols, vitamins A and E, and other nutrients.

NUTRITION INFORMATION

Choices/Exchanges:
1 nonstarchy vegetable,
2 lean protein, 2 fat

Per Serving:

Calories	200
Calories from fat	120
Total fat	13 g
Saturated fat	2.7 g
Trans fat	0 g
Cholesterol	190 mg
Sodium	320 mg
Potassium	490 mg
Total carbohydrate	7 g
Dietary fiber	2 g
Sugars	4 g
Added sugars	0 g
Protein	14 g
Phosphorus	215 mg

french lentil salad

Garbanzo beans (chickpeas) seem to be getting all of the love these days. But lentils are another pulse that deserves their day in the spotlight. So show them off! Make this lemony dressed lentil salad when you need a satisfying side. It's got such appealing texture. The duo of carrots and dill is a highlight, and the combination of protein and fiber is so satisfying. Since this is no wimpy salad, it keeps well in the fridge for several days. Plan it into a couple meals—or even enjoy as a stand-alone snack!

1	cup dry French green lentils, rinsed and drained
1	(32-fluid-ounce) carton low-sodium vegetable broth
3	tablespoons bottled lemon juice (not from concentrate)
1	tablespoon extra-virgin olive oil
1/2	teaspoon sea salt
1	cup shredded carrots
1/4	cup packed fresh dill fronds (feathery leaves)

KITCHEN TOOLS

- Mesh strainer
- Microplane zester/grater
- Large saucepan with lid
- Dry measuring cups
- Cooking spoon
- Measuring spoons
- Large mixing bowl
- Whisk

party sorghum salad with
arugula & pistachios
page 224

no-brainer bean burrito wrap
page 128

sweet cherry milkshake
page 312

savory tzatziki-style yogurt
page 110

sheet pan zucchini, red pepper
& tofu "stir-fry"
page 156

no-bake cheesecake-in-a-glass
page 302

three-minute skillet
beans & greens
page 142

"steak" fajitas
page 152

serves: 6 | serving size: 2/3 cup salad
prep time: 8 minutes | cooking time: 30 minutes
(plus cooling time)

DIRECTIONS

1. In a large saucepan, add the lentils and broth. Bring to a boil over high heat. Reduce heat to medium low and simmer, partially covered, until the lentils are tender, about 25 minutes. Drain any excess broth.

2. In a large bowl, whisk together the lemon juice, oil, and salt. Add the hot lentils (do not rinse) and the carrots and stir to combine. Set aside to cool for about 30 minutes. Stir, then chill in the refrigerator until ready to serve. Stir the dill into the lentil salad just before serving.

EASY TIP!

You don't need to pull out the cutting board and chef's knife for dill prep; simply pinch off the feathery dill leaves using your fingers.

GOT EXTRA BROTH?

In this recipe, you'll drain any excess broth used for lentil preparation. When you have extra broth, make a plan for it. Perhaps drizzle it over other meal components for extra scrumptiousness. Otherwise, cool it, then freeze it in ice cube trays. Once frozen, store the broth cubes in a freezer container for later use, such as plopping into the cooking liquid for whole grains.

NUTRITION INFORMATION

Choices/Exchanges:
1 starch, 1 nonstarchy vegetable, 1 lean protein

Per Serving:

Calories	140
Calories from fat	20
Total fat	2.5 g
Saturated fat	0.4 g
Trans fat	0 g
Cholesterol	0 mg
Sodium	270 mg
Potassium	440 mg
Total carbohydrate	21 g
Dietary fiber	8 g
Sugars	4 g
Added sugars	0 g
Protein	8 g
Phosphorus	195 mg

fast fattoush salad

The first leafy salad I remember trying was *fattoush*. I loved the name of it (and still do!), which added to its appeal. *Fattoush* is a traditional Lebanese salad that features cucumber, fresh mint (my favorite herb!), and toasted Middle Eastern flatbread pieces. It's an excellent way to use day-old pita bread, kind of like how stale bread is used in Italian panzanella salad. But here, you don't need stale bread; just buy packaged whole-grain pita chips. Or, if you'd like to make this *fattoush* extra special, bake a batch of DIY Pita Chips (page 74).

3	tablespoons bottled lemon juice (not from concentrate)
2	tablespoons extra-virgin olive oil
1	(6-inch) piece English cucumber, unpeeled, thinly sliced into coins
1	(5-ounce) package chopped romaine lettuce
1	cup grape tomatoes (6 ounces)
1/4	cup packed fresh mint leaves
24	whole-grain pita chips

KITCHEN TOOLS

- Cutting board
- Chef's knife
- Large mixing bowl
- Measuring spoons
- Whisk
- Tongs

serves: 4 | **serving size:** 2 cups salad
prep time: 8 minutes | **cooking time:** 0 minutes

DIRECTIONS

1. In a large bowl, whisk together the lemon juice and oil.

2. Add the cucumber, lettuce, tomatoes, mint, and pita chips to the bowl, and toss well with tongs to fully combine. Serve.

EASY TIP!

For mint prep, simply pinch off the whole mint leaves using your fingers; there's no need to chop them. The whole leaves become part of the salad greens.

BEYOND ORDINARY CUCUMBERS

Since their skin isn't tough, I prefer English cucumbers rather than standard cucumbers. In most recipes, you can use all parts of the English cucumber, no peeling or seed removal required. If you'd like to experiment, try Persian cucumbers. They're thin skinned and soft seeded as well. Since they're small (up to 6 inches long), the entire cucumber is easily used in recipes. No leftovers!

NUTRITION INFORMATION

Choices/Exchanges:
1 starch, 1 nonstarchy vegetable, 1 1/2 fat

Per Serving:

Calories	160
Calories from fat	90
Total fat	10 g
Saturated fat	1.2 g
Trans fat	0 g
Cholesterol	0 mg
Sodium	140 mg
Potassium	300 mg
Total carbohydrate	17 g
Dietary fiber	3 g
Sugars	3 g
Added sugars	0 g
Protein	3 g
Phosphorus	55 mg

four-ingredient bean salad

After you make this bean salad once or twice, you won't need the recipe anymore. It's that easy! It's tasty, too. Beans and fresh herbs are dressed with a two-ingredient red wine vinaigrette. By using regular beans and rinsing them, you'll get plenty of flavor without the need to add salt. (Hint: Rinsing may remove as much as 40% of the sodium!) You'll still get a double whammy of protein and fiber, too. Making this with the cannellini bean and basil combo provides Italian flair to any meal. Or pick your own bean-and-herb variation to personalize this salad as you wish.

2	tablespoons red wine vinegar
1	tablespoon extra-virgin olive oil
1	(15-ounce) can cannellini beans or beans of choice, rinsed and drained
3	tablespoons chopped fresh basil leaves or herbs of choice

KITCHEN TOOLS

- Can opener
- Strainer
- Cutting board
- Chef's knife
- Measuring spoons
- Medium mixing bowl
- Whisk
- Large spoon

serves: 3 | serving size: 1/2 cup salad
prep time: 5 minutes | cooking time: 0 minutes

DIRECTIONS

1. In a medium bowl, whisk together the vinegar and oil.

2. Add the beans and herbs, stir, and serve.

EASY TIP!

Add 1/2 cup of red wine vinegar and 1/4 cup of extra-virgin olive oil to a jar. Seal and store in the fridge. Shake, then drizzle onto salads all week long, including drizzling 3 tablespoons of it into this recipe.

BEAN-AND-HERB PAIRINGS

For this bean salad, use whatever beans and fresh herbs you have on hand—or choose based on a specific global influence. Besides cannellini beans and basil, try these other pairings: black or pinto beans and cilantro; kidney beans and parsley; or garbanzo beans and mint or dill.

NUTRITION INFORMATION

Choices/Exchanges:
1 starch, 1 lean protein, 1/2 fat

Per Serving:

Calories	140
Calories from fat	45
Total fat	5 g
Saturated fat	0.7 g
Trans fat	0 g
Cholesterol	0 mg
Sodium	180 mg
Potassium	340 mg
Total carbohydrate	18 g
Dietary fiber	5 g
Sugars	0 g
Added sugars	0 g
Protein	7 g
Phosphorus	115 mg

mesclun salad with beans

Eating beans regularly is a healthy habit. This is because beans are nutrient-rich, full of fiber, and a notable plant-based source of protein, which is especially beneficial if you're trying to cut back on meat—or completely eliminating meat from your diet. That said, you want to make sure you find enjoyment in eating beans regularly. This versatile recipe can help you do just that! You'll toss together garbanzo beans, mint, and mesclun with lemon juice and olive oil for quick-n-easy Mediterranean appeal. You can switch up the ingredients to meet your individualized flavor preferences, too.

3	tablespoons bottled lemon or lime juice (not from concentrate)
2	tablespoons extra-virgin olive oil
1	(15-ounce) can garbanzo beans (chickpeas) or beans of choice, rinsed and drained
1/4	cup packed chopped fresh mint leaves or herbs of choice
1	(5-ounce) package fresh mesclun

KITCHEN TOOLS

- Can opener
- Strainer
- Cutting board
- Chef's knife
- Measuring spoons
- Large mixing bowl
- Whisk
- Tongs

serves: 4 | **serving size:** 1 1/2 cups salad
prep time: 6 minutes | **cooking time:** 0 minutes

DIRECTIONS

1. In a large bowl, whisk together the lemon juice and oil.

2. Add the beans and herbs and toss with tongs to combine. Add the mesclun and toss to combine. Serve.

EASY TIP!

If you don't have bottled lemon or lime juice, know that 1 whole lemon typically provides about 3 tablespoons of juice and 1 whole lime typically provides about 2 tablespoons of juice.

WORLDLY SALAD

Try these other global cuisine–inspired ingredient trios in this recipe. Mexican: black or pinto beans, cilantro, and lime juice. American: kidney beans, parsley, and lemon juice. Italian: cannellini beans, basil, and lemon. Asian: black soybeans, Thai basil, and lime.

NUTRITION INFORMATION

Choices/Exchanges:
1 starch, 1 nonstarchy vegetable, 1 1/2 fat

Per Serving:

Calories	170
Calories from fat	80
Total fat	9 g
Saturated fat	1.1 g
Trans fat	0 g
Cholesterol	0 mg
Sodium	200 mg
Potassium	310 mg
Total carbohydrate	19 g
Dietary fiber	5 g
Sugars	4 g
Added sugars	0 g
Protein	6 g
Phosphorus	120 mg

fresh watermelon & cucumber salad

Fresh fruit salad is nutritious but can put your carb count over the top. This salad shows one way to enjoy fruit that has a high glycemic index in a diabetes-friendly way. By adding cucumber, you'll get fewer carbs per cup, but you'll still get delightful fruity sweetness. By adding healthy fat, it might help reduce the watermelon's impact on your blood glucose level since dishes that contain fat are converted into sugar more slowly. The pinch of sea salt used in the recipe helps to balance all the flavors. For a bonus kick in the palate, try a sprinkling of minced hot chile pepper, too.

2	tablespoons bottled lemon juice (not from concentrate)
2	tablespoons extra-virgin olive oil
1/4	teaspoon sea salt
1	(12-inch) English cucumber, unpeeled, cut into quarter-moon slices
4	cups seedless watermelon cubes
1/4	cup packed fresh mint leaves, finely chopped

KITCHEN TOOLS

- Cutting board
- Chef's knife
- Large mixing bowl
- Measuring spoons
- Dry measuring cups
- Whisk
- Large spoon

serves: 8 | serving size: 1 cup salad
prep time: 8 minutes | cooking time: 0 minutes

DIRECTIONS

1. In a large bowl, whisk together the lemon juice, oil, and salt.

2. Add the cucumber, watermelon, and mint, gently toss to combine, and serve.

EASY TIP!

See page 24 for "How to cut a cucumber."

WATERMELON? "YES, WAY!"

Because it's considered "sugary," some say "no way" to watermelon. But when served like this salad, or paired with foods containing protein and fat, like grilled salmon, its impact on blood glucose is blunted. Plus, by enjoying watermelon, you'll get lycopene, which may help reduce the risk of diabetic retinopathy. (Hint: Buy watermelon already cubed rather than an entire melon.)

NUTRITION INFORMATION

Choices/Exchanges:
1/2 fruit, 1/2 fat

Per Serving:

Calories	60
Calories from fat	30
Total fat	3.5 g
Saturated fat	0.5 g
Trans fat	0 g
Cholesterol	0 mg
Sodium	75 mg
Potassium	170 mg
Total carbohydrate	8 g
Dietary fiber	1 g
Sugars	6 g
Added sugars	0 g
Protein	1 g
Phosphorus	20 mg

SAVORY SIDES

southern black-eyed peas

Too many people (even some chefs!) consider side dishes more like an afterthought. Personally, I think they deserve as much love and attention as any other part of the meal. That means this recipe may be the most intriguing part of your lunch or dinner. Equally intriguing is the fact that black-eyed peas are technically beans—and they're considered "good luck" on New Year's in the South. But on any day, you'll appreciate the result here. This dish is rather brothy, so savor the flavorful broth along with the black-eyed peas—or drizzle it over other parts of your meal.

2	teaspoons extra-virgin olive oil
1	small or 1/2 large red onion, finely diced
2	garlic cloves, minced
2	cups thawed frozen black-eyed peas
1	cup chicken broth
1/2	teaspoon freshly ground black pepper

KITCHEN TOOLS

- Cutting board
- Chef's knife
- Medium saucepan with lid
- Measuring spoons
- Dry measuring cups
- Liquid measuring cup
- Cooking spoon

serves: 4 │ **serving size:** 2/3 cup
prep time: 10 minutes │ **cooking time:** 18 minutes

DIRECTIONS

1. In a medium saucepan, heat the oil over medium heat. Add the onion and cook while stirring until softened, about 5 minutes. Add the garlic and cook while stirring until fragrant, about 1 minute.

2. Add the thawed black-eyed peas, broth, and pepper, and bring to a boil over high heat.

3. Reduce heat to low, cover, and simmer until the black-eyed peas are cooked through and tenderly crisp, about 8 minutes. Taste and adjust seasoning as needed, then serve.

EASY TIP!

See page 22 for "How to mince garlic" and "How to dice an onion."

QUICK-SOAKING DRY BLACK-EYED PEAS

If you can only find dry black-eyed peas, use this quick soaking method so they're recipe ready. Add them to a saucepan, cover with water by several inches, and boil. After a couple minutes of boiling, turn off the burner, cover with a lid, and let the black-eyed peas soak for 1 hour. Then use them in recipes like this.

NUTRITION INFORMATION

Choices/Exchanges:
1 1/2 starch, 1 lean protein

Per Serving:

Calories	150
Calories from fat	25
Total fat	3 g
Saturated fat	0.5 g
Trans fat	0 g
Cholesterol	0 mg
Sodium	170 mg
Potassium	410 mg
Total carbohydrate	23 g
Dietary fiber	4 g
Sugars	2 g
Added sugars	0 g
Protein	8 g
Phosphorus	115 mg

saucy caribbean beans

Beans are often served along with other key ingredients, as in the popular pairing of beans and rice. Here, they're so full of appeal—with their garlicky goodness and stewed essence—that they can be the star of the meal all by themselves. The trade secret is that the liquid from the canned beans helps create its sauciness! As a bonus, lime juice offers zing, and cilantro provides a lovely, herbal fragrance to complete this bean dish.

1	(15-ounce) can no-salt-added black beans (do not drain or rinse)
2	large garlic cloves, peeled and finely chopped
1/4	teaspoon plus 1/8 teaspoon sea salt
2	scallions, green and white parts, thinly sliced
1/4	cup fresh cilantro leaves with tender stems
1/2	lime, cut into 4 wedges

KITCHEN TOOLS

- Can opener
- Cutting board
- Chef's knife
- Medium saucepan with lid
- Measuring spoons
- Cooking spoon

serves: 4 | **serving size:** about 1/2 cup
prep time: 8 minutes | **cooking time:** 8 minutes

DIRECTIONS

1. In a medium saucepan, stir together the beans (with bean liquid), garlic, and salt. Bring to a boil over high heat. Reduce heat to medium low, stir in the scallions, cover, and cook until flavors are combined, about 5 minutes.

2. Transfer to a serving bowl, sprinkle with the cilantro leaves and stems, and serve with the lime wedges.

EASY TIP!

Instead of measuring, you can simply just tear off a handful of cilantro from the leaf end of a bunch. The tender stems are 100% edible.

A DIABETES SUPERFOOD

The American Diabetes Association considers beans to be a diabetes superfood! Beans are beneficial for health promotion and disease prevention. They're rich in vitamins and minerals, antioxidants, and fiber. Beans' soluble fiber can have a significant, beneficial impact on blood glucose level management. And their notable nutrient duo of protein and soluble fiber can boost satiety to help you feel full.

NUTRITION INFORMATION

Choices/Exchanges:
1 starch

Per Serving:

Calories	90
Calories from fat	0
Total fat	0 g
Saturated fat	0.1 g
Trans fat	0 g
Cholesterol	0 mg
Sodium	230 mg
Potassium	270 mg
Total carbohydrate	16 g
Dietary fiber	5 g
Sugars	2 g
Added sugars	0 g
Protein	6 g
Phosphorus	120 mg

lemony freekeh protein pilaf

Simple whole-grain side dishes are occasionally bland. Not here. This pilaf has a star ingredient that offers taste-bud excitement. What's that ingredient? A unique grain called freekeh. To further entice you, this pilaf offers a simple way to punch up the plant-protein content of your meal by 5 grams. The sneaky addition of hemp seeds also contributes protein to this lemon-accented side. Serve it just like rice, though cracked freekeh is higher in protein, fiber, and iron than traditional brown rice—and cooks in half the time! Try this side with Pesto Grilled Shrimp (page 176).

1/2	cup uncooked cracked freekeh
1 1/2	cups cold water
3	tablespoons raw shelled hemp seeds or flaxseeds
2	teaspoons bottled lemon juice (not from concentrate)
2	teaspoons extra-virgin olive oil
1/4	teaspoon plus 1/8 teaspoon sea salt

KITCHEN TOOLS

- Dry measuring cups
- Liquid measuring cup
- Medium saucepan with lid
- Measuring spoons
- Cooking spoon

serves: 4 | serving size: about 1/2 cup
prep time: 5 minutes | cooking time: 23 minutes
(plus standing time)

DIRECTIONS

1. Add the freekeh and water to a medium saucepan. Bring to a boil over high heat. Reduce heat to low, cover, and simmer until the freekeh is tender, about 20 minutes, or according to package directions.

2. Remove from heat, stir in the hemp seeds, lemon juice, oil, and salt. Let stand for 5 minutes, then serve.

EASY TIP!

For freekeh and hemp seed recommendations, see page 326 for "Ingredients of Choice."

WHAT'S FREEKEH?

Freekeh is young, green wheat with a low glycemic index. It contains resistant starch, which is a diabetes-friendly carbohydrate. I find its taste complex with a smoky essence since it's roasted before being crushed. Though it's an ancient grain with roots in Middle Eastern cuisine, savor this "supergrain" as part of your present-day whole-grain repertoire. It's great in any type of cuisine.

NUTRITION INFORMATION

Choices/Exchanges:
1 starch, 1 fat

Per Serving:

Calories	150
Calories from fat	50
Total fat	6 g
Saturated fat	0.7 g
Trans fat	0 g
Cholesterol	0 mg
Sodium	200 mg
Potassium	180 mg
Total carbohydrate	16 g
Dietary fiber	4 g
Sugars	1 g
Added sugars	0 g
Protein	6 g
Phosphorus	230 mg

vegan farrotto

Don't have the patience for making risotto? Here's the answer: a risotto-style dish that's made with ease and served as a side. It's called "farrotto" for fun. Where does it get its creaminess? From light coconut milk, which also gives it a hint of Thai-like luxuriousness. Do have a plan for the remaining coconut milk so it doesn't go to waste, such as splashing it onto Three-Minute Skillet Beans & Greens (page 142). Serve the farrotto as a side for fish, chicken, or a stir-fry, like Ginger, Tempeh & Snow Pea Stir-Fry (page 144).

1	cup quick-cooking (10-minute) farro (uncooked)
3	cups cold water
1/3	cup canned light organic coconut milk
1/4	teaspoon plus 1/8 teaspoon sea salt
1/4	cup fresh cilantro leaves

KITCHEN TOOLS

- Dry measuring cups
- Liquid measuring cup
- Medium saucepan with lid
- Mesh strainer
- Measuring spoons
- Cooking spoon

serves: 4 | **serving size:** 1/2 cup
prep time: 5 minutes | **cooking time:** 15 minutes

DIRECTIONS

1. In a medium saucepan, add the farro and water. Bring to a boil over high heat. Reduce heat to low, cover, and simmer until tender, about 10 minutes or according to package directions. Drain excess liquid using a strainer.

2. Transfer the farro back into the dry saucepan. Stir in the coconut milk and salt, place over low heat, and cook while stirring until most of coconut milk is absorbed, about 2 minutes.

3. Sprinkle with the whole cilantro leaves. Serve.

EASY TIP!

For coconut milk and farro recommendations, see pages 324 and 326, respectively, for "Ingredients of Choice."

GOT REGULAR FARRO?

If you're unable to find quick-cooking (10-minute) farro, you can still make this recipe. In step 1, prepare 3/4 cup of regular, uncooked farro in 4 cups of water in a large saucepan, simmering for 30 minutes or according to package directions. Drain the excess liquid. Then follow the rest of the recipe exactly as written.

NUTRITION INFORMATION

Choices/Exchanges:
2 starch

Per Serving:

Calories	160
Calories from fat	20
Total fat	2 g
Saturated fat	1.1 g
Trans fat	0 g
Cholesterol	0 mg
Sodium	220 mg
Potassium	150 mg
Total carbohydrate	30 g
Dietary fiber	3 g
Sugars	0 g
Added sugars	0 g
Protein	5 g
Phosphorus	145 mg

orange-pistachio couscous

Couscous can be a pile of plain-tasting carbs. Or it can be a whole-grain food offering plenty of flavor, texture, and color. Luckily the latter is what you get by making this recipe. Whole-wheat couscous is a tiny-sized pasta that offers whole-grain goodness, including fiber and iron. Orange zest provides citrusy fragrance without extra carbohydrates. And the pistachios add colorful crunch along with the satisfying trio of plant-based protein, healthy fats, and fiber. It's a delight when paired with poultry or fish, such as Spice-Rubbed Salmon (page 168).

1 1/4	cups cold water
1	cup dry whole-wheat couscous
2	scallions, green and white parts, thinly sliced
1	teaspoon grated orange zest
1/2	teaspoon sea salt
1/3	cup shelled, roasted, salted pistachios or slivered almonds

KITCHEN TOOLS

- Cutting board
- Chef's knife
- Microplane zester/grater
- Medium saucepan with lid
- Liquid measuring cup
- Dry measuring cups
- Measuring spoons
- Large fork

serves: 6 | serving size: 1/2 cup
prep time: 6 minutes | cooking time: 5 minutes
(plus standing time)

NUTRITION INFORMATION

Choices/Exchanges:

1 1/2 starch, 1/2 fat

Per Serving:

Calories	140
Calories from fat	30
Total fat	3.5 g
Saturated fat	0.4 g
Trans fat	0 g
Cholesterol	0 mg
Sodium	210 mg
Potassium	130 mg
Total carbohydrate	24 g
Dietary fiber	3 g
Sugars	1 g
Added sugars	0 g
Protein	6 g
Phosphorus	80 mg

DIRECTIONS

1. In a medium saucepan, bring water to a boil over high heat. Stir in the couscous, cover, and remove from heat. Let stand 5 minutes to complete the cooking process. Or prepare according to package directions.

2. Add the scallions, orange zest, salt, and pistachios. Stir and fluff with a fork. Serve.

EASY TIP!

To save time, buy the pistachios already shelled. For a pistachio recommendation, see page 325 for "Ingredients of Choice."

GETTING ZESTY

To get 1 teaspoon of orange zest, grate half of a naval orange (while it's still whole) or one entire mandarin orange using a Microplane zester/grater. A tiny bit of zest provides intense citrus flavor . . . plus antioxidants. Be sure to scrub the orange under running water before zesting. And do enjoy the remaining orange or mandarin orange another way the same day.

mexican cilantro rice

The fragrant rice served at Mexican-style restaurants is often made with white rice. And there's a good chance that it's overloaded with sodium. But you don't need to give up Mexican-style rice. Give this recipe a go instead. You'll still get plenty of aromatic Mexican flair in a better-for-you way by using brown rice and you'll get a just-right amount of sodium from the salsa verde. Plus you'll get an extra little punch of protein and "good" fats from the unique addition of hemp seeds, which might help reduce rice's effect on blood glucose since it'll be converted into sugar more slowly.

1	cup uncooked brown rice
2/3	cup preservative-free salsa verde
1 1/3	cups cold water
1/3	cup fresh cilantro leaves with tender stems
2	tablespoons raw shelled hemp seeds or flaxseeds

KITCHEN TOOLS

- Dry measuring cups
- Liquid measuring cup
- Medium saucepan with lid
- Cooking spoon
- Measuring spoons

serves: 6 | serving size: 1/2 cup
prep time: 5 minutes | cooking time: 45 minutes
(plus standing time)

DIRECTIONS

1. Add the rice, salsa, and water to a medium saucepan. Bring to a boil over high heat. Reduce heat to low, cover, and simmer until rice is tender, about 40 minutes. Remove from heat and let stand covered for 10 minutes to complete the cooking process.

2. Tear the cilantro leaves with stems into small pieces. Stir the cilantro pieces and hemp seeds into the rice. Serve.

EASY TIP!

For salsa verde, hemp seed, and rice recommendations, see pages 325 and 326 for "Ingredients of Choice."

RICE PAIRINGS

This Mexican-inspired rice is not meant to be a stand-alone recipe. What should you pair it with? You can't go wrong by pairing rice with beans, like Saucy Caribbean Beans (page 246). It's a great match for "Steak" Fajitas (page 152)—just drop the tortillas and swap in this rice. Try it with Sheet Pan Chile-Lime Shrimp & Peppers (page 178), too.

NUTRITION INFORMATION

Choices/Exchanges:
1 1/2 starch, 1/2 fat

Per Serving:

Calories	140
Calories from fat	20
Total fat	2.5 g
Saturated fat	0.4 g
Trans fat	0 g
Cholesterol	0 mg
Sodium	120 mg
Potassium	190 mg
Total carbohydrate	26 g
Dietary fiber	3 g
Sugars	1 g
Added sugars	0 g
Protein	4 g
Phosphorus	145 mg

pan-roasted sweet bell peppers

I love sweet bell peppers for so many reasons. You can generally find them all year long. They're easy to prepare. You can enjoy the peppers in a myriad of ways, including raw, grilled, or roasted. They've got natural sweetness and savoriness in every bite. They add lively color to the plate. Bell peppers count as nonstarchy veggies. They're a nutritious source of carotenoids and an excellent source of vitamin C. And you can make this scrumptious (and versatile) side with them! (Hint: Pick a colorful trio of peppers for this recipe, such as red, yellow, and green.)

3	large bell peppers (various colors), cut into 4–5 pieces each
2	teaspoons extra-virgin olive oil
1/4	teaspoon sea salt

KITCHEN TOOLS

- Cutting board
- Chef's knife
- Large mixing bowl
- Measuring spoons
- Large rimmed baking sheet

serves: 3 | **serving size:** 4–5 pieces
prep time: 5 minutes | **cooking time:** 12 minutes

DIRECTIONS

1. Preheat oven to 475°F.

2. In a large bowl, toss together the bell pepper pieces, oil, and salt. Arrange the pieces, skin side down, in a single layer on a large rimmed baking sheet.

3. Roast in the oven until browned on the bottom (skin side), about 12 minutes; no flipping over needed. Serve.

EASY TIP!

See page 23 for "How to slice a bell pepper."

PEPPER PAIRINGS

This recipe is delicious served warm right after roasting. It's tasty when cool, too. Either way, the versatile roasted peppers pair well with egg, chicken, or bean dishes. Try them with Herbed Soft Scrambled Eggs on Toast (page 118) or Herbs de Provence Roasted Chicken Breasts (page 190). Double the batch, roasting on two baking sheets, for enjoyment throughout the week.

NUTRITION INFORMATION

Choices/Exchanges:
2 nonstarchy vegetable, 1/2 fat

Per Serving:

Calories	70
Calories from fat	30
Total fat	3.5 g
Saturated fat	0.5 g
Trans fat	0 g
Cholesterol	0 mg
Sodium	190 mg
Potassium	370 mg
Total carbohydrate	11 g
Dietary fiber	3 g
Sugars	6 g
Added sugars	0 g
Protein	2 g
Phosphorus	45 mg

tomato & sweet onion stovetop okra

Need a comforting side dish for a family gathering? Make this! How about for a super-sized gathering? Double this recipe! And no need to tell anyone it's easy to fix . . . they'll never believe you anyway. This okra dish tastes like it's been slowly stewed for hours; that's partly because you'll use the flavorful liquid from canned diced tomatoes. If you're new to okra, this is a great way to try it out. If you like flexibility, you can prepare this recipe with other varieties of canned diced tomatoes, such as petite diced tomatoes with jalapeños and cilantro (if cooking for spice fans).

1	tablespoon avocado oil or sunflower oil
1	large Vidalia or other sweet onion, thinly sliced
2	garlic cloves, minced
1	(16-ounce) package frozen sliced okra, thawed
2	(10-ounce) cans diced tomatoes with green chilies (do not drain)
3/4	teaspoon dried thyme leaves

KITCHEN TOOLS

- Cutting board
- Chef's knife
- Can opener
- Measuring spoons
- Large saucepan
- Cooking spoon

DIRECTIONS

1. Heat the oil in a large saucepan over medium-high heat. Add the onion and cook while stirring until lightly golden, about 5 minutes. Add the garlic and cook while stirring until fragrant, about 1 minute.

2. Stir in thawed okra, canned tomatoes (with liquid), and thyme, and cook uncovered until liquids are reduced to desired consistency, about 5 minutes, stirring occasionally. Serve.

EASY TIP!

See page 22 for "How to slice an onion" and "How to mince garlic."

OKRA DESERVES THE SPOTLIGHT

Okra is called "ladies' fingers" by some. Brainiacs call it *abelmoschus esculentus*. I call it okra! Some studies suggest that okra may play a role in lowering blood glucose levels due to a beneficial effect on absorption rates. Myricetin, a flavonoid found in okra (and berries, tea, and red wine!), may have something to do with it.

NUTRITION INFORMATION

Choices/Exchanges:
2 nonstarchy vegetable, 1/2 fat

Per Serving:

Calories	60
Calories from fat	20
Total fat	2 g
Saturated fat	0.2 g
Trans fat	0 g
Cholesterol	0 mg
Sodium	220 mg
Potassium	340 mg
Total carbohydrate	10 g
Dietary fiber	3 g
Sugars	4 g
Added sugars	0 g
Protein	2 g
Phosphorus	55 mg

grilled sesame asparagus

Asparagus is definitely one of my favorite veggies. If it's not yours, it just might be after you take a taste of this recipe. Grilling imparts those distinctive grill marks and a delicious, natural smokiness to the spears. Because they're first tossed with toasted sesame oil and then finished with toasted sesame seeds, you'll get a double dose of sesame goodness with an Asian twist. Grill this up along with shrimp, tofu, or chicken for your next cookout (or cook-in!). You might not even miss the burgers and hot dogs.

12	ounces asparagus spears, ends trimmed (about 24 spears)
2	teaspoons toasted sesame oil
1/8	teaspoon sea salt
1/2	teaspoon toasted sesame seeds

KITCHEN TOOLS

- Grill or grill pan
- Cutting board
- Chef's knife
- Measuring spoons
- 9 × 13-inch dish
- Long-handled tongs

serves: 2 | serving size: about 12 spears
prep time: 5 minutes | cooking time: 6–8 minutes

DIRECTIONS

1. Preheat an outdoor grill or grill pan.

2. Add the asparagus spears and oil into a 9 × 13-inch dish. Toss with tongs to coat.

3. Grill the asparagus (in batches, if necessary) over direct medium-high heat until just cooked through and lightly browned, about 6–8 minutes total, rotating only as needed.

4. Place the spears into the dish, sprinkle with the salt and sesame seeds, and serve.

EASY TIP!

Weigh asparagus on the scale at your market so you've got exactly what you need at recipe prep time. See page 24 for "How to prep asparagus."

SAVOR THOSE SPEARS

I suggest including asparagus as a regular part of your eating repertoire. That's because the nonstarchy vegetable is chock-full of nutrients, including folate and vitamin K, and will give you a boost of antioxidants in a calorie-friendly and tasty way. Plus, animal research finds that asparagus extract may have an antidiabetic effect. That's a promising thing!

NUTRITION INFORMATION

Choices/Exchanges:
1 nonstarchy vegetable, 1 fat

Per Serving:

Calories	70
Calories from fat	45
Total fat	5 g
Saturated fat	0.7 g
Trans fat	0 g
Cholesterol	0 mg
Sodium	150 mg
Potassium	290 mg
Total carbohydrate	6 g
Dietary fiber	3 g
Sugars	3 g
Added sugars	0 g
Protein	3 g
Phosphorus	80 mg

easy middle eastern green beans

The short name for a Lebanese dish that I grew up on is *loubieh*. It's a fragrant, comforting, stewy green bean and tomato dish. My mom usually made it with cubes of beef as well, though I always preferred it without the beef—and still do! While this easy recipe is not *loubieh*, it's my inspired, loose interpretation of it. It's simply green beans and grape tomatoes cooked with a just-right amount of extra-virgin olive oil and seasoned with cinnamon and sea salt. I hope it makes you smile as much as it does me.

2	teaspoons extra-virgin olive oil
8	ounces fresh green beans, stem ends trimmed
1	cup grape tomatoes (6 ounces)
1/4	teaspoon ground cinnamon
1/8	teaspoon sea salt

KITCHEN TOOLS

- Kitchen shears/scissors
- Measuring spoons
- Large cast-iron or other stick-resistant skillet with lid
- Dry measuring cups
- Tongs

serves: 2 | **serving size:** about 1 1/2 cups
prep time: 6 minutes | **cooking time:** 12 minutes

DIRECTIONS

1. Heat the oil in a large cast-iron or other stick-resistant skillet over medium heat. Add the green beans and tomatoes, cover, and cook until the green beans are crisp-tender and tomatoes are fully softened, about 10 minutes, tossing with tongs a couple times throughout the cooking.

2. Sprinkle with the cinnamon and salt, toss to combine, and serve.

EASY TIP!

Weigh green beans on the scale at your market so you've got exactly what you need at recipe prep time. Or look for packaged trimmed fresh green beans—no snipping will be needed.

RECIPE EXTRAS

I enjoy this recipe's simplicity. But absolutely add your own special touch, if you like. For a nutty accent, sprinkle with pan-toasted pine nuts or sliced almonds. For a generous side, combine with steamed whole grains, like farro, freekeh, or brown rice, then squirt with lemon. For extra pops of color, use a colorful variety of grape tomatoes. Or for a Mexican-style interpretation, sprinkle with cumin and chili powder instead of cinnamon.

NUTRITION INFORMATION

Choices/Exchanges:
2 nonstarchy vegetable, 1 fat

Per Serving:

Calories	90
Calories from fat	45
Total fat	5 g
Saturated fat	0.7 g
Trans fat	0 g
Cholesterol	0 mg
Sodium	150 mg
Potassium	340 mg
Total carbohydrate	11 g
Dietary fiber	4 g
Sugars	4 g
Added sugars	0 g
Protein	3 g
Phosphorus	50 mg

steamy baby kale with raisins

Cooking in a microwave makes getting food to the table go so quickly. By using the right combination of ingredients, it can be so tasty, too. This side dish is definitely both of those things! Lemon juice along with the sweetness of the raisins delightfully balances the natural bitterness of kale. And the olive oil helps ensure you absorb as much good nutrition from the kale as you can. By the way, you can still make this green side if you don't have a microwave; simply toss all the ingredients in a large skillet over medium heat until the kale is wilted.

2	tablespoons seedless raisins
1	(5-ounce) package fresh baby kale
2	teaspoons extra-virgin olive oil
2	teaspoons bottled lemon juice (not from concentrate)
1/8	teaspoon sea salt
1/8	teaspoon crushed red pepper flakes

KITCHEN TOOLS

- Measuring spoons
- Large microwave-safe bowl
- Tongs

serves: 2 | **serving size:** 3/4 cup
prep time: 4 minutes | **cooking time:** 1 minute 30 seconds

DIRECTIONS

1. Add the raisins and kale to a large microwave-safe bowl. Sprinkle with the oil, lemon juice, salt, and crushed red pepper flakes.

2. Microwave on high for 1 minute 30 seconds or until the kale is wilted.

3. Toss with tongs to combine. Serve.

EASY TIP!

Use any dried fruit bits you have on hand in this recipe. You can also chop up larger dried fruits, such as dried plums (prunes), figs, or unsulfured apricots.

KALE, YEAH!

Research finds that eating kale at a meal may help to suppress a blood glucose spike after eating the meal. One of the reasons is likely kale's fiber content.
So when in doubt for what to fix for a side, keep this green, leafy, nonstarchy veggie (and this recipe!) top of mind.

NUTRITION INFORMATION

Choices/Exchanges:
1/2 fruit, 1 nonstarchy vegetable, 1 fat

Per Serving:

Calories	100
Calories from fat	45
Total fat	5 g
Saturated fat	0.7 g
Trans fat	0 g
Cholesterol	0 mg
Sodium	170 mg
Potassium	420 mg
Total carbohydrate	14 g
Dietary fiber	3 g
Sugars	7 g
Added sugars	0 g
Protein	3 g
Phosphorus	75 mg

cauliflower "mashed potatoes"

Mashed potatoes are the ultimate comfort food. Even if you have diabetes or prediabetes, it's OK to have a small portion of them when properly planned into your meal. Better yet, make this velvety, potato-free variation on mashed potatoes. It's made with cauliflower, a nonstarchy veggie. Don't worry, it's still got plenty of flavor, thanks in part to garlic and chives. And by using a just-right amount of butter, this puréed cauliflower tastes rich while still meeting health goals.

1	cup cold water
2	garlic cloves, peeled
1 1/2	pounds small cauliflower florets (6 cups packed)
1/4	cup plain 0% fat Greek yogurt
1	tablespoon unsalted butter
1/4	teaspoon plus 1/8 teaspoon sea salt
1	tablespoon minced fresh chives or scallions

KITCHEN TOOLS

- Cutting board
- Chef's knife
- Large saucepan with lid
- Liquid measuring cup
- Dry measuring cups
- Measuring spoons
- Large strainer
- Food processor
- Large spoon or spatula

serves: 7 | **serving size:** 1/2 cup
prep time: 10 minutes | **cooking time:** 22 minutes

DIRECTIONS

1. Add the water and garlic cloves to a large saucepan. Bring to a boil over high heat. Add the cauliflower, cover, reduce heat to medium low, and cook until the cauliflower is fully softened, about 20 minutes.

2. Drain excess liquid from cauliflower and garlic. Add the cauliflower, garlic, yogurt, butter, and salt to a food processor. Cover and purée on high speed until velvety, about 2 minutes.

3. Transfer to a serving bowl, sprinkle with chives, and serve.

EASY TIP!

If you prefer, snip chives using kitchen shears directly over the puréed cauliflower at serving time.

CAULIFLOWER FINDS

Buy a 2-pound cauliflower head. It'll produce the 6 cups of cauliflower used in this recipe. You can pick various colors of cauliflower, such as purple, for a colorful plate. Or, to save a little prep time, look for cauliflower that's already cut into florets from your supermarket's pre-prepped produce section or salad bar. You can also shave several minutes off the cooking time by using frozen florets.

NUTRITION INFORMATION

Choices/Exchanges:
1 nonstarchy vegetable, 1/2 fat

Per Serving:

Calories	45
Calories from fat	20
Total fat	2 g
Saturated fat	1.2 g
Trans fat	0.1 g
Cholesterol	2 mg
Sodium	150 mg
Potassium	310 mg
Total carbohydrate	5 g
Dietary fiber	2 g
Sugars	2 g
Added sugars	0 g
Protein	3 g
Phosphorus	55 mg

caramelized riced cauliflower

It looks kind of like rice. And you can enjoy it just like rice. But this recipe has fewer carbs and a wealth of plant nutrients. It's got plenty of flavor thanks in part to black pepper and turmeric. Plus the browning kicks up cauliflower's natural, savory sweetness. So don't get antsy and cook this for just a few minutes—go for the full 10 minutes. Serve as is. Or, if you want to further jazz it up, stir in your favorite herb, such as fresh cilantro when pairing it with Mexican dishes.

1	pound cauliflower florets (4 cups packed)
2	teaspoons avocado oil or sunflower oil
1/4	teaspoon sea salt
1/4	teaspoon freshly ground black pepper
1/4	teaspoon ground turmeric

KITCHEN TOOLS

- Cutting board
- Chef's knife
- Dry measuring cups
- Food processor
- Measuring spoons
- Large, deep, cast-iron or other stick-resistant skillet
- Cooking spoon

serves: 4 | serving size: 1/2 cup
prep time: 8 minutes | cooking time: 12 minutes

DIRECTIONS

1. Add the cauliflower florets to a food processor. Cover and pulse until it resembles rice.

2. Heat the oil in a large, deep, cast-iron or other stick-resistant skillet over medium-high heat. Add the riced cauliflower, salt, pepper, and turmeric, and cook while stirring until cooked through and lightly browned, about 10 minutes. Serve.

EASY TIP!

Look in your supermarket's pre-prepped produce section or freezer department for cauliflower that's already riced. Use 4 cups of riced cauliflower in this recipe.

TURMERIC PLUS PEPPER

Turmeric gives this cauliflower side dish a rich, golden-yellow color. That's actually an indicator of curcumin, which may have an antidiabetic effect. Black pepper contains a phenolic compound called piperine. Research suggests that if you enjoy turmeric with black pepper, your ability to absorb turmeric's curcumin may be 2,000% greater, thanks to pepper's piperine!

NUTRITION INFORMATION

Choices/Exchanges:
1 nonstarchy vegetable, 1/2 fat

Per Serving:

Calories	50
Calories from fat	20
Total fat	2.5 g
Saturated fat	0.4 g
Trans fat	0 g
Cholesterol	0 mg
Sodium	170 mg
Potassium	340 mg
Total carbohydrate	6 g
Dietary fiber	2 g
Sugars	2 g
Added sugars	0 g
Protein	2 g
Phosphorus	50 mg

SOUPS & STEWS

spring pea soup

Whenever you want to slurp up some springy goodness, this aromatic pea soup will surely satisfy . . . any time of the year. You'll love that it can be served as a brothy soup with rustic texture from the ingredients or as a sophisticated puréed soup that you can partake in, served either hot or chilled. Whichever way you plan to (politely!) slurp it, ideally do so before a meal. It may just help prevent you from overeating that meal. Try it!

2	teaspoons extra-virgin olive oil
1	small or 1/2 large white onion, diced
1	(16-ounce) package frozen peas, thawed, or 3 cups fresh peas
1	(32-ounce) carton low-sodium chicken broth or mushroom broth
1/4	cup packed fresh mint leaves, finely chopped
1/4	teaspoon plus 1/8 teaspoon sea salt

KITCHEN TOOLS

- Cutting board
- Chef's knife
- Measuring spoons
- Large saucepan
- Measuring cups
- Cooking spoon

DIRECTIONS

1. Heat the oil in a large saucepan over medium heat. Add the onion and cook while stirring until softened and lightly browned, about 8 minutes.

2. Add the peas, broth, mint, and salt, and bring to a boil over high heat.

3. Reduce heat to medium low and simmer, uncovered, until the peas are softened, about 3 minutes. Serve.

EASY TIP!

See page 22 for "How to dice an onion."

VELVETY INTRIGUE

For a velvety textured soup, purée it in the saucepan after simmering using an immersion (wand) blender—or purée in a blender, in batches, using the "hot fill" line as a guide. When puréed, this soup has a gorgeous, springy green color. It's delicious served hot or chilled.

NUTRITION INFORMATION

Choices/Exchanges:
1 starch, 1/2 fat

Per Serving:

Calories	100
Calories from fat	20
Total fat	2 g
Saturated fat	0.3 g
Trans fat	0 g
Cholesterol	0 mg
Sodium	260 mg
Potassium	300 mg
Total carbohydrate	12 g
Dietary fiber	4 g
Sugars	5 g
Added sugars	0 g
Protein	8 g
Phosphorus	120 mg

italian tomato-basil soup

Tomato purée is the key ingredient in this thick and vibrant soup. And it's why the soup is loaded with lycopene, a carotenoid with powerful antioxidant abilities. But don't just have a cup of this tomato-basil soup because it's good for you; have it because it's tasty. Dip a little whole-grain Italian bread into it to savor the flavor. And don't stop there . . . let this soup do double duty. Serve as a no-sugar-added marinara sauce, using the recipe exactly as it's written—or stir in minced garlic and crushed red pepper flakes for extra punch.

2	teaspoons extra-virgin olive oil
1	small or 1/2 large red onion, diced
1	(28-ounce) can no-salt-added tomato purée
1	cup low-sodium vegetable broth (from carton)
1/4	teaspoon sea salt
1/3	cup packed fresh basil leaves, thinly sliced
2	teaspoons balsamic vinegar

KITCHEN TOOLS

- Cutting board
- Chef's knife
- Can opener
- Measuring spoons
- Large saucepan
- Liquid measuring cup
- Cooking spoon or ladle

DIRECTIONS

1. Heat the oil in a large saucepan over medium heat. Add the onion and cook while stirring occasionally until fully softened, about 8 minutes.

2. Add the tomato purée, broth, and salt, and bring to a boil over high heat. Reduce heat to medium low and simmer, uncovered, until flavors are combined, about 5 minutes. (Hint: For a thinner soup, drizzle in more broth.) Stir in the basil and vinegar.

3. Ladle into bowls. Serve hot or chilled.

EASY TIP!

Stack up large, fresh basil leaves, up to eight leaves high. Roll them up tightly into a long roll, then thinly slice. Sprinkle the thinly sliced basil (it's called "chiffonade") on top of each serving to garnish.

SOUP SALTINESS

Soups are usually salty. Frankly, salt is what makes soup taste like soup. But you can still get great taste without shaking in excess salt. Instead, splash soup with a culinary acid, like lemon or lime juice or vinegar—or add more if there's acid already in the recipe. Balsamic vinegar matches the rich tomatoey-ness here. Sprinkle in more if you wish!

NUTRITION INFORMATION

Choices/Exchanges:
4 nonstarchy vegetable, 1/2 fat

Per Serving:

Calories	110
Calories from fat	20
Total fat	2.5 g
Saturated fat	0.4 g
Trans fat	0 g
Cholesterol	0 mg
Sodium	230 mg
Potassium	970 mg
Total carbohydrate	22 g
Dietary fiber	5 g
Sugars	12 g
Added sugars	0 g
Protein	4 g
Phosphorus	110 mg

tex-mex tortilla soup

Is it a soup? Or is it an entrée? It's both! The black beans, with their plant protein and fiber, make this soup satisfy like an entrée. The splash of lime juice eliminates the need for excess salt. In fact, you can sprinkle with extra lime juice for a soup that seems saltier. This soup is fun topped with crisp tortilla chips, which are awesome as they soak up the broth. What's more, you can transform this soup into a speedy stew by adding cooked chicken or turkey with the beans— or topping with avocado for bonus nutrient richness and decadence.

1	(10-ounce) can diced tomatoes with jalapeños and cilantro (do not drain)
1	(15-ounce) can no-salt-added black beans, drained
3	cups low-sodium chicken broth (from carton)
1/4	teaspoon sea salt
2	tablespoons bottled lime juice (not from concentrate)
1	ounce tortilla chips, whole or crushed
1/4	cup fresh cilantro leaves with tender stems

KITCHEN TOOLS

- Can opener
- Mesh strainer
- Large saucepan
- Liquid measuring cup
- Measuring spoons
- Cooking spoon or ladle

serves: 4 | **serving size:** 1 1/3 cups soup plus garnish
prep time: 8 minutes | **cooking time:** 12 minutes

DIRECTIONS

1. In a large saucepan, add the canned tomatoes (with liquid), beans, broth, and salt. Bring to a boil over high heat. Reduce heat to medium low and simmer, uncovered, until flavors are combined, about 8 minutes. Stir in the lime juice.

2. Ladle into bowls. Top with the tortilla chips and cilantro. Serve.

EASY TIP!

Simply tear off a small handful of cilantro leaves with stems from the top of the bunch; it'll equal about 1/4 cup. The tender stems are 100% edible.

PICK A CAN

Can't find canned diced tomatoes with jalapeños and cilantro? Use 1 1/4 cups of another, similar variety of tomatoes. Look for diced tomatoes with just jalapeños or other chilies. Or go with a plain or fire-roasted option. For extra spice, simply add a splash of hot pepper sauce or taco sauce to your soup.

NUTRITION INFORMATION

Choices/Exchanges:

1 1/2 starch, 1 lean protein

Per Serving:

Calories	160
Calories from fat	20
Total fat	2.5 g
Saturated fat	0.3 g
Trans fat	0 g
Cholesterol	0 mg
Sodium	520 mg
Potassium	560 mg
Total carbohydrate	24 g
Dietary fiber	4 g
Sugars	3 g
Added sugars	0 g
Protein	11 g
Phosphorus	180 mg

ramen-style ginger chicken noodle soup

Chicken soup is apparently good for the soul. It's also good when you're not feeling so swell. This version is ideal if you're feeling a tad queasy, since it's made with fresh ginger, which research (and personal experience!) suggests may help settle your stomach. It's loaded with comforting noodles, too. Try it with brown rice udon noodles and enjoy with chopsticks (and a big soup spoon) as the main dish feature of a soup-n-salad meal. Accessorize it with nutritious goodies, like extra thinly sliced red hot chile peppers, if you wish, too.

5	cups low-sodium chicken broth (from carton)
1	tablespoon grated fresh gingerroot
3/4	teaspoon plus 1/8 teaspoon sea salt
2	cups cubed, pre-cooked chicken breast meat (from 2 rotisserie chicken breasts)
6	ounces dry whole-grain noodles of choice (such as no-salt-added brown rice udon)
1	(5-ounce) package fresh baby spinach
1/3	cup packed fresh cilantro leaves with tender stems

KITCHEN TOOLS

- Cutting board
- Chef's knife
- Spoon or peeler (for peeling ginger)
- Microplane zester/grater
- Liquid measuring cup
- Measuring spoons
- Large saucepan
- Dry measuring cups
- Kitchen scale
- Cooking spoon or ladle

DIRECTIONS

1. Add the broth, grated ginger, and salt to a large saucepan, and bring to a boil over high heat.

2. Stir in the chicken and noodles, bring back to a boil, then reduce heat to medium and cook, uncovered, until the noodles are desired texture, about 8 minutes. Stir in the spinach.

3. Ladle into bowls. Sprinkle with the cilantro. Serve.

EASY TIP!

See page 23 for "How to grate fresh gingerroot."

EXTRA GOODIES

Make your ramen-style soup bowl playful and extra nutritious. Try any of these toppings: avocado, boiled egg halves, scallions, mung bean sprouts, shiitake mushroom caps, toasted sesame seeds, lime, extra thinly sliced red hot chile peppers, or hot pepper sauce. (Hint: If you plan ahead, you can splash with reduced-sodium soy sauce in place of some of the salt in the recipe, too.)

NUTRITION INFORMATION

Choices/Exchanges:
1 1/2 starch, 2 lean protein

Per Serving:

Calories	180
Calories from fat	15
Total fat	1.5 g
Saturated fat	0.6 g
Trans fat	0 g
Cholesterol	35 mg
Sodium	580 mg
Potassium	520 mg
Total carbohydrate	23 g
Dietary fiber	3 g
Sugars	1 g
Added sugars	0 g
Protein	19 g
Phosphorus	260 mg

tuscan turkey sausage stew

Sure, you could travel to Tuscany for a comforting bowl of stew. Or simply set aside a few minutes (and only a few dollars!), and your taste buds will be transported there. You've got everything you need in one satisfying bowl here. This ribollita-style stew features big bread cubes, hearty beans, nutrient-rich kale, and scrumptious turkey sausage. (Hint: It's OK to use chicken sausage.) It's an excellent use for day-old bread. Do finish it with Parmesan cheese—it does triple duty, providing cheesiness, savoriness, and saltiness. Hopefully you won't feel the need to add any salt.

1	(14.5-ounce) can no-salt-added diced tomatoes (do not drain)
1	(32-ounce) carton low-sodium chicken broth
2	(3-ounce) links pre-cooked natural or organic turkey sausage, sliced into coins
1	(10-ounce) package chopped fresh kale (8 cups packed)
4	ounces day-old whole-wheat Italian baguette, cut into 3/4-inch cubes
1	(15-ounce) can no-salt-added cannellini beans, drained
1/4	cup grated Parmesan cheese

KITCHEN TOOLS

- Can opener
- Cutting board
- Chef's knife
- Extra-large saucepan or stockpot
- Kitchen scale
- Dry measuring cups
- Cooking spoon

serves: 8 | **serving size:** 2 cups
prep time: 12 minutes | **cooking time:** 15 minutes

DIRECTIONS

1. Add the canned diced tomatoes (with liquid) and chicken broth to an extra-large saucepan and bring to a boil over high heat.

2. Stir in the sausage, kale, bread cubes, and beans, and bring back to a boil.

3. Reduce heat to medium low and simmer, uncovered, until the sausage is fully heated and flavors are well combined, about 8 minutes. Sprinkle with the Parmesan cheese. Serve.

EASY TIP!

Instead of Italian bread, use a whole-wheat bagel from a bakery, bagel store, or the bakery department of your local market; it's likely around 4 ounces (or a little more).

USING BABY KALE

I created this recipe using regular curly kale. It's full of texture and holds up well in stews. But baby kale is increasingly popular and readily available. It's delicate for a stew; however, if you prefer baby kale instead of curly kale, simply stir it in here during the last minute of simmering.

NUTRITION INFORMATION

Choices/Exchanges:
2 starch, 2 nonstarchy vegetable, 3 lean protein

Per Serving:

Calories	320
Calories from fat	60
Total fat	7 g
Saturated fat	2.1 g
Trans fat	0 g
Cholesterol	35 mg
Sodium	620 mg
Potassium	1200 mg
Total carbohydrate	39 g
Dietary fiber	10 g
Sugars	7 g
Added sugars	0 g
Protein	29 g
Phosphorus	435 mg

sporty halftime chili

Pre-prep all of your ingredients, and this speedy bowl of chili can be ready in 15 minutes flat! Yep, that means you can make it during the halftime break while watching your favorite football team (like my Ohio State Buckeyes!). It's basically a bean chili with extra beans. That makes it extra hearty—and an awesome source of soluble fiber. (Check out its fiber stats!) The chili hits the spot as is. But you can finish it with extra thrill, such as diced green pepper, minced jalapeño, or fresh cilantro. It's a bowl of fun any which way.

2	(15-ounce) cans no-salt-added kidney beans, drained (do not rinse)
1	(14-ounce) can crushed tomatoes with chilies (do not drain)
1 1/4	cups vegetable broth
1	tablespoon chili powder
1/4	teaspoon ground cinnamon
3	scallions, green and white parts, thinly sliced

KITCHEN TOOLS

- Can opener
- Large strainer
- Cutting board
- Chef's knife
- Liquid measuring cup
- Measuring spoons
- Large saucepan
- Cooking spoon

serves: 4 | **serving size:** 1 1/4 cups
prep time: 8 minutes | **cooking time:** 15 minutes

DIRECTIONS

1. To a large saucepan, add the beans, tomatoes (with liquid), broth, chili powder, and cinnamon; stir to combine, and bring to a boil over high heat.

2. Stir in the scallions, reduce heat to medium, and cook, uncovered, until desired consistency, about 10 minutes, stirring occasionally. Serve.

EASY TIP!

If you're unable to find canned crushed tomatoes with chilies, use regular canned crushed tomatoes and add a small minced jalapeño pepper or a few shakes of hot pepper sauce.

TRANSFORM CHILI INTO A MEAL

Try these three concepts! Transform it into a Mexican salad bowl. Stuff it into roasted bell pepper "cups." Or create an inspired Cincinnati-style chili by adding a pinch each of unsweetened cocoa powder and cinnamon to the recipe, then enjoying on spiralized zucchini "noodles" (zoodles!).

NUTRITION INFORMATION

Choices/Exchanges:
2 starch, 2 nonstarchy vegetable, 1 lean protein

Per Serving:

Calories	240
Calories from fat	20
Total fat	2.5 g
Saturated fat	0.4 g
Trans fat	0 g
Cholesterol	0 mg
Sodium	340 mg
Potassium	840 mg
Total carbohydrate	44 g
Dietary fiber	12 g
Sugars	11 g
Added sugars	0 g
Protein	14 g
Phosphorus	255 mg

CONDIMENTS

fruit-sweetened bbq sauce

Some people absolutely don't want to know a world without barbecue sauce! Since so many sauces on the market contain added sugars, this recipe comes in handy if you can't find a fruit-sweetened or no-sugar-added BBQ sauce in the market. It's also super easy to make—simply stir everything together. That's it!

1/4	cup fruit-sweetened or no-sugar-added ketchup
3	tablespoons unsweetened applesauce
1	teaspoon apple cider vinegar
1/2	teaspoon freshly ground black pepper
1/2	teaspoon smoked paprika

KITCHEN TOOLS

- Liquid measuring cup
- Measuring spoons
- Spoon or small spatula

serves: 4 | **serving size:** 2 tablespoons
prep time: 5 minutes | **cooking time:** 0 minutes

DIRECTIONS

In a liquid measuring cup, stir together all ingredients.
Serve, or store in a sealed jar in the refrigerator for up to 1 week.

EASY TIP!

For a ketchup recommendation, see page 325 for "Ingredients of Choice."

BBQ BEWARE

Backyard barbecues or cookouts are an awesome way to enjoy family, friends, and food all together! However, a calorie and carb overload may result. Watch out for these popular but calorie- and carb-heavy dishes: 8 ounces of barbecue ribs (690 calories, 27 grams of total carbohydrate), 1 cup of creamy macaroni salad (430 calories, 48 grams of total carbohydrate), and 1 cup of potato salad (360 calories, 28 grams of total carbohydrate).

NUTRITION INFORMATION

Choices/Exchanges = 0

Per Serving:

Calories	15
Calories from fat	0
Total fat	0 g
Saturated fat	0 g
Trans fat	0 g
Cholesterol	0 mg
Sodium	105 mg
Potassium	60 mg
Total carbohydrate	4 g
Dietary fiber	0 g
Sugars	2 g
Added sugars	0 g
Protein	0 g
Phosphorus	5 mg

cheese-free pesto

Pesto used to be rather taboo in America when following a healthy diet. Luckily, that's changed! If you overdo it, the calories in this recipe will still add up. But when used by the tablespoon, not the cupful, it's a scrumptious, Mediterranean-style highlight for healthful dishes like Turkey Meatballs Arrabbiata (page 206) and Pesto Grilled Shrimp (page 176). And when you whirl up this version, it's not weighed down by Parmesan cheese. (Hint: If you like to play with your food as I do, add a couple pinches of my personal recipe twists: grated lemon zest, smoked paprika, and crushed red pepper flakes.)

2	cups packed fresh basil leaves
2	large garlic cloves
1/2	cup raw or roasted pine nuts, pistachios, or walnut pieces
1/3	cup extra-virgin olive oil
1	tablespoon bottled lemon juice (not from concentrate)
1	large ice cube
1/4	teaspoon sea salt

KITCHEN TOOLS

- Dry measuring cups
- Liquid measuring cup
- Measuring spoons
- Food processor

serves: 8 | **serving size:** 2 tablespoons
prep time: 5 minutes | **cooking time:** 0 minutes

DIRECTIONS

In a food processor, purée together all ingredients. Serve, or store in a sealed jar in the refrigerator for up to 3 days.

EASY TIP!

Freeze extra pesto in an ice cube tray. Once frozen, transfer the pesto cubes to a sealable freezer container for up to 3 months. Thaw individual cubes in the fridge as needed.

DINING OUT?

Though pesto can be a healthful part of Mediterranean or diabetes-friendly eating plans, skip oversized restaurant pesto dishes that are off the charts for calories and carbs, like Rigatoni with Creamy Pesto Sauce at Olive Garden (1,250 calories, 92 grams of total carbohydrate) or Orecchiette Chicken Pesto at Maggiano's Little Italy (1,570 calories, 130 grams of total carbohydrate)! If you want a pesto dish when dining out Italian, pair the flavorful pesto with simple grilled salmon, shrimp, or chicken. If that's not available, skip the pesto and try picks like a lunch-sized portion of chicken margherita or a salad topped with salmon and dressing on the side.

NUTRITION INFORMATION

Choices/Exchanges:
3 fat

Per Serving:

Calories	140
Calories from fat	140
Total fat	15 g
Saturated fat	1.7 g
Trans fat	0 g
Cholesterol	0 mg
Sodium	70 mg
Potassium	130 mg
Total carbohydrate	2 g
Dietary fiber	1 g
Sugars	0 g
Added sugars	0 g
Protein	2 g
Phosphorus	60 mg

easy dijon vinaigrette

Sure, you can take a trip to the supermarket to buy a bottle of Dijon-style salad dressing. In that bottle you might find vinegar, oil, and Dijon mustard, but possibly also sugar, honey, modified food starch, calcium disodium EDTA, and caramel color. Eek! Or you can shake together Dijon mustard, red wine vinegar, and extra-virgin olive oil in a jar within the next 3 minutes. And in that jar will just be Dijon mustard, red wine vinegar, and extra-virgin olive oil—no surprise ingredients. I choose the 3-minute approach any day. How about you? It doesn't get much easier than that!

1/3	cup Dijon mustard
1/3	cup red wine vinegar
1/3	cup extra-virgin olive oil

KITCHEN TOOLS

- Liquid measuring cup
- 1 (8-ounce-capacity) jar with lid

serves: 8 | **serving size:** 2 tablespoons
prep time: 3 minutes | **cooking time:** 0 minutes

DIRECTIONS

Add all ingredients to a jar. Seal and shake. Serve, or store in the sealed jar in the refrigerator for up to a month.

EASY TIP!

For a mustard recommendation, see page 325 for "Ingredients of Choice."

DRIZZLE IT

This vinaigrette is versatile and adds vivacious flavor to any cuisine. Use it as a marinade for chicken or a grilling sauce for fish. Drizzle it onto simple cooked vegetables, like asparagus, carrots, and leafy greens. Add it as the vinaigrette of choice in grain salads. And absolutely enjoy it with the Niçoise-Inspired Salad recipe (page 230).

NUTRITION INFORMATION

Choices/Exchanges:
2 fat

Per Serving:

Calories	90
Calories from fat	80
Total fat	9 g
Saturated fat	1.2 g
Trans fat	0 g
Cholesterol	0 mg
Sodium	220 mg
Potassium	20 mg
Total carbohydrate	2 g
Dietary fiber	0 g
Sugars	1 g
Added sugars	0 g
Protein	0 g
Phosphorus	10 mg

simple italian vinaigrette

The first bottled salad dressing I ever knew was an Italian vinaigrette. For years, I didn't even know there was another option for salad. Then I became a teenager, and leafy salads became my thing—and so did experimentation with salad dressings. I haven't stopped that experimentation! Regardless, there's always a place for Italian vinaigrette in my kitchen. This is my super-quick version that's better for you and seriously more enjoyable than most of the bottled stuff on the market. Try it on your next salad . . . and more!

1/2	cup red wine vinegar
1/2	cup extra-virgin olive oil
1/8	teaspoon garlic powder
1/8	teaspoon dried oregano
1/8	teaspoon sea salt
1/8	teaspoon freshly ground black pepper

KITCHEN TOOLS

- Liquid measuring cup
- Measuring spoons
- 1 (8-ounce-capacity) jar with lid

serves: 8 | **serving size:** 2 tablespoons
prep time: 5 minutes | **cooking time:** 0 minutes

DIRECTIONS

Add all ingredients to a jar. Seal and shake. Serve, or store in the sealed jar in the refrigerator for up to a month.

EASY TIP!

In a small jar, add 1/2 teaspoon each of garlic powder, dried oregano, sea salt, and black pepper. Seal, then label it "vinaigrette seasoning." Use 1/2 teaspoon of it each time you make this recipe.

BEYOND LEAFY SALAD

Italian vinaigrette is a multipurpose culinary ingredient. Stir with fresh diced tomatoes to make an Italian-style salsa or bruschetta topping. Toss with white beans for a two-ingredient bean salad. Use as a marinade or grilling sauce for vegetable kebabs, chicken, or shrimp. Dip raw veggies into it anytime. And definitely drizzle it into the Italian Rotini Pasta Salad recipe (page 158).

NUTRITION INFORMATION

Choices/Exchanges:
3 fat

Per Serving:

Calories	120
Calories from fat	130
Total fat	14 g
Saturated fat	1.9 g
Trans fat	0 g
Cholesterol	0 mg
Sodium	40 mg
Potassium	5 mg
Total carbohydrate	0 g
Dietary fiber	0 g
Sugars	0 g
Added sugars	0 g
Protein	0 g
Phosphorus	0 mg

grape tomato pico de gallo

Better than any ol' jar of tomato salsa, this super-fresh pico de gallo is a quick, mild, and tasty spin on traditional fresh Mexican salsa (also called salsa fresca). Using scallion instead of onion makes it speedy. Since it's made with fresh ingredients and served freshly prepared, it's more refreshing than jarred salsa—and you don't have to worry about any of those pesky chemical additives that are found in some salsas. You can count it as part of your daily nonstarchy veggie servings, too. Your taste buds will want you to make this often.

1	cup grape tomatoes, halved or quartered
1	scallion, green and white part, thinly sliced
1	tablespoon packed small fresh cilantro leaves
1	tablespoon bottled lime juice (not from concentrate)
1/8	teaspoon sea salt

KITCHEN TOOLS

- Cutting board
- Chef's knife
- Dry measuring cups
- Measuring spoons
- Medium bowl
- Large spoon

serves: 4 | serving size: 1/4 cup
prep time: 5 minutes | cooking time: 0 minutes

DIRECTIONS

1. In a medium bowl, stir together all ingredients.

2. Serve, or store in a sealed jar or container in the refrigerator for up to 3 days.

EASY TIP!

It's not necessary to cut the cilantro or pull off leaves one at a time. Estimate what looks like the total number of leaves needed, then twist off that amount. You can use the tender cilantro stems, too.

ENJOYMENT VERSATILITY

Enjoy pico de gallo with tortilla chips or alternative chips, like DIY Pita Chips (page 74) or plantain chips. Try it as a topper for avocado toast, grilled chicken, or eggs, as in the Fried Egg Taco with Pico de Gallo recipe (page 112). Or stir it into black beans for a simple salad, or savor it as a sandwich condiment.

NUTRITION INFORMATION

Choices/Exchanges = 0

Per Serving:

Calories	10
Calories from fat	0
Total fat	0 g
Saturated fat	0 g
Trans fat	0 g
Cholesterol	0 mg
Sodium	70 mg
Potassium	105 mg
Total carbohydrate	2 g
Dietary fiber	1 g
Sugars	1 g
Added augars	0 g
Protein	0 g
Phosphorus	10 mg

NEED MORE SIMPLE SALAD DRESSING IDEAS?

You can make a quick and easy salad dressing with a few simple ingredients you have on hand. In addition to the dressing recipes in this chapter, try these tasty combos if you're in a pinch:

- Make a fruity vinaigrette using fruit that's starting to get mushy: Blend together 1/4 cup each of extra-virgin olive oil, apple cider vinegar, and your fruit of choice (like mushy strawberries or peaches).
- Go herbal with this easy dressing: In a jar, shake together 1/4 cup each of extra-virgin olive oil and white balsamic vinegar, plus 2 tablespoons of chopped fresh herbs of choice (such as basil or mint leaves).

For extra flavor, add a pinch each of sea salt and black pepper to homemade dressings.

DESSERTS & DRINKS

warm banana "pudding" with vanilla whip

Enjoying a piece of fruit can count as dessert, but it doesn't always seem that dessert-like. So meet Warm Banana "Pudding" with Vanilla Whip. Just a little bit of heat transforms the banana from snack to sweet treat! It's not pudding, but it seems pudding-like as you savor it! The topping is really cool, too—it's creamy and vanilla-y without added sugar. So enjoy a little bit of whip with every naturally sweet banana bite. And don't forget to add the cacao nibs or peanuts for a crunchy contrast.

1	tablespoon Neufchâtel (light cream cheese)
2	teaspoons plain 0% fat Greek yogurt
1/4	teaspoon pure vanilla extract
1	medium fully ripened banana, peeled and sliced into coins
3/4	teaspoon cacao nibs or finely chopped roasted, salted peanuts

KITCHEN TOOLS

- Cutting board
- Paring or chef's knife
- Measuring spoons
- Small bowl
- Spoon
- 1 (1-cup-capacity) microwave-safe ramekin or small dish

DIRECTIONS

1. In a small bowl, stir together the Neufchâtel, yogurt, and vanilla until smooth.

2. Arrange the banana coins in a 1-cup-capacity microwave-safe ramekin. Microwave on high for 30 seconds, or until hot. Carefully remove the ramekin from the microwave.

3. Top with the vanilla whip and cacao nibs. Serve.

EASY TIP!

For easier stirring, set the Neufchâtel out at room temperature for 15 minutes before beginning step 1.

WHAT ARE CACAO NIBS?

They're fermented, dried, and roasted (or raw) cacao beans that are crushed into bits. Crunchy yet light textured, they provide chocolatey taste without added sugar. It's not like eating semi-sweet chocolate chips. But when paired with a naturally sweet food, like banana, the pleasantly bitter nibs seem dessert-like! (Hint: Look for Navitas Organics Cacao Nibs.)

NUTRITION INFORMATION

Choices/Exchanges:
2 fruit, 1 fat

Per Serving:

Calories	170
Calories from fat	45
Total fat	5 g
Saturated fat	2.7 g
Trans fat	0 g
Cholesterol	10 mg
Sodium	60 mg
Potassium	480 mg
Total carbohydrate	29 g
Dietary fiber	4 g
Sugars	16 g
Added sugars	0 g
Protein	4 g
Phosphorus	65 mg

single-serve peach cobbler with pecans

Got a few minutes? Make peach cobbler! Yes, you can enjoy peach cobbler all year round, and prepare it in a really fast and healthy way! One quick trick is using frozen peaches—they're packaged at their peak of ripeness, nutritional value, and flavor. If it's summertime, use 1 1/2 cups of diced, fully ripened fresh peaches (remove the seed, but keep on the peel for extra fiber). A bit of butter provides a just-right richness, and granola and pecans provide the crunch. (Hint: If you plan ahead, dollop with a small scoop of a natural, no-sugar-added vanilla ice cream or no-sugar-added yogurt!)

1	(10-ounce) package frozen sliced peaches, thawed, roughly chopped
1	teaspoon pure vanilla extract
2	teaspoons cold unsalted butter, finely diced
1/4	cup Homemade Fruit-Sweetened Granola (page 106) or no-sugar-added granola
1/4	cup pecan pieces
1/8	teaspoon ground cinnamon
1/8	teaspoon sea salt

KITCHEN TOOLS

- Cutting board
- Chef's knife
- Medium mixing bowl
- Measuring spoons
- Dry measuring cups
- Large spoon
- 4 (3/4-cup- or 1-cup-capacity) microwave-safe ramekins

serves: 4 | **serving size:** 1 (6-ounce) cobbler
prep time: 10 minutes | **cooking time:** 1 minute 30 seconds

DIRECTIONS

1. In a medium bowl, stir together the peaches (along with any juices) and vanilla. Transfer the mixture equally into 4 ramekins, about 1/3 cup each.

2. Sprinkle each with 1/2 teaspoon butter, 1 tablespoon granola, 1 tablespoon pecans, and a dash each cinnamon and salt.

3. Microwave all 4 cobblers on high for 1 minute 30 seconds, or until steaming hot. Carefully remove the dishes from the microwave and serve.

EASY TIP!

Don't take the time to chop up perfect pecan halves; buy pecan pieces. These smaller bits of pecan are ideal as dessert toppers—and usually cost less than whole pecan halves.

A PINCH OF CINNAMON

Recent research suggests that using cinnamon may be helpful in addition to medications when treating type 2 diabetes. It seems to offer a slight antidiabetic effect, potentially helping to reduce fasting blood glucose and A1C levels. So go ahead, add a sprinkling of cinnamon to your dessert—and beyond! And discuss its use with your diabetes healthcare provider.

NUTRITION INFORMATION

Choices/Exchanges:
1/2 fruit, 2 fat

Per Serving:

Calories	120
Calories from fat	70
Total fat	8 g
Saturated fat	1.7 g
Trans fat	0.1 g
Cholesterol	5 mg
Sodium	75 mg
Potassium	180 mg
Total carbohydrate	10 g
Dietary fiber	2 g
Sugars	6 g
Added sugars	0 g
Protein	2 g
Phosphorus	50 mg

no-bake cheesecake-in-a-glass

You'll adore this inspired, upside-down strawberry cheesecake-in-a-glass! It's based on a mixture of Greek yogurt and Neufchâtel, which creates a naturally lighter cream cheese. Make it with any strained yogurt, like Icelandic-style skyr; it doesn't need to be Greek. Either way, the thicker the yogurt, the better the result. Surprisingly, using frozen rather than fresh strawberries creates a more desirable result in this recipe. Make these personalized desserts in advance and chill so that they're ready and waiting right after dinner—just wait until serving time to sprinkle with granola for crust-like crunch.

1	(10-ounce) package frozen whole strawberries, thawed (2 cups)
1	tablespoon bottled lemon juice (not from concentrate), divided
4	ounces Neufchâtel (light cream cheese)
1/2	cup plain 0% fat Greek yogurt
2	tablespoons fruit-sweetened apricot fruit spread (jam)*
1 1/4	teaspoons pure vanilla extract
1/3	cup Homemade Fruit-Sweetened Granola (page 106) or no-sugar-added granola

*Note: Ideally, choose a fruit spread without added sugars.

KITCHEN TOOLS

- Medium bowl
- Measuring spoons
- Spoon
- 6 juice glasses or other 5 1/2-ounce-capacity glasses
- Large mixing bowl
- Dry measuring cups
- Electric mixer

serves: 6 | **serving size:** 1 juice glass
prep time: 15 minutes | **cooking time:** 0 minutes

DIRECTIONS

1. In a medium bowl, stir together the strawberries with 1 teaspoon lemon juice. Spoon into juice glasses, about 1/3 cup each.

2. In a large mixing bowl, add the Neufchâtel, yogurt, fruit spread, vanilla, and remaining 2 teaspoons lemon juice. Blend with an electric mixer on medium speed until fluffy. Spoon on top of the strawberries, about 3 tablespoons each.

3. When ready to serve, sprinkle with the granola, about 1 tablespoon each.

EASY TIP!

Go thicker. Add 3/4 cup of Greek yogurt to an unbleached paper towel–lined mesh strainer and strain over a bowl in the refrigerator overnight for more of a cream cheese–like yogurt.

PIPE IT

Add the cheesecake mixture to a quart-sized freezer bag. Seal it. Then snip off one of the bottom corners to create a small opening. Working from the top, squeeze the mixture down toward the open corner. Then pipe out the mixture onto the strawberries in the juice glasses. Otherwise, if you've got one, use a pastry bag.

NUTRITION INFORMATION

Choices/Exchanges:
1/2 fruit, 1 lean protein, 1 fat

Per Serving:

Calories	110
Calories from fat	45
Total fat	5 g
Saturated fat	2.5 g
Trans fat	0 g
Cholesterol	15 mg
Sodium	85 mg
Potassium	150 mg
Total carbohydrate	12 g
Dietary fiber	2 g
Sugars	7 g
Added sugars	0 g
Protein	4 g
Phosphorus	75 mg

flourless peanut butter cookies

Every once in a while, anyone might need a little cookie fix. I do! So here's a nutty-tasting, chewy cookie with balanced sweetness that you'll feel good about eating. Instead of white sugar, this updated spin on classic peanut butter cookies is sweetened with coconut sugar—also known as coconut palm sugar. It's derived from coconut palm sap, and it tastes and cooks like granulated brown sugar, not coconut. Research suggests it has a low glycemic index, making it more diabetes-friendly than white sugar. Now, go plan a cookie break. And slowly savor every bite of your cookie!

1/2	cup granulated coconut sugar
1/3	cup creamy, natural, unsweetened peanut butter
2	tablespoons ground flaxseeds
1	large egg
1 1/2	teaspoons pure vanilla extract
1/8	teaspoon flaked or coarse sea salt

KITCHEN TOOLS

- Large baking sheet
- Unbleached parchment paper
- Large mixing bowl
- Dry measuring cups
- Measuring spoons
- Electric mixer
- Cooling rack

serves: 12 │ **serving size:** 1 cookie
prep time: 12 minutes │ **cooking time:** 15 minutes

NUTRITION INFORMATION

Choices/Exchanges:

1/2 carbohydrate, 1 fat

Per Serving:

Calories	80
Calories from fat	40
Total fat	4.5 g
Saturated fat	0.7 g
Trans fat	0 g
Cholesterol	15 mg
Sodium	30 mg
Potassium	125 mg
Total carbohydrate	8 g
Dietary fiber	1 g
Sugars	6 g
Added sugars	6 g
Protein	3 g
Phosphorus	40 mg

DIRECTIONS

1. Preheat oven to 350°F. Line a baking sheet with unbleached parchment paper.

2. In a large mixing bowl, blend together the coconut sugar, peanut butter, flaxseeds, egg, and vanilla using an electric mixer on medium speed until creamy.

3. Drop the cookie batter by the measuring tablespoon onto the baking sheet.

4. Bake until firm, about 15 minutes. Immediately sprinkle with the sea salt. Cool the cookies completely in the pan on a cooling rack and serve.

EASY TIP!

Since the texture of peanut butter can vary, the texture of the cookie dough can vary as well. If your batter is more like a dough, consider rolling it into 12 smooth balls instead of dropping it on a cookie sheet by the tablespoon.

SHOPPING FOR COCONUT SUGAR

You can find coconut sugar at natural markets, like Whole Foods Market. Or shop for it online, at sites such as thrivemarket.com or amazon.com. Look for Bob's Red Mill Organic Coconut Sugar or Wholesome Organic Coconut Palm Sugar. Can't find it? Use turbinado sugar instead, like Sugar in the Raw.

cocoa-dusted nut-stuffed dates

Do you like chocolate-covered peanut butter cups? Well, meet these chocolate-covered peanut butter cup–inspired after-dinner treats. They double as sweet snacks and will fit better into a healthful diabetes eating plan than regular peanut butter cups. The dates provide delightful, no-sugar-added sweetness; the peanuts or pistachios provide a crunchy, 100% nutty filling; and the cocoa powder provides chocolatiness in a nutrient-rich way. The nuts help reduce the impact of dates on your blood glucose since they'll be converted into sugar more slowly; but still remember to stick with a three-date serving. When this trio of ingredients is enjoyed all together, this better-for-you bite is rather candy-like!

12	pitted dates
24	shelled, roasted, salted peanuts or pistachios
1	teaspoon unsweetened cocoa powder

KITCHEN TOOLS

- Measuring spoons
- Luncheon-sized plate
- Small mesh strainer

DIRECTIONS

1. Stuff each date with 2 peanuts or pistachios. Do not cut the dates open. Place on a plate.

2. Gently add the cocoa powder to a strainer. Shake it over the dates by lightly tapping on the rim of the strainer with the palm of your hand to lightly coat them. Serve.

EASY TIP!

Look for a hole (pit) in each date from where the seed was removed. That's where you'll stuff the nuts. To finish, just coat one side of the dates with cocoa powder.

STUFF 'EM GOOD

While enticingly sweet, dates don't have added sugars. But, like any carb-rich food, it's helpful to pair them with foods containing healthy fats or protein—or both—so that the dates are converted into sugar more slowly. That means stuffing them with nuts, like peanuts or pistachios, is a great idea. Beyond nuts, consider stuffing dates with Neufchâtel (light cream cheese) for an occasional treat, too.

NUTRITION INFORMATION

Choices/Exchanges:
1 fruit, 1/2 fat

Per Serving:

Calories	90
Calories from fat	25
Total fat	3 g
Saturated fat	0.4 g
Trans fat	0 g
Cholesterol	0 mg
Sodium	45 mg
Potassium	180 mg
Total carbohydrate	17 g
Dietary fiber	2 g
Sugars	14 g
Added sugars	0 g
Protein	2 g
Phosphorus	35 mg

peppermint chocolate nice cream

Meet my favorite flavor duo: chocolate and mint! And meet this creamy dessert. There's no dairy here, so technically it's not ice cream. Since it's made with good-for-you ingredients, the name "nice cream" works like a charm. Bananas provide its delectable creaminess and sweetness. As you're puréeing the nice cream, it starts out looking crumbly—and you might not think it's going to work. Just be patient. It'll all of a sudden become velvety smooth. Oh, and then there's fun crunch from the cacao nibs—which also provide antioxidants with no added sugar in sight.

2	medium fully ripened bananas, peeled, sliced into coins, and frozen
3	tablespoons unsweetened cocoa powder
1/2	teaspoon pure vanilla extract
1/4	teaspoon pure peppermint extract
1	tablespoon cacao nibs

KITCHEN TOOLS

- Cutting board
- Paring or chef's knife
- Measuring spoons
- Food processor
- Flexible spatula

serves: 3 | **serving size:** about 1/2 cup | **prep time:** 10 minutes
(plus freezing time) | **cooking time:** 0 minutes

DIRECTIONS

1. Add the frozen banana coins, cocoa powder, and extracts to a food processor. Cover and pulse 10 times to chop the bananas. Then process on high speed until creamy, about 2 1/2 minutes, while stopping and scraping down the inside of the food processor container about every 30 seconds of processing. Add the cacao nibs, and pulse 3 times to combine.

2. Enjoy the nice cream immediately, soft-serve style. Or freeze until solid—then at serving time, set it out for 15 minutes to soften, scoop, and serve.

EASY TIP!

For a cacao nibs recommendation, see page 323 for "Ingredients of Choice."

HOW TO FREEZE BANANAS

Peel the fully ripened bananas. Slice crosswise into coins. Arrange the banana coins on an unbleached parchment paper–lined rimmed baking sheet, cover, and freeze for at least 4 hours or overnight. Use in the recipe. Or transfer the frozen banana coins into a sealable freezer bag or container for later use.

NUTRITION INFORMATION

Choices/Exchanges:
1 1/2 fruit, 1/2 fat

Per Serving:

Calories	110
Calories from fat	20
Total fat	2.5 g
Saturated fat	1.5 g
Trans fat	0 g
Cholesterol	0 mg
Sodium	0 mg
Potassium	410 mg
Total carbohydrate	24 g
Dietary fiber	5 g
Sugars	11 g
Added sugars	0 g
Protein	2 g
Phosphorus	70 mg

english cucumber, basil & strawberry sorbet

This isn't any ordinary sorbet. It's special enough for a special occasion. And it's definitely a unique treat with its hint of vegetable goodness and herbal flair. But don't worry, it's still got enough sweetness from the combination of strawberries and raspberry fruit spread to satisfy, while carbs are kept in check. Just be sure to plan ahead for the freezing time that this sorbet needs before serving. And if you like, garnish with petite basil sprigs.

1	(12-inch) English cucumber, unpeeled, chilled, cut into coins
10	large fresh basil leaves
2	tablespoons fruit-sweetened raspberry fruit spread (jam)*
1 1/2	teaspoons white balsamic or champagne vinegar
1	(16-ounce) bag frozen strawberries (do not thaw), divided

*Note: Ideally, choose a fruit spread without added sugars.

KITCHEN TOOLS

- Cutting board
- Chef's knife
- Measuring spoons
- Blender
- Flexible spatula
- 8-inch round cake pan
- Fork
- Ice cream or cookie scoop

serves: 8 | **serving size:** 1/2 cup | **prep time:** 12 minutes
(plus freezing time) | **cooking time:** 0 minutes

DIRECTIONS

1. Add the cucumber, whole basil leaves, fruit spread, vinegar, and half the frozen strawberries to a blender. Cover and purée. Add the remaining frozen strawberries. Cover and purée until smoothie-like, scraping down the inside of the blender container as needed.

2. Pour the mixture into an 8-inch round pan. Freeze for 30 minutes. Scrape up the sorbet with a fork. Spread back out into an even layer. Freeze until desired texture is reached, about 30 more minutes. Scrape up with a fork again.

3. Scoop into dessert dishes or glasses to serve.

EASY TIP!

Make this sorbet before dinner so it'll be ready soon thereafter. But don't wait too long; it may turn into a solid block of ice if you freeze too long.

STRAWBERRIES ARE HEALTH PROMOTERS

Strawberries contain bioactive compounds, such as anthocyanins, flavonoids, and phenolic acid, which may offer protection from inflammation-related conditions, obesity, heart disease, and more. Research suggests strawberry polyphenols may play a beneficial role in insulin sensitivity, potentially reducing the risk of diabetes. Plus, in women, lower strawberry intake has been associated with higher A1C levels, potentially increasing the risk of diabetes.

NUTRITION INFORMATION

Choices/Exchanges:
1/2 fruit

Per Serving:

Calories	35
Calories from fat	0
Total fat	0 g
Saturated fat	0 g
Trans fat	0 g
Cholesterol	0 mg
Sodium	0 mg
Potassium	160 mg
Total carbohydrate	9 g
Dietary fiber	2 g
Sugars	5 g
Added sugars	0 g
Protein	1 g
Phosphorus	20 mg

sweet cherry milkshake

This isn't one of those super-sized, extra sweet, overly rich, extremely decadent milkshakes. But it does still count as a shake! The base of this shake is plain Greek yogurt (that's the "milk" part) and the sweetness comes naturally from fruit, so you've got a truly smart, diabetes-friendly beverage. Personally, I'm a geeky fan of its vibrant fuchsia color and its 8 grams of protein. Consider it dessert . . . it's that enjoyable!

1	cup frozen pitted dark sweet cherries (do not thaw)
2/3	cup plain 0% fat Greek yogurt
1	teaspoon bottled lemon juice (not from concentrate)
2	large ice cubes

KITCHEN TOOLS

- Dry measuring cups
- Measuring spoons
- Blender
- Flexible spatula

serves: 2 │ **serving size:** 3/4 cup
prep time: 4 minutes │ **cooking time:** 0 minutes

DIRECTIONS

1. Add the frozen cherries, yogurt, lemon juice, and ice cubes to a blender. Cover and purée.

2. Pour into glasses. Serve.

EASY TIP!

You can make this milkshake in advance and chill it in the refrigerator for hours. It stays pretty thick!

BE SWEET ON SWEET CHERRIES

Cherries contain anthocyanins, which are polyphenol plant nutrients that give cherries their rich color. Research suggests that these powerful pigments may help boost insulin and lower the risk of diabetes complications. Anthocyanins are found in many other fruits and veggies. Look for vivid purple, blue, and red produce; the bright color is often an indicator of anthocyanins.

NUTRITION INFORMATION

Choices/Exchanges:
1/2 fruit, 1/2 fat-free milk

Per Serving:

Calories	100
Calories from fat	0
Total fat	0 g
Saturated fat	0.1 g
Trans fat	0 g
Cholesterol	5 mg
Sodium	30 mg
Potassium	260 mg
Total carbohydrate	15 g
Dietary fiber	2 g
Sugars	12 g
Added sugars	0 g
Protein	8 g
Phosphorus	115 mg

blueberry chia smoothie

Smoothies are so easy—just toss everything into a blender and hit a button! This fruity smoothie is a sweet treat, and it's got great nutritional benefits! Blueberries provide a punch of antioxidants, natural sweetness, and purplish color. Banana offers the nutritious creaminess—no dairy needed. Unsweetened vanilla almond milk provides a dairy-like quality in a calorie-friendly way. Chia seeds add some protein and texture intrigue. And lemon juice balances the taste along with providing its notable citrus flair. It's a refreshing delight! By the way, you can try this smoothie with any frozen fruit of your choice.

1	cup frozen blueberries (do not thaw) (5 ounces)
1	small banana, peeled and broken into 4 pieces
3/4	cup unsweetened vanilla almond milk, chilled
1	tablespoon bottled lemon juice (not from concentrate)
2	teaspoons chia seeds

KITCHEN TOOLS

- Dry measuring cups
- Liquid measuring cup
- Measuring spoons
- Blender

DIRECTIONS

1. Add all ingredients to a blender. Cover and purée for about 2 minutes on high speed.

2. Pour into glasses. Serve.

EASY TIP!

If using plain instead of vanilla unsweetened almond milk, add 1/4 teaspoon of pure vanilla extract to this smoothie. For a chia seed recommendation, see page 326 for "Ingredients of Choice."

SUPER SEEDS

White and black chia seeds are super nutritious—and super cool. They create a gel when in liquid for about 15 minutes. So if you make this smoothie in advance, the seeds further thicken the smoothie as they become less crunchy and more gel-like. Choose white chia seeds for a prettier appearance here. Bonus: Chia seeds are a great source of fiber and protein. This can help prevent sharp spikes in blood glucose since these nutrients can help whatever foods the seeds are paired with convert into sugar more slowly in the body.

NUTRITION INFORMATION

Choices/Exchanges:
1 1/2 Fruit, 1/2 Fat

Per Serving:

Calories	120
Calories from fat	30
Total fat	3.5 g
Saturated fat	0.4 g
Trans fat	0 g
Cholesterol	0 mg
Sodium	70 mg
Potassium	320 mg
Total carbohydrate	24 g
Dietary fiber	5 g
Sugars	13 g
Added sugars	0 g
Protein	2 g
Phosphorus	65 mg

sparkling refresher

Even with all of the fun and functional beverages available today, enjoying a plain ol' glass of water several times a day is still one of the best ways to hydrate. So here's some water with a little more fragrance and fizz! The fresh grated gingerroot adds zing. And the fresh mint provides aromatic delight. By first rolling up and twisting the mint leaves with your fingers, the natural flavor essence is released, so don't skip that step. Count this refresher as part of your water intake for the day. Double the recipe on a sweltering hot day!

5	fresh mint leaves
1/2	teaspoon grated fresh gingerroot
1	cup lemon-lime sparkling water, chilled

KITCHEN TOOLS

- Spoon or peeler (for peeling ginger)
- Microplane zester/grater
- Measuring spoons
- Liquid measuring cup (optional)
- Beverage glass

serves: 1 | **serving size:** 1 cup
prep time: 5 minutes | **cooking time:** 0 minutes

DIRECTIONS

1. Stack up the mint leaves, roll up, and twist while squeezing a few times to release their flavor.

2. Add the mint, grated ginger, and sparkling water to a beverage glass. Serve with or without ice.

EASY TIP!

See page 23 for "How to grate fresh gingerroot."

SHOULD YOU SIP WITH A PLASTIC STRAW?

If you're aiming to be eco-conscious, the answer is "No!" In America, we may be using over 500 million plastic straws daily! Unfortunately, many of the discarded straws wind up polluting the ocean and potentially killing fish and other marine life. So go straw-less—or buy reusable straws. You can find out more at strawlessocean.org.

NUTRITION INFORMATION

Choices/Exchanges = 0

Per Serving:

Calories	5
Calories from fat	0
Total fat	0 g
Saturated fat	0 g
Trans fat	0 g
Cholesterol	0 mg
Sodium	5 mg
Potassium	25 mg
Total carbohydrate	1 g
Dietary fiber	0 g
Sugars	0 g
Added sugars	0 g
Protein	0 g
Phosphorus	0 mg

thai-style vegetable juice cocktail

I started creating this drink as a loose interpretation of a Bloody Mary. The end result is nothing like the classic cocktail . . . it's better. It's got exciting worldly appeal, too. And don't worry, while some cocktails and other alcoholic beverages can be quite caloric and carb-heavy due to sugary mixers, it's more difficult to go overboard when you start with a vegetable juice. Use whatever vegetable juice you like, but aim for one without added salt for the healthiest sip.

1/2	teaspoon grated fresh gingerroot
1 1/2	ounces 80-proof vodka, chilled
2 1/2	ounces 100% vegetable juice of choice (such as beet or carrot), chilled
1/2	teaspoon bottled lime juice (not from concentrate)
1	ounce lemon-lime sparkling water, chilled
5	fresh cilantro leaves

KITCHEN TOOLS

- Spoon or peeler (for peeling ginger)
- Microplane zester/grater
- Measuring spoons
- Liquid measuring cup or jigger
- Cocktail shaker with strainer
- Cocktail glass

serves: 1 | **serving size:** 1 (5.25-ounce) cocktail
prep time: 5 minutes | **cooking time:** 0 minutes

DIRECTIONS

1. Add the ginger, vodka, juice, and lime juice to a shaker container filled with several ice cubes. Cover and shake well.

2. Strain into a cocktail glass, add the sparkling water, top with the cilantro leaves, and serve.

EASY TIP!

See page 23 for "How to grate fresh gingerroot."

THE PROOF

Getting 100 is a better score than an 80 on a test. But not when it comes to the calorie content of vodka or other spirit. The lower the proof, the lower the calories! Basically, a 1 1/2-ounce shot of 80-proof vodka provides 100 calories, 90-proof vodka provides 110 calories, and 100-proof vodka provides 120 calories. So aim for 80!

NUTRITION INFORMATION

Choices/Exchanges:
1 nonstarchy vegetable, 1 alcohol

Per Serving:

Calories	130
Calories from fat	0
Total fat	0 g
Saturated fat	0 g
Trans fat	0 g
Cholesterol	0 mg
Sodium	55 mg
Potassium	250 mg
Total carbohydrate	7 g
Dietary fiber	1 g
Sugars	3 g
Added sugars	0 g
Protein	1 g
Phosphorus	35 mg

pomegranate mimosa

A mimosa is traditionally equal parts champagne and orange juice. Here it's given a juicy makeover with pomegranate juice. Because it's served in a champagne glass, calories are kept in check by its petite size. And you'll be finishing it with a sprig of mint or basil to make it extra special. Keep the herb in the glass to get a lovely scent with every sip. The herb stem can act as a stirrer, too! And don't waste the herb leaves after your last sip of mimosa; add it to food that you're enjoying along with your drink.

> 2   ounces 100% pomegranate juice, chilled
> 2   ounces Prosecco or other sparkling wine, chilled
> 1   sprig fresh mint or basil

KITCHEN TOOLS

- Liquid measuring cup
- Champagne flute

serves: 1 | **serving size:** 1 (4-ounce) mimosa
prep time: 2 minutes | **cooking time:** 0 minutes

DIRECTIONS

1. Pour the juice into a champagne flute. Add the Prosecco.

2. Place the sprig of mint into the flute, like it's a floral bouquet. Serve.

EASY TIP!

Stand a champagne flute on a kitchen scale and pour in the juice and Prosecco based on weight—no measuring cup necessary.

A BEVERAGE WITH BENEFITS

You can get big benefits in a small amount of juice, such as 100% pomegranate juice. Pomegranate juice offers polyphenol antioxidants, such as anthocyanins and ellagitannins, which fight free radicals. Related to diabetes health, the pomegranate has anti-inflammatory effects and plays a protective role. Research suggests that properties of the pomegranate show the most potential for benefit on diabetes, cardiovascular diseases, and metabolic syndrome.

NUTRITION INFORMATION

Choices/Exchanges:
1/2 fruit, 1/2 alcohol

Per Serving:

Calories	80
Calories from fat	0
Total fat	0 g
Saturated fat	0 g
Trans fat	0 g
Cholesterol	0 mg
Sodium	10 mg
Potassium	180 mg
Total carbohydrate	10 g
Dietary fiber	0 g
Sugars	9 g
Added sugars	1 g
Protein	0 g
Phosphorus	15 mg

INGREDIENTS OF CHOICE

This is a selected list of food brands that I personally like—and that also meet the nutritional standards I used in this cookbook, such as products with no added sugars or no artificial ingredients. These are not the only brands/products you can use when preparing dishes from the book—and the American Diabetes Association does not specifically endorse any of the products on this list. This is simply a guide to the types of ingredients suggested for use in the recipes.

Applesauce
Santa Cruz Organic Applesauce

Barbecue Sauce
Primal Kitchen Organic Unsweetened Classic BBQ Sauce

Beans
365 Everyday Value Beans (Any Variety)
Amy's Organic Vegetarian Traditional Refried Beans, Light in Sodium
Eden Organic No Salt Added Beans (Any Variety)

Bread/Buns
Ezekiel 4:9 Sprouted Whole Grain Bread
Ezekiel 4:9 Sprouted Whole Grain Burger Buns

Broths
365 Everyday Value Organic Broths (Vegetable, Chicken, and/or Low Sodium)

Cacao Nibs
Navitas Organics Cacao Nibs

Cheese Alternatives

Kite Hill Almond Milk Ricotta

Treeline Treenut Aged Artisanal
　　Nut Cheese—Classic

Treeline Treenut Creamy Soft French-Style
　　Cheese—Herb-Garlic

Chia Seeds (see Seeds)

Chicken

Bell and Evans Organic Boneless, Skinless
　　Chicken Thighs

Coleman Organic Chicken Breasts

Chickpea Snacks

Biena Chickpea Snacks—Sea Salt

Coconut Milk

365 Everyday Value Organic Light
　　Coconut Milk

Native Forest Unsweetened Organic Light
　　Coconut Milk

Coconut Sugar

Bob's Red Mill Organic Coconut Sugar

Dried Fruit

Now Real Food Certified Organic
　　Unsweetened Apricots

Egg Alternative

Follow Your Heart VeganEgg

Farro (see Whole Grains)

Fish

Australis All-Natural Barramundi (Frozen)

Wild Planet Albacore Wild Tuna Single-
　　Serve Pouch—No-Salt-Added

Freekeh (see Whole Grains)

Fruit Spread (Jam)

Crofter's Organic Just Fruit Spread
　　(Various Flavors)

Polaner All Fruit Spreadable Fruit
　　(Various Flavors)

Granola

Wildway Grain Free Granola

Hemp Seeds (see Seeds)

Hot Pepper Sauce

Franks RedHot Original Cayenne
　　Pepper Sauce

NYC Hot Sauce Company

Hummus

Hope Organic Original Recipe Hummus

Tribe Organic Classic Hummus

Juices

Santa Cruz Organic Pure Lemon Juice

Santa Cruz Organic Pure Lime Juice

Pom Wonderful 100% Pomegranate Juice

Ketchup

Primal Kitchen Organic Unsweetened
Ketchup

Marinara Sauce

Newman's Own for the Common Good
Organic Marinara Pasta Sauce

Rao's Homemade Arrabbiata Sauce

Thrive Market Organic Marinara
Tomato Sauce

Mayonnaise

Primal Kitchen Mayo with Avocado Oil

Mustard

Annie's Organic Dijon Mustard

Nuts

Nuts.com Pecan Pieces

Wonderful No Shells Pistachios

Nut Butters

365 Everyday Value Almond Butter—
Creamy, No Sugar Added

365 Everyday Value Organic Peanut
Butter—Creamy, Unsweetened, No Salt

Smucker's Natural Creamy Peanut Butter

Pastas/Noodles

Barilla Whole Grain Rotini

Eden Organic Spelt & Buckwheat Gemelli

Eden Selected 100% Buckwheat Soba

Explore Cuisine Pastas and Noodles
(Any Variety)

Tolerant Organic Red Lentil Rotini

Pecans (see Nuts)

Pesto Sauce

Kitchen & Love Basil Pesto Sauce

Pistachios (see Nuts)

Pita Chips

Athenos Whole Wheat Baked Pita Chips

Quinoa (see Whole Grains)

Rice (see Whole Grains)

Salad Dressing

Primal Kitchen Greek Vinaigrette & Marinade

Primal Kitchen Italian Vinaigrette & Marinade

Primal Kitchen Ranch Dressing

Salsas

365 Everyday Value Roasted Verde Salsa

Green Mountain Gringo Salsa—Mild, Medium, or Hot

Sausage
Applegate Organics Sweet Italian Chicken Sausage
Wellshire Farms Smoked Turkey Andouille Sausage

Seeds
Mamma Chia Organic Chia Seed
Manitoba Harvest Hemp Hearts

Soup
Imagine Creamy Broccoli Soup
Imagine Creamy Portobello Mushroom Soup

Tahini
365 Everyday Value Organic Tahini

Tofu
Nasoya Organic Sprouted Super Firm Tofu

Tortillas
Ezekiel 4:9 Sprouted Whole Grain Tortillas

Tuna (see Fish)

Whole Grains
365 Everyday Value Organic Italian Farro (Quick Cooking)
Bob's Red Mill Organic Farro
Freekehlicious Cracked Freekeh
Lundberg California Brown Basmati Rice
Lundberg Organic Quinoa—Tri-Color Blend

Yogurt/Skyr
Wallaby Organic Aussie Greek Plain Nonfat Yogurt
Icelandic Provisions Plain Skyr

INDEX